Musical Ethics and Islam

Musical Ethics and Islam

The Art of Playing the Ney

BANU ŞENAY

UNIVERSITY OF ILLINOIS PRESS
Urbana, Chicago, and Springfield

1 2 3 4 5 C P 5 4 3 2 1
∞ This book is printed on acid-free paper.

Library of Congress Cataloging-in-Publication Data
Names: Şenay, Banu, author.
Title: Musical ethics and Islam: the art of playing the ney / Banu Şenay.
Description: Urbana: University of Illinois Press, 2020. | Includes bibliographical references and index. |
Identifiers: LCCN 2019037836 (print) | LCCN 2019037837 (ebook) | ISBN 9780252043024 (cloth) | ISBN 9780252084881 (paperback) | ISBN 9780252051883 (ebook)
Subjects: LCSH: Music—Religious aspects—Islam. | Music—Moral and ethical aspects—Turkey. | Nāy—Instruction and study—Turkey. | Maqām—Turkey.
Classification: LCC ML3921.6.I85 S4 2020 (print) | LCC ML3921.6.I85 (ebook) | DDC 788.3/509561—DC23
LC record available at https://lccn.loc.gov/2019037836
LC ebook record available at https://lccn.loc.gov/2019037837

This book is dedicated to the musicians and apprentices at Hezarfen.

Contents

Acknowledgments

MUSICAL ETHICS AND ISLAM has been composed over many years. Myriad relationships, both professional and personal, have contributed to its development. Although there is no way to adequately thank all those who have helped bring this book about, there remains the pleasant duty of expressing my gratitude and appreciation to those individuals and institutions who generously supported its completion.

I owe my teacher Neyzen Salih Bilgin more than I can say. He introduced me to the nurturing world of the ney and fostered my learning through the transformative experience of musical apprenticeship. From him, I learned the value of dwelling on a single note—the gift of producing good sound—and to appreciate the skill of crafting small things well. The book could not have been crafted without him. I am immensely grateful for his welcome and guidance at Hezarfen Ney School, where he made a musical home. As Salih Hoca says, "Musical style in the first instance involves a style of living."

A million thanks also to the apprentices and fellow learners at Hezarfen for their hospitality and friendship. It was a pleasure to apprentice music with them (and from them). I am thankful, too, for their willing participation in interviews, for their insightful conversations, and for making Salih Hoca's lessons available to me while I was in Australia. For better or for worse, this book would not exist without them. I am deeply grateful to the hundred or more ney students and ney teachers in Istanbul and in other cities for sharing their knowledge with me.

My research in Istanbul was aided by constant acts of kindness and goodwill. Among the many ney musicians and masters who have encouraged this research and opened up new avenues of inquiry, I want to acknowledge Niyazi Sayın, Ömer Erdoğdular, Süleyman Erguner, Sadrettin Özçimi, Yılmaz Kale, Bülent Özbek, Ali Tan, Ali Tüfekçi, Aziz Şenol Filiz, Burcu Karadağ, Kudsi Erguner, Ahmet Kaya, Ercan Irmak, Eyüp Hamiş, Ahmet Şahin, Ayça Arın, Hakan Alvan and Ahmet Toz. I offer sincere thanks to tanbur musicians Hakan Talu and Birol Yayla, Neyzen Hüseyin Özkılıç, and Hattat (calligrapher) Efdaluddin Kılıç for their generous sharing of their knowledge. I have attempted to accurately represent all their perspectives in these pages.

The MacArthur Fellowship of the University of Melbourne generously supported research in Istanbul between 2012 and 2014. Fellowships from Macquarie University in Sydney and the German Orient-Institute in Istanbul contributed to additional research, writing, and the completion of the book manuscript. The Orient-Institute provided not only library and working space but also friendships. I thank Martin Greve for companionship and commentary, and Alexandre Toumarkine for exchange of ideas. The Center for Advanced Studies in Music at Istanbul Technical University also provided library support and a stimulating research environment. There I thank Songül Karahasanoğlu for her friendship and support, and Robert Reigle for the opportunity to share my research with the center's graduate students.

At Macquarie University, I thank my colleagues in the Department of Anthropology for intellectual support and for giving me the freedom in my teaching schedule to complete this book. Selvaraj Velayutham, Kalpana Ram, Lisa Wynn, Norbert Ebert, Eve Vincent, Alison Leitch, Robbie Peters, Payel Ray, and the late Joel Kahn have each contributed to this book in a variety of ways. Many friends invited me to colloquia and contributed to the ideas that appear in these pages. I am indebted to Michael Jackson and Martin Stokes for reading the entire manuscript, for sharing their insights, and for offering me valuable feedback on how to revise it. In different ways, they have both been a reference point and inspiration, opening new directions of thinking and dwelling in anthropology.

Laurie Matheson at the University of Illinois Press welcomed the book from the beginning, and I am deeply indebted to her work and support in editing the manuscript. I also thank Julie Gay, Jennifer Argo, Julie Laut, and the entire editorial team for their efforts in improving this book. For tightening my loquacious prose, I am grateful to Jim Houston. Credit also goes to Max Harwood and Tomas Wilkoszewski for their patient assistance on the manuscript's images.

There are other publishers to thank. Versions of chapter 1 appear in *Ethnomusicology Forum* (23 [2014]: 405–24) and *European Journal of Cultural Studies* (18 [2014]: 52–69). A version of chapter 5 appears in the *Journal of the Royal Anthropological Institute* (21 [2015]: 524–41).

My friends Dilek Çilingir, Burcak Muraben, and Faik Gür provided thoughts on the book at various points, and I thank them for keeping me well fed and in fine conversation with their companionship. Thanks also to the Mevlevis in Melbourne, in particular to Sheikh Abdul Aziz, for allowing me to play the ney in their ceremonies. My family in Turkey, Gönül Şenay and Erdal Şenay, and my family in Australia, Jim Houston, Marjorie Houston, Nick Houston, and Isabelle Gakavian, were supportive throughout the process. I am particularly indebted to my father, Erdal Şenay, for planting the seed of my love of music.

My partner Christopher Houston sustained me, while somehow sustaining himself, throughout the writing of this book. He patiently listened to every idea, graciously endured re-reading through far too many drafts of the manuscript, and took time away from his own book to help me when I most needed it. I thank him for standing by me and for his insights and unconditional support, which shaped and refined all of the pages that follow.

And finally, I acknowledge my deep gratitude to my first (and beloved) master, Halit Kefeli (1920–2009)—also a tanbur artist—who taught me the *ud* (short-necked plucked lute) during my childhood in a small north Aegean town in Turkey. In weekly lessons he acquainted me with the lineaments of Ottoman classical music. Even more, and unbeknownst to me until I began this ney research, he also gave me my first experience of musical apprenticeship, a privilege for which I feel truly grateful.

I visited the grave of my master,
And washed his headstone with my tears.

Musical Ethics and Islam

Introduction

THIS BOOK IS AN ETHNOGRAPHY about musical craftsmanship. For Richard Sennett, craftsmanship involves "the skill of making things well" (2009, 8), and one of this book's goals is to present an ethnographic account of the processes involved in becoming a *neyzen*—that is, a master player of the *ney*. Commonly referred to in English as the Sufi-flute or reed-flute, this instrument has been intimately connected with Sufism both in the Ottoman Empire and, for better or worse, in modern secular Turkey, although also long used throughout the Middle East and North Africa. After enduring a checkered social life during the Turkish Republic's twentieth century, today in a more Islam-friendly political environment the ney once again occupies a significant place in the country's public soundscape. How it emerged from neglect and censure to find recent fame and renown is only one of the fascinating dimensions of the story.

At root, the book documents the lifetime of preparation required to become an expert player of the ney. It is no easy undertaking. As is the case with all enskillment, the experience of learning an art or craft proficiently is an embodied event, demanding a reworking of existing "ready-made" bodily habits and perceptions. To get a grasp on a new practice, novices engage in acts of "phenomenological modification" (Husserl 1970), taking up new sensory-motor skills and perceptive capacities through repeated efforts. But this is only part of the event. As I show in this book, crafting oneself as a neyzen also involves developing a certain way of living. Ney competency is a fulsome activity requiring learners to enter a particular engagement with a suite of "entities," both human and nonhuman, as well to form new ways of relating to other selves. Among other things, it involves cultivating a particular way of inhabiting the city and making competent use of its urban affordances. It also involves, in the words of Neyzen Salih Bilgin, "becoming a good citizen [*vatandaş*]." This participation in a guided shaping of one's life entails ethical change, including in the first place a new valuing of craftsmanship in diverse areas of practice.[1]

And yet there is no one method of becoming a neyzen in Turkey, a land where pedagogies, educational practices, curricula, artistic genres, and cultural production have always been heavily politicized. Ceaseless endeavor to redefine, reformulate, and restructure these fields of activity has been a feature of state politics in Turkey since the inception of the Republic in 1923 (and even earlier). In examining the skill-based practices that enable one to become a neyzen, the ethnographic inquiry in this book takes as its focus one particular way of learning music, and that is through the slow-learning process of *meşk*.

Rooted in the long-term master-apprentice learning relationship (*usta-çırak; hoca-talebe*), meşk refers to imitative learning based on repetition and memorization (Behar 2012). By establishing a context in which the learner's connection to the artistic tradition is strongly mediated through the master, the pedagogy grafts the apprentice into a certain lineage (*silsile*) through which a particular style (*üslub*), repertoire, and techniques of the craft can be acquired. This oral teaching and learning method formed the primary means of transmission in the art world of Ottoman classical music (and of other artistic traditions such as calligraphy[2] and miniature) up until the beginning of the twentieth century, when the use of Western notation gradually became accepted and adopted in the educational and performance settings of this musical practice. Although today meşk no longer retains its essentially oral features, it has nevertheless remained—and/or has been revived—as a preferred method of teaching and learning, at least among some circles of Ottoman-Turkish classical musicians over the course of the twentieth and twentieth-first centuries.[3] As the biographical evidence about the artistic disciplining of the ney musicians examined in this book shows, it has also facilitated the continuity of some of the key lineages of ney artists in Turkey at a critical time when the instruction of Ottoman classical music received no support from the newly founded state of the Turkish Republic.

In more precise terms, then, this book provides an ethnographic account of the crafting of oneself as a neyzen through a particular means of pedagogy at a particular place and time. The place is Hezarfen Ney School in Istanbul's old suburb of Üsküdar (formerly Scutari). Tucked away in a narrow, crooked street

FIGURE 1.1 Neyzen Niyazi Sayın (on the left) and Neyzen Salih Bilgin, 2016. Courtesy of Salih Bilgin.

behind the eighteenth-century Valide-i Cedid Mosque, this vibrant arts hub was opened in early 2012 by Neyzen Salih Bilgin (b. 1960), whom I refer to throughout this book using the honorific title Salih Hoca. Bilgin's professional career as a leading ney artist in Turkey has spanned more than thirty years, including long years of teaching practice at the Istanbul State Conservatorium as well as at various private music schools, in addition to his continuing performance as chief neyzen with the Presidential Turkish Classical Music Choir.[4] Salih Hoca's choice of Üsküdar for the school was not arbitrary. For him, Üsküdar was a "spiritual" (*maneviyatlı*) suburb, a place that had been home to a large number of dervish *tekkes* (lodges), including one of the city's five Mevlevi lodges, as well as numerous old mosques and cemeteries from the Ottoman era. The tomb of a highly revered seventeenth-century Sufi, Mahmud Hüdâyi of the Celveti order, was only a few minutes' walk away from the ney school. "The Sufi saints [*ehl-i tasavvuf*] of Üsküdar are its real neys," Salih Hoca used to say. In his "sacred geography," Üsküdar was important for another reason: some of the key members of his lineage (for example, Neyzen Salim Bey, Neyzen Aziz Dede) were either born in or had spent most of their lives in this old Bosporus suburb, including his own master, the great Neyzen Niyazi Sayın (b. 1927), who continues to live there today and who occasionally visited Hezarfen. Üsküdar was a place that nurtured neyzens.

Designed as both an atelier and a teaching space, Hezarfen (literally, "a thousand sciences") both gave instruction and engaged in a wide range of creative practices. Indeed, its aims are partly revealed in its very name: to craft persons knowledgeable in many skills. On a typical day, one could find Salih Hoca working on the lathe, converting a piece of hardwood into a ney mouthpiece (*başpare*), or cooking with/for his students in the atelier section, which resembled a carpentry workshop with its workbenches, tools, and bundles of reeds left drying before their metamorphosis into neys. The long table in the middle of the room turned the atelier into a social space that glued people together not only through work but also through *sohbet* (conversation), music-making, and commensality. Indeed, the workshop was a meeting place for ney musicians and students alike, and for many faithful practitioners of Ottoman classical music, where they could chat as well as explore and improvise music. Within a year of its opening, it had become a complex hub where willing students could take up training in a variety of other pleasurable activities, from playing the classical *kemençe* (*politiki* lyra) and *tanbur* (long-necked lute) to writing Islamic calligraphy. And there were ney lessons, of course.

Taking this vibrant community of practice in contemporary Istanbul as an ethnographic anchor point while drawing on my own experience of musical apprenticeship at Hezarfen under the guidance of Salih Hoca, I examine in this book the transformative power of this musical practice to change selves. I draw on the Husserlian concept of "intentional modification" as a vital analytical tool for understanding and describing what this experience of change might entail. Accordingly, a fundamental phenomenological question that guides the analytical inquiry concerns the kinds of modifications—physical, perceptual, and ethical—enabled by the core methods of the music pedagogy at work here. What new repertoire of sensory and affectual capacities, and modes of perception does enskillment in the ney cultivate in novices? In what ways does learning foster certain ways of being and acting in the world, shaping skilled practitioners in moral ways? And what kind of Muslim moral subjectivity is in the making here? These questions motivate the present study.

To answer them, I have divided the book into seven chapters. Chapters 2, 3, and 4, which should be treated as one extended discussion, examine the core skills and perceptual modifications that musical apprenticeship demands from ney learners: producing good sound; mastery of tonal relationships; and the art of improvisation (*taksim*). Competent execution of each one of these skilled actions essentially requires, among other things, developing new forms of hearing and listening that are different from those acquired earlier in life (what Husserl called the "natural attitude"). Drawing an analogy from Alessandro Duranti's work on musical training in jazz, we can describe this process as developing an Ottoman classical music "way of hearing." As Duranti notes, learning to become skillful in jazz demands from its players "special kinds of 'listening'" so that new aural perceptions—a "jazz way" of hearing, in this instance—can be cultivated (2009, 210).[5] Thereafter one may not be able to "remember" their prior modes of hearing. In the case of ney learning, too, becoming attentive to the musical and affective force of melodic modes (*makam*) and discerning the right pitch relations conducive for effectively producing a mode is only possible if novices experience a series of intentional modifications in how they hear. I discuss this topic in chapters 3 and 4.

As many have noted, skills are instilled bodily through observation, copying, and repetition (Ingold 2001; Marchand 2008; 2009). Only through imitation and repetitive practice can novices gradually transform their bodily movements to align with the master's playing body, so that thereafter fluidity and dexterity emerge. Yet mimetic learning does not characterize all aspects of apprenticeship in the ney. A further vital dimension of the learning practice I examine here involves the masterful performance of poetic speech, gifted to students through the speech event of sohbet (in the first instance, conversation). As an essentially Sufi disciplinary practice with a long trajectory in Islam (Algar 1992; Silverstein 2008), sohbet has a vital pedagogical, affective, and ethical force in ney learning. Pedagogically, what is crucial here is that learners' act of listening is not restricted to the musical demonstrations of their hoca. They listen to a wide range of orally expressed knowledge, musical and extramusical, communicated to students through different rhetorical styles, from anecdotes to scene narratives.

This importance bestowed on listening and the recourse to "talk" as a tool of scaffolding in the ney practice contrasts with many other case studies of craft apprenticeship that anthropological studies have examined. Teaching is often said to be "silent" and implicit, implicating a tacit "acquisition of unarticulated bodily-sensorial knowledge" (Weidman 2012, 217) where "on-site communication is non-propositional" (Marchand 2008, 249; see also Keller and Keller 1999). By contrast, masterful speech is accorded so much value in the pedagogical practices of Ottoman classical music that for many musical masters, "*meşk* cannot be done without *sohbet*" (tanbur artist Hakan Talu). What is it about sohbet that makes it such a compelling vehicle for musical education? To answer this question, chapter 5 presents a number of key processes that the pedagogy of sohbet is designed to facilitate in learners: new skills of hearing and musical understanding; extramusical sensibilities germane to becoming a neyzen; and communal affections (an affect of intimacy) between those participating in the listening act.

Finally, chapters 6 and 7 shift our attention to consider the ethical modifications that this apprenticeship-style learning fosters in skilled practitioners. This learning method transcends "mere" musical technique in profound ways. *Talebes* receive an education in myriad practices that are in many respects extramusical and have entailments both for enskilling them in musical knowledge and for shaping their sensibilities as Muslims, a topical concern to which I will return at the end of this introductory chapter. Before proceeding further, though, I should say something about the broader social context of the ney in Turkey.

The Fall and Rise of the Ney

Ney playing has experienced a major revival over the past ten years in Turkey. The instrument's growing popularity is not just limited to Istanbul, a city that has always been the heartland of musical production in Turkey, but is occurring in other urban centers too, including small towns all over the country, leading to an exponential growth of ney performances and a huge demand for ney learning. This striking popularity of the ney carries more weight once we consider the explosive Kemalist legacies impinging upon the social life of the instrument and its devotees in the early twentieth century.

In the years immediately following the founding of the Turkish Republic in 1923, the ney had a rather difficult public career. Taken as a whole, the sweeping "secularizing" reforms (*devrimler* or *inkilaplar*) implemented by the Kemalist nation-builders in the 1920s and 1930s—an event that also came to be known as a "Cultural Revolution"—intended to transform the Islamic-Ottoman life-world and to fabricate a new "national" culture. These state-induced changes took as their target not only the legal, political, and institutional realms but also the prime habits of everyday life, as they aimed to imbue citizens with new embodied skills, tastes, and knowledge.

Nothing better illustrates this than the state's heavy-handed intervention in music. As music historian İlhan Tekelioğlu (1996) notes, from the moment the Republic was formed, the sonic field of music became a prime concern for the Kemalist culture brokers as part of their project of social engineering. A "revolution in music" (*musiki inkilabı*) was put into effect (see chapter 1). In it, certain musical forms were hailed as genuine expressions of the "national (*milli*) culture," others demonized for not being truly "authentic/Turkish." Similarly, particular performance practices became the object of state sponsorship and promotion, while others became the target of its censorship. New music schools and repertoires were created, even as older institutions and musical genres were transmuted into official history, artifacts pronounced as "obsolete" to be heard as museum pieces or, worse, simply silenced—like Kurdish music.[6] Whether they fully succeeded in these intentions or not, such enactments of the "pedagogical state" (Kaplan 2006), undertaken both in the pristine period of "High Kemalism" (1923–1950) and thereafter routinely and extraordinarily in periods of state activism (for example, under the military junta government during 1980–1983), were influential in creating a transformed musical landscape.

How might this antagonistic Kemalist legacy be relevant for the ney, an instrument that remains strikingly underresearched in the ethnomusicological literature? An end-blown reed flute, the ney is the beloved wind instrument of Ottoman classical music[7] (*Osmanlı klasik musikisi*, today also known as Turkish classical music), a *makam* (melodic mode)-based music that developed in the late sixteenth century and continues to prove its vitality today (Behar 2015; 1993; 1987; Feldman 1996). Among all instruments of Ottoman music, it was the ney in particular that enjoyed an intimate relationship with Sufi orders, among which the Mevlevi order, instituted following the thirteenth-century Sufi mystic Mevlâna Celaleddin Rumî (1207–1273), was most significant. By the eighteenth century, the majority of neyzen in the Ottoman capital were either dervishes or sympathizers (*muhib*) of this order, while their lodges (known as *tekke, dergâh*, or *zaviye*) performed the role of conservatoria in Ottoman cities, constituting primary sites for the teaching of the ney. When the radical reforms of the Kemalist state targeted Ottoman classical music, the ney, as a leading sound of this artistic tradition, endured a series of hostile reforms directed at the institutions teaching its music. Most crucially, in 1925 the Turkish state outlawed Sufi orders and closed down their lodges in an attempt to establish its own monopoly over Islam. In the same year, the Kemalists proscribed the teaching of Ottoman music in all primary and secondary schools, followed by the closure in 1926 of the Eastern Music Section of *Darül Elhan* (House of Tunes), the first official conservatorium of the late Ottoman (and Republican) era. These institutional changes inflicted a major blow upon Ottoman and Istanbul music even if such measures failed to bring its skilled teaching to a final end. Despite the absence of any official support for the instruction of Ottoman classical music—the first state conservatorium reteaching it opened in Istanbul only in 1975—the transmission of this musical tradition survived in the hands of individual masters, who taught students in their own homes while continuing the master-student learning relationship. The artist lineage that is the focus of this book provides us with a biographical case study through which both musical continuities and ruptures might be traced between old and current teaching methods, including the ethical values and principles underpinning them.

This book takes up the ney's story from the past two decades (since 2000), analyzing its remarkable revival in Turkey and its popularity globally. Since the turn of the twenty-first century, the opening up of both private workshops and council-sponsored ney classes has been a striking phenomenon in Turkey's urban centers. Willing students, mostly adults, now take lessons in a range of pedagogical sites, from ney studios and private music schools to religious associations, university clubs, and local mosque organizations. Ney lessons are available as a lunchtime activity at Istanbul's corporate office spaces. Neys are bought and exchanged as gifts between friends and between partners; the instrument's sound fills an eclectic range of urban spaces, from the museum-converted Mevlevi convents to jazz festivals, from yoga studios to private hospital wards used for therapeutic purposes. The ney is "hot."

Why this remarkable new interest in it? What is facilitating its wide circulation in networks of musical performance, pedagogy, and markets, both nationally and transnationally? Indeed, what makes ney consumption increase so rapidly that in recent years local authorities in Turkey's southern city of Hatay have been forced to organize "special protection" for the reed canes[8] growing in their area? "The issue is not the remarkable increase in reed-cutting alone," explained the governor of Samandağ, a town nestled beside the border with Syria where the Asi River meets the Mediterranean Sea, famous for its fertile reed-beds. "The un-informed [*bilinçsiz*] harvesting of the reed is the main problem," he clarified, pointing out how, in the face of mounting competition, large amounts of reeds are now cut off from their riverbed before they are ready.

A local, Saho, one of the first reed harvesters (*kamışçı*) in Samandağ and well known to many ney ateliers in Istanbul, is also unhappy with the situation. "Reed cutting is not as straightforward as it seems," he noted in our interview. "You must have an eye for the ideal diameter of the reed's body and how well balanced it contracts at each node; you must know how much moisture is left in the cane before cutting it, and discern which reed is suitable for which tuning of ney. I can tell a good reed even with my eyes closed." From a pile stacked in the courtyard of his house, he pulls out a few samples to demonstrate. Yet Saho is pessimistic about the future of this small economic enterprise that has given his family a livelihood for nearly thirty years. In the past, only two local families were involved in reed cutting. Now the competition is intense, leading to fears that soon there will be no reeds left to make neys from.

Far away from Samandağ, in Istanbul's bourgeoning ney workshops, trouble in finding reeds suitable for ney making also figures as a common problem. And so does the striking increase in reed prices. "Ten years ago a reed wouldn't even cost five liras, but now the price range changes between 30–60 liras," one owner in Istanbul's Kadıköy region reported.

The complex shifts experienced by sound-producing objects in the face of myriad sociocultural, economic, political, and technological forces have been of intense concern in ethnomusicology, exploring how, in the contemporary world, "old instruments" find themselves in "new contexts" (Neuenfeldt 1998).[9] The recent public life of the ney is an exemplary case, revealing a huge growth of ney music, both live and recorded, and a hunger for ney learning among urban dwellers. Although the constituencies of learners are as diverse as their teaching sites, "a quest for spirituality [*maneviyat*]"[10] is often identified as one key motive in this popular re-creation of ney learning.

But what might be meant by spirituality anyway? It is a well-established critique in the social sciences that the term "spirituality" is "vague," "floating," and far too all-embracing, one that obscures diverse and even contradictory meanings (King 1996).[11] This diversity is also expressed in the variations of "spiritual" talk surrounding the ney. For example, for some players the ney is hailed as an "instrument of the soul," supposedly endowed with a natural ability to express the inner voice of the individual. The material form of the instrument serves as one primary proof of this metaphoric association. Given its reed structure, the ney is celebrated for its "simplicity," its "naturalness" and its "purity," qualities that appear to make it ideal for achieving "wholeness" and "inner transformation." For some serious Muslims, the ney's intrinsic spirituality is revealed in its thin, vertical shape, melded with *alif*, the first letter of the Arabic alphabet, with its symbolic reference to the oneness of God. Here, ney playing unlike, say, piano music, constitutes an activity conducive to deeper piety. Its sound is said "to arouse a desire to worship" and "to draw oneself closer to God," as one learner described it. Similarly, the world music artist Omar Faruk Tekbilek claims that "the ney plays the breath of God" (Bessman 2002).

Although the ney's spiritual associations have a clear historical genealogy in its long service to the musical practices of Sufi orders, its recent recontextualization as a spiritual tool also has other important, interwoven facets. As a growing body of writing in ethnomusicology has observed, other flute traditions (but not all) have been entangled in similar processes of "spiritualization." Take the Japanese *shakuhachi*, for example. Jay Keister explains that "a key factor in the overseas success of the *shakuhachi* is precisely its historical links to Buddhism and the ease with which philosophical ideas based on Zen can be articulated or felt through the instrument." The outcome, he says, is that the shakuhachi "now leads a dual existence" (2004, 100). While it continues to be a key instrument of Japanese classical music, its second mode of existence outside Japan relates to its social life as a spiritual tool.

What Keister claims for the shakuhachi can also go for the ney. Yet unlike the former, it is not just non-Turkish enthusiasts who appreciate the ney's spiritual status. Although the ney has been long endowed with a mystical charisma, its symbolism and spiritual associations have come to resonate so strongly for Turks that, according to several masters, they seem to have drowned out the instrument's musical qualities.[12] While no one narrative captures the ney's changing meanings, a number of contemporary developments do stand out.

Anthropological investigation has highlighted the discursive construction of "tradition," "spirituality," and "authenticity" in world music.[13] A similar close connection can be discerned between the "spiritualization" of the ney and recent artistic and commercial developments in the global and Turkish music industry. As I discuss in chapter 1, following the successful marketing of Turkish "Sufi music" as a subgenre of "world music" in the mid-1990s, the ney has become insinuated into a disparate variety of musical styles that are labeled "Sufi." This new revitalized "Sufi music" comprises a highly eclectic assortment of musical forms, aesthetic styles, sonic practices, and repertoire, from its "world music"[14] expressions to an even more varied collection of musical performance burgeoning within popular music parlance in Turkey. No single or unifying musical signature or artistic style seems to define a distinct genre of Sufi music. Yet the use of ney sound appears to be one vital aural element shared by this disparate set of musical products in which a "spiritual" dimension is claimed as a marketing strategy. As Bohlman notes, one issue at stake here is the shifting ownership of Sufi musical practice. Unlike in the past, its ownership no longer belongs to members of a Sufi order or derives from their devotional sites but has now passed to the consumer, transforming what was once an essentially religious music to "spiritual music" (1997, 67; on Sufi music, see During 1999; Qureshi 2013).

Yet consumers are not the only "owners" of this re-created Sufi music that finds appeal today. Turkish state actors, too, have claimed possession. Ironically, despite the continuing prohibition of Sufi orders by law, today the Ministry of Culture and Tourism appears to be one of the most vigorous promoters of Mevlevi-inspired Sufi music. The state-sponsored annual *sema* ceremonies showcased each December in Konya where Mevlâna's tomb and the central Mevlevi dergâh are located have turned the city into a must-see tourist destination in Turkey for domestic and foreign crowds alike. In chapter 1, I trace out how the ney's entanglement in the touristification, commodification, and nationalization of Mevlevi-inspired practices sponsored by both private and state actors in Turkey constitutes an important social context wherein it interacts with its audiences.

"In the Ney We Find Ourselves"

2014. Inside the newly built and gigantic presidential palace in Ankara, a prize ceremony honors the recipients of the annual Presidential Arts and Culture Award. As host, President Recep Tayyip Erdoğan delivers the keynote speech, recognizing the exemplary contribution that each one of the four eminent award recipients has made to the nation's cultural and intellectual life in the areas of music, literature, cinema, and history. Along with the celebratory notes, he strikes an aggrieved tone as well:

> For too long, we have heard the claim that "no artist, scholar, or intellectual emerges from us." But despite all their efforts to blunt the soul of our nation and our civilization, despite their aiming at the veins of our knowledge, wisdom and morals, they could not stop our arts and artists from growing. The seed has been thrown upon the soil with such genuine feelings and prayers that, regardless of any storms or droughts, it continues to flourish. . . . Thanks be to God. Despite their endeavor to estrange us from ourselves [*yabancılaştırma*] we still have masters who know themselves, their nation, and their civilization. . . . How ungrateful would it be to orphan our old [*kadim*] music, our art of calligraphy, paper-marbling [*ebru*], and [the Islamic arts of illumination] *tezhip* and *tezyin*, just because they are not appreciated and recognized in certain parts of the world.[15]

In the category of music, the artist selected is Niyazi Sayın, proclaimed by Erdoğan as "the pole [*kutup*] of all neyzens." Acknowledging Sayın's exceptional contribution to Turkish classical music (*Türk klasik müziği*) as well as to Sufi music (*tasavvuf müziği*), Erdoğan also expresses his gratitude for Sayın's dedication, not only to the ney but at the same time to "our classical art forms." "May God bless him," Erdoğan concludes, "for he expresses us to ourselves" (*bize bizi anlattığı için*).

What is at issue in the AKP's wooing of the ney? And who—foreigners? secularists?—is it who claims "we" cannot foster the development of great artists? Which "them" and "we" are implicated here? Similarly, what or whom does

Erdoğan hear in Sayın's ney that moves him to assert that its sound "expresses us to ourselves"? And how is it that the ney's sonic qualities express this "collective self"?

By now there is a long acknowledgement of Tayyip Erdoğan's tendency to employ "us versus them" rhetoric in his speeches. Sometimes "us and them" are implied, leaving it to his primed audiences to fill in the terms for themselves. At other times, the naysayers or the alien others are named, either Turkey's "laicists" or (behind them) the "crusader West," each charged with betraying or denigrating the "us" or "we." Thus his accusative rhetoric conjoins with praise of the self, generated through an imaginative discourse of a superior Ottoman civilizational heritage, projected as the source of the "real" traditions, cultural values, and morality of a Turkish-Muslim national community. Jenny White claims that this "new Turkish identity," or "Muslim nationalism" is "that of a pious Muslim Turk whose subjectivity and vision for the future is shaped by an imperial Ottoman past overlaid onto a republican state framework, but divorced from the Kemalist state project" (2013, 9).[16] Taken as a whole, Erdoğan's speech articulates with this Muslim nationalism, as it seeks to induce in listeners' intensification of their mood. The affect at work is Muslim Pride: "We, too, raise up great artists."

Chapters 6 and 7 explore various discourse about which collective self the sound of the ney may express. To be sure, the ney has long been a "natural symbol" in Sufism. The "expressive powers" of the reed flute have constituted a fertile motif in the literary texts of Sufi Islam, embroidered into its poetry and prose (Schimmel 2005, 1980). What more eloquent example than the poetry of Mevlâna Celâleddin Rumî? Rumi's twenty-six-thousand-verse magnum opus, the *Mesnevi-ya Ma'navi* (Doublets of Meaning), which the great Persian Sufi poet Jami (d. 1492) famously described as "the Qur'an in the Persian tongue," is *the* book that immortalizes the ney as the "Perfect Human" (*insan-ı kamil*) in whom divine attributes are embodied. Rumi opens his masterwork with the following lines:

> Listen to the reed how it tells a tale, complaining of separation
> Saying: "Ever since I was parted from the reed-bed, my lament has caused man and woman to moan.
> I want a bosom torn by severance, that I may unfold the pain of love-desire.
> Every one who is left far from his source wishes back the time when he was united with it . . ."[17]

In Rumi's allegory just as the reed is now parted from its reed-bed, so the human soul is separated from its original source: each yearns "for reunification." For Rumi it is this archetypal longing and love for the Beloved that the wailing sound of the ney expresses. And just as the reed-flute needs the breath of its neyzen, the "human-ney" seeks the breath of its Creator; only then does sound/music emerge. The ney in Rumi's "language-game" is nothing other than the human being: each is an instrument in the neyzen's/God's hands.

In Turkey the influence of Rumi's spiritual teachings and of the Mevlevi tradition is not new. And despite the order's historic suppression by the Republic, in the current context of proliferating consumerist practices that take advantage of the Mevlevi spiritual imagery (Vicente 2007), fragments of Rumi's poetry circulate more widely than ever in the public sphere. The president's award ceremony is no exception. Citing selected lines from the *Mesnevi*, Erdoğan also produces suggestive meanings about "us" and the beloved ney: "This noise of the reed is fire, it is not wind: whoso hath not this fire, may he be naught!" An irony emerges. While Sufism keeps the referential and aural meanings of the ney universal—the ney speaks to/for all suffering humanity—in the communal self-instituting discourse of Erdoğan this expansive vision is displaced by a contracting one. Rumi hears the voice of the ney as expressive of the human condition, while the president claims its voice for an *imaginary* collective Turkish-Muslim self.

In response, eighty-seven-year old Sayın walks onto the podium, modestly greeting the audience in the "dervish style," right hand pressed against the heart, head bowed, eyes cast toward the ground. Master of the stage, he delivers a few words:

> Due to my age I can no longer play the ney. But this award bestowed on me by our honorable president is a spiritual [*manevi*] award, a composition, the most beautiful composition that I will ever get to play, even an *ayin-i şerif*,[18] and that I will strive to play not with my body [*bedenen*] but with my heart *inşallah* [*the audience applauds*] . . .
>
> There is a Qur'anic verse inscribed on the coffin: "*Küllu Nefsin Zaiketu'l-Mevt*" [Every soul shall have a taste of death].[19] The *nefs* dies, it says, but not the human being [*insan*]. *İnsan* never dies, and *insan* will never die, because it is the most excellent of all works of the Supreme Being. From God we expect everything. We are meant to know ourselves and then know the one that is to be known. As you know, there is a hadith saying, "*Men Arefe Nefsehu Fekad Arefe Rabbehu*" [He who knows himself knows God].

Concluding suddenly, he exits the stage.

Sayın voices a contradictory position and embodies a contrary mood to that of Erdoğan, even if he does not explicitly disagree with him. He makes no effort to reinforce the "voice of cultural intimacy" (Stokes 2010) that devout Muslim Turks, who feel belittled by the Kemalist state, hear in the sound of the ney. Nor does he seek to cultivate political resentment at historic treatment or express vindication through "our ability to produce artists," unlike Erdoğan. Conspicuous by its absence is any reference to a communal subjectivity. What is at stake for Sayın is not privileging a Turkish-Muslim identity but a notion of self that is at once universal and individual and whose ontic status is ascribed to God. To put it another way, he presents us an Islamic but not an Islamizing and/or nationalizing discourse in which the art of ney playing—or, more generally, those art traditions often dubbed as "Islamic," "traditional,"[20] or "classical arts" (*geleneksel/klasik sanatlar*)—is envisioned as a tool for inculcating individuals into a self-serving and inward-looking political collectivity ("our nation," "our civilization"). Instead, he constructs a contrasting normative meaning for/about Islam, articulating what he recognizes as being important about Islam: namely, the fundamental Sufi idea that that all creation/selves are a manifestation of the Supreme (the Akbarian concept of *vahdet-i vücud*—literally, oneness or unity of being); and the importance of self-knowledge as a means for attaining Divine knowledge.[21] Both ideas are digested in and efficaciously communicated through the famous hadith that is a Sufi motto, recited in his speech: "*He who knows himself knows God.*"[22]

In short, the same ney and its biography allows Erdoğan and Sayın to indicate very different understandings of being and living as a Muslim. Indeed, the differences gestured to in their speeches testify to serious incompatibilities between versions of Islam that revealed themselves in my fieldwork with ney musicians. Although this book's primary concern is the lifetime of "sweet servitude" required for becoming a skilled practitioner of the ney, the larger context and one core aspect of this learning experience is the creative engagement of this musical practice with Islam (a *musical Islam*). As we will see throughout this book, this pedagogy brings music, through myriad ways, into a mutually effecting relationship with Islam (as well as with other spheres of social life). This is most explicitly manifested in Salih Hoca's spoken language, which, with its rich metaphoric texture, crisscrosses between music and various Sufi epistemological ideas all the time, inviting in his listeners analogous relations and reasoning between musical and other kinds of knowledge.

In chapter 7 I discuss how this intertwining of music and Islam differs strikingly from many other forms of Muslim music-making that has become the primary focus of recent anthropological scholarship on music and Islam. In those music endeavors we often find a mobilizing urge to communicate a religious message through the artistic practice, or an explicit intention to transform individual subjects into "better" Muslims. There is a strong tendency in many studies of music practices engaged in by Muslims to link such music-making to a legalistic mode of Islamic discourse and then to privilege piety as a primary object of study.

This tendency is perhaps most evident in one particularly influential strand of anthropological research on Islam that focuses on Muslim "piety movements" and ethical "self-fashioning," crystallizing around the work of Saba Mahmood (2005) and Charles Hirschkind (2006). Along with other scholars (Schielke 2009; Mittermaier 2012), my uneasiness with anthropology's engagement with the study of Muslim ethics, to which Mahmood's and Hirschkind's studies have made important contributions, is that this research program has become increasingly characterized by the privileging of one particular form and practice of Islam that is oriented toward its discursive and legal traditions. Insufficient attention, in turn, is given to a broad array of other ways of becoming Muslim where the prescriptive projects of Islamic law are not high on people's agenda.

In chapters 6 and 7 I examine how Hezarfen's musical discourse on Islam and/or its Islamic discourse on music is oriented toward a goal other than the authorization or prescription of "correct" practice. I find Shahab Ahmed's (2016) idea of "explorative discourse" useful for revealing how music and Islam intertwine in this learning environment. For Ahmed, the distinction between the prescriptive and explorative discourses of Muslims reside in their position toward authority: "Whereas the proponent of prescriptive authority views his authority as a license to prescribe to another, the bearer of explorative authority views his authority as a license to *explore* (by) himself" (283, original emphasis).[23] Sayın's gnomic words above, too, epitomize this valuing of the task of exploration for he emphasizes self-knowledge as a means for reaching the Divine: "*He who knows himself knows God.*"

Ethical Modification

For the dedicated group of practitioners with whom I worked, participation in meşk-style learning is a transforming (*dönüştürücü*) experience. This transformation occurs not only in learners' physical skills and sensory capacities (in other words, modes of hearing the world) but also entails learning a new way of being-in-the-world. Meşk is fundamentally a process of self-change, even if that may not be the intent of those novices who take it up.

The approach I take in this book to explore the relationship between enskillment and subject formation builds on insights from the anthropological literature that credits the self-making potential of apprenticeship-style learning. Mastering a musical instrument, a craft, a form of dance, or a martial art "involves the body in ways beyond technical competence" (Qureshi 2000, 808), entailing the crafting of a particular kind of embodied subject (see Marchand 2008; 2009; Weidman 2012). Emphasizing the situatedness of learning that requires one's full participation in a community of practice, Lave and Wenger suggest an understanding of learning that takes into account "the historical production, transformation and change of persons" (1991, 51) enabled by systems of relations: "learning involves the whole person; it implies not only a relation to specific activities, but a relation to social communities—it implies becoming a full participant, a member, a kind of person" (1991, 53). Apprenticeship, in this sense, is akin to a practice of ethical character formation.

For instance, in an anthropological analysis of learning the *saz*, a type of long-necked lute iconic of folk music in Turkey, Rebecca Bryant argues that to become good at the saz, one must "become the type of person who can play the saz," involving, among other things, learning to "become a good Turk of a particular type, one capable of displaying in behavior and comportment a masculine Turkishness" (2005, 224–25). Bryant describes this "self-conscious self-making" realized through a music discipline as "empersonment." Similarly, the relationship between musical apprenticeship and selfhood is also the focus of Denise Gill's recent work on present-day Ottoman classical musicians in Turkey. Analyzing the ways in which melancholy and a narrative of "death of Ottoman music" play a role in the shaping of musicians' moral subjectivities, Gill discerns that "to be a competent, participating musician of this genre, one must adopt and circulate a narrative discourse of loss that constitutes one's personhood as a melancholic modality" (2017, 58). By contrast, I found that in Hezarfen the primary affect informing ethical self-change is not melancholic so much as activist, in the sense that it encourages a crafting of one's life to the best of one's ability, just as becoming a musician involves doing the best one can do. As Salih Hoca always said, "*Allah* loves the doers of good,"[24] an ethic that applied to living in the city, to understanding its affordances, and to the taking of pleasure from its qualities as well as from its material craft objects (chapter 6).

These insights into musical apprenticeship perceived as an event of self-alteration are useful for thinking about the particular transformative potential of meşk and how it shapes learners' ethical dispositions and conduct. To capture this process, I use the term "ethical modification" as an analytical device. Unlike the idea of "empersonment" or fabrication of "personhood" (Yen 2005), ethical modification does not suggest that a new ethical subject is re-born through the skilled practice. My concern here is to avoid overemphasizing the efficacy of the skilled practice in fashioning radically different moral selves or to avoid imputing a more totalistic reconstruction of selfhood. Selves are rarely formed by single causes. In the rapidly changing, globalized yet nationalistic city of Istanbul, individual ney-learners' intentions toward the world are conditioned by a range of social forces that also seek to deposit in them certain ethical sensibilities, affectual capacities, and modes of apprehension and perception. In the case of modern Turkey, actors' perceptions of the world, of spirituality, of living a modern life, of nationalism, and so on, can also be partially attributed to the work of efficacious experience-constituting state institutions such as the Turkish military, the nationalist education system, state-sanctioned historiography, patriarchy, private mass media, and the Republic's urban practices and design of cities (see Houston 2005), all of which seek to condition inhabitants' spatial experiences, affective loyalties, and everyday practices. Recognizing that selves are made by multiple, and even contradictory moral horizons, ethical modification provides a more modest take on the process of self-change. More important, a focus on ethical modifications helps us grasp the temporality of change, as it understands subject constitution as articulating (complementing or contradicting) with existing ethical dispositions and sensibilities, including the gradual reshaping of them through long-term engagement with a practice.

In what ways is meşk inducive to transforming the moral character of ney learners? Chapter 6 delineates dual processes through which learners modify their ethical sense. The first is via the musical training itself. The ethical dispositions orienting this artistic practice (for example, humility, surrender, an ethos of responsibility and service, and the like) inhere in concrete music practices—that is, in learning to play the ney in a certain style. A wide range of actions, from obtaining a ney, learning a certain repertoire, and mastering modes to imitating the movements of a master's hand and discerning listening are implicated as ethical concerns. Musical technique and comportment—ways of sitting, speaking, and so on—have ethical import or substance. Ethical virtues preside over each step of the corporeal investment that goes into gaining technical mastery. The Aristotelian tradition of ethics, which has also been taken up by a number of pioneering anthropological works on Muslims' piety and ethical self-fashioning (for example, Mahmood 2005) is instructive here, as it gives attention to the way internal virtuous capacities may be acquired through external practices (rather than through individuals' following of general societal rules).[25]

Second, the ethnographic material in this book guides us to think through an approach to ethics that goes beyond a self-contained subject "caring" for themselves (to channel Foucault) to consider more fully the intersubjective and relational dimensions of "'self'-making." Learning through meşk is fundamentally about learning a relationship. For the people I worked with, meşk implies more than just doing a lesson with one's hoca—it essentially means *rabıta* (relation, bond). This intense learning relationship relies on strong affective ties, mobilizing "fantastic fidelities," as Weidman (2006) notes, for the Indian *guru-shishya*, including, first and foremost, the talebe's surrender (*teslimiyet*) and loyalty (*sadakât*) to his or her hoca, which then opens up a possibility for the talebe to become a member of that lineage of musicians. As autobiographical reflections from ney artists in the following chapters reveal, the learning institution of hoca-talebe translates as a lifetime of learning. The relationship continues on even after one's hoca has died.

Further, the intersubjective nature of learning and ethical becoming extends beyond the master-student relationship, encompassing participation in the sociality of the broader community of practice. As we will see in chapter 6, "lessons" at Hezarfen spill over into other spheres of everyday life, inviting learners to participate in a wide range of extramusical activities, from visiting Istanbul's Muslim places and going around the city's secondhand markets to cooking, all done with/in the presence of others. Embedded in a rich web of social interaction and exchange, the ney pedagogy fosters new forms of urban competencies and sensibilities in skilled practitioners, enabling in them certain ways of being and acting in the world. Learning is not merely a matter of acquiring skills but involves intersubjective exchange with other skilled practitioners.

This view of learning as a process of participation is often missing in conceptualizations of meşk where the analytical trope of "transmission" (*intikâl*) appears to be the de facto explanatory model to describe the process by which musical knowledge and morals are inherited: "socio-cultural codes" (Behar 2012, 73–100; Karakayalı 2010, 347), "ethical principles" (*ahlâki kaideler*) or "patterns of mentality" (*zihniyet kalıpları*) (Ayas 2015, 81), and "cultural attributes" are said to be passed down through chains of transmission (Gill-Gürtan 2011, 616). This framing of enskillment as a means for "cultural reproduction and transmission" (Karakayalı 2010, 344) misrecognizes the fundamental connection between learning, knowing, and discovering. Knowledge is reduced here to preexisting cultural content that gets reproduced over time. As Marchand says, and as the ethnography here shows, knowledge is not something "received" through a "hierarchical and methodical transfer"; rather, it is *made* through "a dialogical and constructive engagement between people, and between people, things, and environment" (2010, iv). The learner's body, thus conceived, is not a "transmitter" and "receiver" of information of cultural categories but is the wellspring of know-how (Lock 1993, 136).[26] Thus, the approach I take up here does not conceive of ethical practice as knowledge of a corpus of "rules" or "codes" coextensive with a certain culture. Ethical becoming is not an inculcation of moral codes. Rather, by returning to Aristotle, we can take ethical modifications to be inextricably connected to training practices that are intended to transform the practitioner.

Crucially, the analytical task of discerning how efficacious this musical discipline is in shaping practitioners' ethical selves poses a challenge for anthropological fieldwork. Ethical becoming is processual, and human existence and perception is historical, layered through time. Thus there are temporal constraints in studying its unfolding.

But every account of change and subjectivity faces this challenge. For example, the voluminous literature on neoliberalism as public policy in Istanbul claims that it also fosters in people modification of mood and emotion, as well as a change of cognition—the generating of a "neoliberal self." Gökarıksel and Mitchell write that neoliberal governance regulates and disciplines subjects so that they "come to understand their own positions and personhood in ways that are compatible with neoliberal trends towards greater individual autonomy and entrepreneurship" (2005, 149). Similarly, Türken et al. claim that in Turkey, neoliberal governmentality "works by instilling in society a concept of human subject as an autonomous, individualized, self-directing decision-making agent who becomes an entrepreneur of one self, a human capital" (2016, 33). Yet, ironically, their "proof" involves presentation of media discourses on self-development in Turkey, with no examination of their reception. In brief, analysts of neoliberalism (for example, Ong 2006) perceive it as a political project that seeks to fabricate a new "subjectivity" in actors, fostering and reinforcing qualities, dispositions, and motivations that facilitate particular conduct or strategic actions for those engaging with and addressed by the policy regime. In making such claims many critics appear to have a "shallow" conception of the individual self as *primarily* conditioned by particular fields of relations (work, welfare, and educational domains) in which neoliberal policies, performance, and language predominate.

By contrast, as the anthropology of ethics (see Faubion 2011; Robbins 2012; Lambek 2010) shows, people's sentiments, moods, self-understandings, goals, ethics, and acts are constituted in richer spheres of activity and interaction than the analysis (and critique) of neoliberalism allows. One vital concern of this research program has been issues of freedom (see Robbins 2012; Laidlaw 2002), which involves a turn away from presumptions of the conditioning of human behavior by social structures or inculcated modes of perception to a more open exploration of people's exercise of the practice of freedom even in the web of constraining cultural and social relations in which they are placed. Preoccupied too much with questions of social regularity, analyses of the "neoliberal self" does not fully account for how human beings reflect upon and change their categories of practice and ways of perceiving the world.

Apprenticeship as Fieldwork Methodology

All of this discussion on ethics, intersubjectivity, loyalty, and relationships has serious consequences for the issue of my fieldwork methodology, as well as for how that research is rediscovered and re-presented in my ethnographic writing. Much of the material in *Musical Ethics and Islam* derives from two years of fieldwork I conducted in Istanbul between 2012 and 2015, followed by subsequent shorter research trips in 2016, 2017, and 2018. One excellent way to study how one becomes a neyzen—there must be others—is to submit to the transformative potential of the musical practice by becoming a talebe oneself. Thus, an apprentice-style method formed the core activity of my field research in Istanbul, involving my own learning experience of ney playing from Salih Hoca at his Üsküdar school. This was supplemented by observational activity undertaken at a number of other ney teaching sites in Istanbul and by interviews I conducted with ney masters and learners.

Participation in the social life of Salih Hoca's school provided ample opportunity for ethnographic apprenticeship, bringing the excitement of learning the ney through exposure to Salih Hoca's pleasurable lessons as well as a vibrant world of music-making and socializing that facilitated numerous conversations with the performers, aficionados, and dedicated learners of Ottoman classical music. The communal nature of Salih Hoca's meşk practice ensured an inimitable opportunity to learn together with/from my fellow-talebes. During the time I took lessons there were more than eighty people coming to the workshop every week from different parts of the city: roughly half of them had been learning from Salih Hoca for more than five years. The majority of these adult learners (their ages ranging from early twenties to sixties) were active in the workforce (involving medical doctors, IT specialists, accountants, schoolteachers, small-business owners, and so on), including university students as well. Women made up roughly one-third of the students. I am immensely grateful for their offering of insights about their own learning experiences and for their making Salih Hoca's lessons virtually available by recording and sharing them with me when I had to suspend my presence in the "field" due to the other demands of professional life.

Because in apprentice-style methodology the en-minded body becomes the primary site of learning, knowing, and transformation, this approach facilitates for the apprentice fieldworker a kind of relationship with (and intimacy to) the "field" that is somewhat different from other forms of "participant observation" commonly taken up in anthropological investigation. By deliberately subjecting one's own self to the modifications—physical, perceptual, moral—generated by the practice under scrutiny, ethnographic apprenticeship transforms the body into the "field," allowing a peculiar way of knowing from "within." There is no substitute for apprehending the embodied substance and multisensory force of a practice (be it craft, sport, or other aesthetic exercise) than through the experience-centered analysis that this kind of approach affords.[27] Apprenticeship fosters affective ties that connect skilled practitioners to a larger sociality, including the relationships of intimacy that we find in the intersubjective institution of the hoca-talebe.

However, as much as it opens up methodological avenues for examining the slow process by which individuals become experts in a particular skill or specialized knowledge, an apprenticeship approach also brings its own challenges to the anthropological project. Entering into the intersubjective field of meşk extracts certain obligations, which must be accomplished if the researcher is to continue doing fieldwork. Most significantly, it requires deep loyalty and allegiance to one's hoca, a practical value that might hinder other desirable ideals of the anthropological enterprise. For instance, ethnographic fieldwork also requires a "city-wide" familiarity with the larger field of the ney so as to investigate the plural material, pedagogical, and social worlds that the instrument is entangled in. Thus, reconciling my dual subject position as a talebe on the one hand and as an ethnographer on the other was no straightforward task, as the moral obligations constituting these two endeavors were not easily made compatible. Indeed, my survey visits to other ney teaching sites and occasional brief participation in the classes taught by other ney masters were contrary to the ethics expected in Salih Hoca's studio. This tension became an enduring issue in my fieldwork. Yet it also alerted me to the "jealous" gift exchange sponsored in meşk pedagogy and to the significance of the relational bond forged with one's hoca that in the long run cultivates in prospective neyzens an ethic of authority and service (*hizmet*).

Further, tension, struggle, and confrontation are inherent in the social world described in this book, and these are negotiated by talebes as they crawl through the slow-learning process. Not all novices can keep up with the obligations and emotional challenges necessitated by this intense kind of learning, and breakdowns of hoca-talebe relations are not uncommon. Although I write about the contested nature of the hoca-talebe institution in chapter 6, my own situated status as a talebe and the power hierarchies at work within the apprenticeship context are conditions that have inevitably shaped my ethnographic description of the ney-playing world and the authority of the hoca in this learning relationship. Thus, readers might feel that there is a "hagiographic" quality to some of my accounts of Salih Hoca's words and teachings. Yet how could it not be so? In the process of my apprenticeship and in my attempts to faithfully represent its unfolding in writing, I continue in part to perform the condition I analyze, the talebe-hoca relationship.[28]

The ethical sensibilities informing the subject position of a talebe are entailed in the very use of this term. The Arabic roots of this word, *tlb* (to seek, to demand, to request), connotes that learning is an orientation produced by the pupil. The talebe is the one who strives after knowledge, showing in their bearing and actions a willing commitment to learn. Although the "modern" Turkish equivalent of this term, *öğrenci* (pupil), reigned in some other lesson contexts that I came across during fieldwork, learners at Hezarfen were strongly encouraged to perform the role of a talebe. Although both words seem to indicate similar subject positions—one whose duty is to learn—different degrees of agency undergird their shades of meaning. Unlike *talebe*, the word *öğrenci* is imbued with a pragmatic functionality, made linguistically possible by the suffix *-ci*. A "job-like" implication inheres in its use: a student is one whose task is to learn. Linguistically engineered by the state in the Turkish Republic's language revolution (*Dil Devrimi*) enacted in the high period of Kemalism (1920–1940s), the newly coined term *öğrenci* replaced in common speech the word *talebe*. If the systematic expulsion of Arabic and Persian words from the new "Turkish" vocabulary was one vital aim of the language reforms, the consolidation of the new Turkish vocabulary with the invention of new words (or by words borrowed from Western European languages, including French, German, and, increasingly, English) was its other core dimension (Lewis 1999). Language does not merely express or reflect the world, it also generates certain ways of perceiving it. Thus, in musicians' deliberate choice to use the word *talebe*—Salih Hoca is not the only one—can be seen a constituting of a certain relationship between student and teacher, which reveals the structure of exchange between them: students surrender to the authority of their hoca as core aspect of their desire to actively take knowledge from them.

Finally, just as it is imperative to reflect upon the dual roles and demands of apprentice and researcher, I should also underline the dual subject position that lineage masters themselves inhabit within the moral economy of this artistic practice. As I discuss in chapter 6 more fully, being a talebe is not an ethical subject position that one dis-inhabits after becoming fully competent in the art. The most skilled master never ceases to be a talebe vis-à-vis their own hoca. In short, one never stops being both at the same time. Thus, while Salih Hoca's teaching practices appear as the focus of this book, in another way he is also my key informant as a talebe. His students observe his submissive demeanor whenever his own aged master drops into the studio.

In showing himself always to be a student of Niyazi Sayın,[29] Salih Hoca also proves the efficacy of the artistic-ethical modifications that he had gone through as a talebe. His own surrender reveals how the experience of [his] apprenticeship transforms moral selves. Further, if long-term fieldwork can grasp only a portion of a person's development or change, a second proof of the transformative power of this pedagogic practice is revealed in Salih Hoca's own teaching method. The relationship between his own student experience and his current teaching practice is worth considering because of the light it sheds on the efficacy of the virtuous qualities and capacities acquired in his own apprenticeship. His teaching music through the skillful practice of sohbet is itself a consequence of his previous ethical modifications.

Before we take a look at the core skills and perceptual modifications that education in ney music facilitates, in chapter 1 we visit some of the key episodes in the ney's public life in modern Turkey, accentuating the primary moments in the relevant prehistory of its ongoing revival.

CHAPTER ONE

A Biography of the Ney

UNDER THE MEDITERRANEAN SEA, in Turkey's first underwater sculpture museum, a parliament of whirling dervishes showcase their "mystic" ritual for adventurist scuba divers. Opened to the public in 2015, the museum promises its visitors a unique excursion to some 110 installations, clustered according to their "cultural" importance. Ranging from "Mevlevi *neyzens*," "Poseidon," and "Camel Trail" to the "Turkish War of Independence," together these giant sculptures reveal, as one local official reports, "the richness of Anatolian civilization."[1]

How is it that an instrument—the ney—deemed incompatible with the project of Turkish modernity less than a century ago, has come to stand in for Turkey's cultural richness? What contemporary processes entangle it in heritage and tourism? In this chapter I address the checkered public life of the ney as a fulcrum point of interactions between individual, national, and extranational actors and a musical nexus of material, artistic, symbolic, and pedagogical practices and meanings. Eliot Bates's question about "how instruments become contested sites of meaning" (2012, 369) is especially relevant. To explore this, I trace the key shifts in the ney's modern history following the institution of the Turkish Republic in 1923. If the snapshots of ney-centered practices here do not provide us with its complete biography, they do reveal major changes of fortune that have occurred in its "social life" (Bates 2012), from its delegitimization in the single-party period, its survival in the transitional years of its learning, and playing in private house meetings to its re-invigoration in the 1990s.

FIGURE 1.1 The sculptures displayed at Side Underwater Museum.

These episodes underline how the meanings derived from and informing the ney are context bound and historically (socially and politically) constructed. Although in this chapter I focus mainly on the ney, I occasionally shift my focus to foreground Ottoman music: their relationship can be likened, in good Sufi fashion, to that between a reed and a reed bed.

Locating the Ney in the Ottoman Musical Milieu

Ney playing held a central place in the musical life of the Ottoman Empire. As both the primary wind instrument of Ottoman classical music and as a leading sound accompanying the singing voice, the ney contributed to both sacred and profane streams of this urban or, better, city music (*şehir musikisi*),[2] which developed as an independent genre from the late sixteenth century on.[3] Its musical-aesthetic conventions, artistic styles, and repertoire, both vocal and instrumental, continued to mature throughout the seventeenth and eighteenth centuries, retaining much of their characteristic form until the early twentieth century. One quick clarification is necessary here. Although the terms "classical music," "art music," and "court music" rather clumsily imply a kind of an elite or aristocratic musical project bound firmly to the patronage of the imperial palace, the Ottoman court was by no means the only force that fostered the public life and artistic continuity of this aesthetic tradition. In addition to the palace, the performance and skilled instruction of this music emanated from a variety of urban places, from dervish lodges to synagogues, churches, mansions, homes, mosques, and coffeehouses. As Behar underlines in nearly all of his writings on Ottoman music history, this musical tradition had an autonomous capacity to sustain its vitality even in the absence of court patronage and of its propagation by the ruling elite (2015; 1993).

This segues into another important dimension of the Ottoman music world. In Istanbul, the Empire's capital city, this music found a participant audience in a wide spectrum of the urban population, including artisans, bureaucrats, Sufi dervishes, members of the *ulema*, mosque cantors, and so on. Similarly, the genealogies of artist lineages demonstrate wide variety in the social background of master musicians, whose active participation in the compositional, performative, and educational practices of the music cut across both class and ethnoreligious lines. Unlike its transformed version, which under the ethnic project of the Republic came to be known as "Turkish classical music," Ottoman music-making was a multiethnic practice. As Feldman notes, "While several social groups, e.g. Mevlevi dervishes, Jewish synagogue cantors, Greek church psalters and others tended to have distinct lines of musical transmission, none of them was entirely closed to outsiders" (1996, 18). Indeed Jackson's (2011) work on Jewish musical transmission in the late Ottoman period demonstrates the vibrant musical interchange and conviviality that was shared between different ethnoreligious communities of musicians around the communal spaces of Mevlevi lodges, synagogues, and churches. Crucially, her work also foregrounds how this element of cosmopolitanism characterized the social fabric of the historical chains of masters and pupils, vivified by the intimate teaching and learning practice of meşk.

While it was in such diverse social milieus that the art of ney playing matured under the Ottomans, it is no secret that the reed-flute became the companion of one particular influential patron of Ottoman classical music: the Mevlevi dervishes. By the early eighteenth century, the majority of neyzens in Istanbul were either dervishes or sympathizers of the Mevlevi order, a class that took a leading role in the transmission and diffusion of the Ottoman music repertoire, both religious and secular, among the urban population. The ney enjoyed a vibrant public life in the Sufi devotional sites (dergâhs or tekkes), where it was accorded pride of place within the religious discipline and musical practices of dervishes, as indicated by its hailing with the title of *nây-ı şerîf* (sacred ney). The predominance of Sufi masters in the genealogies of neyzen lineages up until the twentieth century is remarkable. The artist lineage central to this book also demonstrates this. "Our way goes back to [Armenian] Oskiyam Efendi," pronounces the great Neyzen Niyazi Sayın during one of our conversations, immediately putting forward his musical-spiritual kinship before his individual being. Although a complete genealogy cannot be recited, Sayın is able to trace his lineage back five generations, revealing a family of neyzen masters, including his own master Halil Dikmen (1906–1964), his teacher Emin (Yazıcı) Dede (1883–1945), his teacher in turn Aziz Dede (1835–1905), Sâlim Bey (1829?-1885), and Neyzen Oskiyam (d. 1870). While Oskiyam, who was well-versed in both the ney and tanbur, was hired to teach at the music school of the palace (known as *Enderun*) during the reign of Mahmud II (1808–1839), the three successive members of this lineage had been initiated into musical mastership primarily through Sufi orders. Sâlim Bey had been attached to the Sâdiyye order, while also being a *muhib* (sympathizer) of the Mevlevi order (Ergun 1943, 502). Üsküdar-born Aziz Dede and his talebe Emin Dede, on the other hand, were both dervishes of the Mevlevi path and were deeply involved in the social life of this order in Istanbul. Having become initiated to musical disciplining at the Cairo Mevlevi lodge (*mevlevihane*), Aziz Dede served as the chief ney player (*neyzenbaşı*) of Istanbul's three Mevlevi lodges (Galata, Üsküdar, and Bahariye). It is reported that every Friday he would offer ney lessons ex gratia in his dervish cell in the Galata *mevlevihanesi* (Ayvazoğlu 2008, 37).[4] Following his death, his apprentice Emin Dede, who was a calligrapher and also employed in the maps section of the Ministry of War, took over the role of neyzenbaşı in Galata, a service that he fulfilled until the closing down of the Sufi tekkes in 1925.[5]

Even this fragment of a single lineage illuminates the intimate relationship between the ney (and Ottoman music more generally) and the Sufi orders, in particular with the Mevlevis, for whom music, unlike with the other *tarikats*, did not merely constitute a means for religious worship but was seen as Divine service in itself (Behar 2015, 143).[6] The historical role of the Mevlevi lodges as centers of music education (as well as of Islamic aesthetics in other art forms, such as calligraphy, literature, and poetry) has been well documented (Ergun 1943; Feldman 1996, 85–192). Extending over a vast region from Belgrade to Baghdad and from Cairo to Salonika, the Mevlevi lodges were key hubs for musical training and performance, offering shared space for hearing new compositions and the exchange of musical ideas. Their likening to modern conservatories attests to this historical function. The liturgical compositions (*ayin-i şerif*) performed during the primary Mevlevi ritual event, *mukabele*, are seen as the most monumental, elaborate, yet also most complex artistic expressions of Ottoman classic music.[7] These compositions became, in the words of the oud master and composer Çinuçen Tanrıkorur (1938–2000), "the school, the book, and the teacher of Ottoman music" in a later era, when, with the instituting of the Turkish Republic, this musical tradition endured a loss of prestige (2003, 30).

Mevlevi *ayin* unfold in an intricate modal, rhythmic, and melodic structure consisting of four composed vocal movements (*selams*), preceded with the recitation of *na't* (poetry in praise of the Prophet Muhammad), an opening improvisation (*taksim*) on the ney, and an instrumental interlude (*peşrev*) set in the *makam* of the ayin. While other instruments are also used, the ney and the percussion instrument *kudûm* have always been considered most essential to the mukabele, which unites music and the cosmic dance (*sema*) of whirling dervishes.[8] The extended ney improvisation performed at the beginning (known as *post taksimi*) is not only an integral part of the ritual ceremony, it is also, as Feldman (1996, 190) says, "a developed and independent art form." What makes this taksim form distinctive? According to the late Halil Dikmen, the opening ney taksimi carries a crucial function as it should bring to life the makam of the ayin in the broadest sense, displaying all melodic possibilities of that mode, and (to do so) spanning fifteen to twenty minutes (cited in Gölpınarlı 1963, 464). Feldman's words on the aesthetic specificity of this improvisational form (see chapter 4 on the taksim genre) are worth quoting at length here:

> Part of this aesthetic is an emphasis on the overtones emitted from the *ney*, and the function of the breath of the player. Some Mevlevi neyzens are articulate about this connection. For example the late Aka Gündüz Kutbay, in his conversations, used to view the breath of the neyzen as a symbol of the mystical syllable *Hû*, which articulated the fact of divine existence in the universe. . . . The *ney* could express these timbral relationships both in solo playing, and through the use of drones (*demkeş*) held by the accompanying neyzens. (1996, 97–98)

The connection between the element of breath and the musical design of the ney taksimi in the Mevlevi ceremony finds different description elsewhere. According to Neyzen Salih Bilgin, the spiritual references of the Mevlevi ayini demand that the player begin the melodic construction by voicing the lowest tones of the ney, known as *dem sesler*, before returning back to this tonal area to bring the sonic journey to a complete end. Bilgin states, "It is unbefitting if the *taksim* finishes in the middle tonal area. The correct thing to do is to bring the melody to a finish in the lowest notes. What I am talking about here is not what is correct musically speaking, but what is appropriate in the *manevi* (spiritual) sense." Bilgin proffers a theory of the affective power of the ney's low notes, a tonal area which, in the ears of many, best retains and expresses the breathy texture of the instrument's idiosyncratic sound. For him, there is something about the ney's low notes that make their particular sound timbre more effective in achieving the intended emotional and spiritual affect of the taksim.

The central place that the reed-flute was accorded in the religious-musical lives of the dervishes also had wide implications for the artistic and material features of the Ottoman/Turkish ney, while also shaping the moral principles organizing its pedagogical practices. For instance, the preference of the Mevlevi neyzens for using longer-size neys (especially the *şah* ney) due to their deeper sound required the Ottoman ney to have an additional mouthpiece (*başpare*) section.[9] Further, a particular style of ney playing known as *tekke tavrı* (tekke style) developed in the dervish lodges, characterized by long, sustained sounds and a plain, un-ornamented melodic structure.[10] Feldman adds that it was again the Mevlevis who were largely responsible for giving the ney a prestigious role in the courtly orchestra which it had never had before, emphasizing that "in the long run, this stylistic development was more influential on Turkish music than any specifically Mevlevi instrumental repertoire" (1996, 97).

In the years immediately following the founding of the Turkish Republic, this long and intimate relationship between the ney and the Sufi orders came to an end. In 1925 the Turkish state abolished Sufi orders and prohibited dervish lodges, resulting in the dissolution of the spatial relationship between ney and tekke and leading to a severely diminished role in its public life. The anti-Ottoman enactments of the Republic not only engendered a forced secularization of these religious built environments (for example, the conversion of the central *mevlevihane* in Konya into a museum) but also left the guardians and descendants of this musical tradition with no option but to make a living through other means. Thus we see Abdülbaki Dede, the last sheikh of the Yenikapı Mevlevihanesi, becoming a teacher of Persian literature at Darü'l Fünun (Istanbul University) (Feldman 2002, 108). Osman Dede, another member of the Yenikapı Mevlevihanesi, memorialized in Neyzen Doğan Özeke's (2000) memoire *Neyzenler Kahvesi* (The Neyzens' Coffeehouse), found himself making (and selling) neys in a coffee shop in Beyazıt. In the 1950s this coffee shop became a key place of musical sociality for Istanbul's neyzens.

Over and beyond its implications for the social life of the ney, the closing down of the Sufi lodges had severe consequences for the social organization of Ottoman classical music, removing one of its key patrons and leading to a loss of repertoire (see Behar 1987, 137–38). Another serious implication was the splitting of the once-close relationship between the religious and nonreligious spheres of Ottoman music-making. This absence of separation between the "religious" and the "secular" forms of musical activity had been a defining aspect of the social ethos of Ottoman musical culture. For one thing, the same groups of music experts composed both the religious and nonreligious repertoire. Prominent Sufi figures such as Hafız Post, a lay member of the Halveti order, and the Mevlevi-affiliated Buhûrîzâde Itrî, Neyzen Osman Dede, and İsmail Dede Efendi (renowned as the greatest composers of the nineteenth century) were also significant composers of the secular repertoire. Neither the aesthetic conventions nor the structural elements (for example, modes and *usûl*) underpinning the repertoire's two forms were different from each other. To become an expert practitioner, one had to master both. Thus it was the norm for secular singers (*hanende*) to commence their musical training with Qur'anic recitation, as is evident in the many mosque cantors (*hafız*) actively involved in the performance of the courtly repertoire (Feldman 1996, 84). This characteristic feature of Ottoman classical music was lost in the face of modernist separations of religious and secular fields under the Turkish Republic.

The Early Republican Era: Music Reforms

Most readers would be familiar with the institution of the modern Turkish Republic in 1923 under the leadership of Mustafa Kemal following the dissolution of the Ottoman Empire. Less well known may be its explicit Cultural Revolution (*Kültür İnkilabı*) (1923–1940s), which set out to cultivate a new national identity quarantined from the cosmopolitan Ottoman legacy (Zürcher 1998; Parla and Davison 2004). The Kemalists claimed the Republic to be radically different from its imperial predecessor in at least two fundamental ways. First, unlike the multiethnic, multireligious, and multilingual social fabric of the imperial era, the new nation-state sought to be ethnically and linguistically homogenous.[11] Second, the reforms implemented in the foundational period of the Republic showed an explicit commitment to transforming Ottoman institutions and lifeworld. This "transformationism"—one of the so-called six arrows of the political practice of Kemalism (Parla and Davison 2004)—entailed a comprehensive program reorganizing a vast range of practices pertaining to every sphere of personal and public life: from dress etiquette, languages, legal codes, education systems, and the arts (music, dance, theater, folklore, painting, sculpture, architecture) to the making of new modernist built environments and public spaces. Characterized by a distaste for religion, all these initiatives of the Kemalist state sought to transform citizens' daily practices and social relations, instilling them with new habits, embodied skills, and ethical sensibilities. Although this radical "civilizing" mission and practice of Kemalism is often inadequately described as a process of "modernization" and "westernization" (see Lewis 1961; Berkes

1964), a much better way of understanding it, following Houston, is to frame it as a "project of self-institution" by which Kemalist reformers "invested selective imaginary significations of Ottoman [and European] society with new meanings" (2012, 259).[12]

This point casts a revealing light on how Ottoman music itself became a target of the reformers in the 1920s and 1930s in their systematic attempts to formalize and disseminate certain musical styles, repertoires, and pedagogies, as well as new aesthetic meanings about "authentic" Turkish music. What was it about this art tradition that so fueled the hostility and intolerance of the Kemalist cultural brokers that they opted for a "revolution in music" (*Musiki İnkilabı*)—and not a revolution in painting or architecture—immediately after the founding of the Republic? And what strategies did they pursue to mute Ottoman music in the soundscape of the new nation and, in doing so, transform places as well as people's embodied experiences of their spatial-sonic environments?[13]

In the face of extensive social science analyses on the Republican music reforms (see Stokes 1992; Tekelioğlu 1996; Ayas 2014; Behar 2008), there is no need for me to repeat their arguments. But let me foreground one particular discursive practice of Kemalism to illuminate the ways in which the reformers invested Ottoman (and Western) music with new meanings.[14] This pertains to the modernist-positivist self-assertions that present Kemalism as a project of enlightenment and radical social transformation ceaselessly targeting superstition and irrationality. This imaginary is reflected in the binary oppositions that the official rhetoric of the music revolution made between "Western" and "Eastern" music, hearing the former as a sonic expression of "universality," "progress," and "science," and the latter as evocative of "backwardness," "irrationality," and the "past." This selective Eurocentrism condemned Ottoman music for lacking a systematic musical structure and pedagogy, as seen most clearly in the criticisms of its (supposedly) monophonic character. For example, in *The Principles of Turkism*, Ziya Gökalp (1923, 130–31), the pioneering ideologue of Turkish nationalism, claims that the "irrationality" and "artificialness" of makam music—as he hears it—lie in its "quarter tones"[15]—that is, in those tones obtained with the dividing of whole and semi-tones into smaller units. Gökalp posits "quarter tones" as a social and dispositional "problem" to be overcome, holding the note system used in Ottoman-Turkish music accountable for its "morbid" melodies.

The German composer and conductor Paul Hindemith (d. 1963) made a similar argument when commissioned by the Kemalist cadres to visit Ankara in the 1930s in order to supervise the founding of the new school of music. In his 1935 report, "The Restructuring of Turkish Musical Life," Hindemith describes Ottoman music as a "species" that had completed its biological evolution, and he recommends the replacement of its microtonal pitch system with the chromatic scale used in Western music as the only way to renew it (2013, 125). He writes:

> Today there are two varieties of music in Turkey. The city music that has been under the influence of Arabs [the second one is folk music] had already reached its peak, completing its evolution. With its concentration on monophonic melodic flow, this music has gradually exhausted its technical possibilities. What it produces today can only be a repetition of the past. . . . The intricate melodic forms of Arab music can never be transformed into pleasurable polyphony: one day every musical development must build some relationship with polyphony. (124)

Striking in Hindemith's evolutionist discourse is a way of talking about an aesthetic practice such as monophony as a symptom of "backwardness" and "lack of progress," something that inevitably becomes en passé as society follows its linear developmental trajectory. Similar modernist assumptions that posit both polyphony (and other features of Western music) as a sign of "social progress" and music reforms as a necessary correlation with "scientific change" were not rare among the reformers. For example, the famous Turkish conductor Hikmet Şimşek remarked, "Pardon me friends, correct me if I am wrong, how could the music of a nation that travels in automobiles and planes be monophonic!?" (Tanrıkorur 2004, 198). On another occasion the Education Minister Hasan Ali Yücel declared at a 1940 parliamentary discussion on the founding of the new conservatorium in Ankara, "To get rid of the *oud* because it fails to express our national sentiments, and to take in the keyboard is a requirement of science and technology" (Ayas 2014, 172). In the same discussion, the violinist Zeki Bey (Üngör) (president of the School for Music Teachers) refers to Ottoman music as music that "cannot be scientifically explained," arguing that its "unscientific" methods of teaching from master to apprentice can have no place in schools (Ayas 2014, 172–73).[16] Likewise similar positivist-modernist arguments were made about the perceived affect of those instruments associated with Ottoman music. The early Republican intellectual Ahmet Ağaoğlu asserted that "the tunes of the *ney*, its complaining, all those '*ah*' [sounds] of the oud, are the moaning of the East oppressed for centuries" (177). For him, it is the "lack of autonomy and individual freedom" in the East that makes the music of those societies generate such moods of grief and numbness.

What state-sponsored initiatives targeting Ottoman classical music happened during the 1920s and 1930s? To summarize briefly, one of the earliest measures was taken in 1925—only two years after the founding of the new nation-state—with the law (the Law on Unification of National Education) prohibiting the teaching of Ottoman music in all primary and secondary schools, while endorsing the reorganization of all music education according to the Western music curriculum. This ban continued to be effective for the next fifty years. A year later, in 1926, the Ministry of Education authorized the closing down of the Eastern music section of *Darül Elhân* (House of Tunes, later the Istanbul Municipality Conservatory), the first official conservatory of the Ottoman and Republican era.[17] Permission was given only for the continuation of repertoire work by a handful of remaining staff.[18] These acts that sought to bring the teaching and learning of Ottoman-Turkish classical music to an end were followed by other prohibitions directed at its public dissemination, including the banning of its broadcasting on the radio twice, briefly in 1928 and later in 1934.

In the meantime, in an endeavor to build up a new institutional field of music-making and pedagogy, the Kemalist reformers established in 1924 the School for Music Teachers to train teachers capable of instructing Western music (note that its curriculum limited instrumental teaching to violin, piano, flute, and cello only), sponsored young talents to take Western music training in European cities, and recruited foreign experts to consolidate classical music education. A range of mobilizing initiatives sought to aurally re-sound public places, attuning people's hearing to polyphonic music: from free performances of symphony orchestras around the country and mass dissemination of classical music repertoire through radio broadcasts to the organizing of ballroom dances to endear the Western dance music to elites and the free music lessons and performances held at *Halk Evleri* (People's Houses), the local community centers that carried out Kemalism's "enlightenment" mission of educating ordinary people from the 1930s to 1950s.[19] Meanwhile, in line with the reformist vision that the folk melodies of Anatolia would serve as the core ingredient of the national music to be created, the Kemalist intelligentsia also directed their energies to the fabrication of a folklore repertoire. Methodologically, this was enabled by fieldwork.[20] The collection, documentation, and publication of a selective body of vernacular folk music considered to be "Turkish" formed the backbone of Kemalist reforms in this area.

To recap: taken as a whole, these selective examples of music reforms can also be understood as a politics of mood, intended to uplift and enliven the nation. Ahmet Adnan Saygun, one of the influential music ideologues of the Republican era, articulates this point clearly when making an assessment of Mustafa Kemal's famous 1928 speech in Sarayburnu, wherein he criticizes "the murmurings" of Eastern music for being "unsophisticated" and for its inability to "feed the needs of the innovative Turkish soul" (Tekelioğlu 1996, 204). According to Saygun (1987, 7), what matters here is not the artistic value of the music in question but rather "its effect on the soul" (*musikinin ruhlar üzerindeki etkisi*). Explicit in both Kemal's and Saygun's statements is a theory of the transformative power or potential of music to engender listeners' mood and affective sensibilities.

This is brilliantly shown in Ahmet Hamdi Tanpınar's iconic 1949 novel, *A Mind at Peace* (*Huzur*). Set in late-1930s Istanbul, the novel captures the anxieties of cosmopolitan urbanites, uneasy and disillusioned with living in a city estranged from its immediate past in the face of its radical sonic and spatial reorganization. This narrative centers on the life of Mümtaz, a young writer and *flâneur* for whom to know oneself, one must also know Istanbul. The lost city, its forsaken objects, its old music and poetry, its sounds (for example, Istanbul's classic ferries with foghorns), and distinct objects (broken marble fountains, antiques, old book bindings) are what make Tanpınar's characters spiritually destitute. As Mümtaz says, "We love our old *mûsiki* and we understand it more or less. It is the key in our hand that can unlock the door to the past." The narrative voice continues: "For Mümtaz, Istanbul's landscape, our whole civilization, our dirt, our rust, our admirable attributes, they all existed in our *mûsiki*" (2010, 170).

For Tanpınar (1901–1962), born and educated in the old Ottoman Empire yet living through the radical transformation of its life-world, *mûsiki* encompasses more than the music itself; it is a way of living, a certain kind of urban experience. Not only Ottoman music but the ney, too, appears as one of the main objects/characters of *Huzur*, an aural signifier of this dimming past. If Mevlâna's ney cries for the soul's separation from God, Tanpınar's ney yearns for the absent sensory environments of the post-Ottoman subject.

New Developments in the Ney's Public Life: The 1950s Onward

Given these serious efforts, how effective was the musical project of the modernist intellectuals? In short, not very. Indeed, it was never likely to be successful in censoring a music that in the early Republican period a large segment of the urban population still preferred to listen to. Although the cumulative effect of the closing down of the dervish lodges and the official banning of the teaching of Ottoman-Turkish music for a period of fifty years—the State Conservatory for Turkish Music did not open until 1975 in Istanbul Technical University—posed a serious peril to its transmission, the music reforms did not effect a complete rupture. The top-down measures of the state were unable to penetrate the efficacious civil domains where musical education and exchange survived.

The traditional pedagogy of meşk rooted in the long-term learning relationship between master-apprentice is the most crucial of these civil realms. By instituting a face-to-face learning context in which the talebe's commitment and loyalty to the musical milieu (repertoire, style, technique) as they received it directly from their master constitutes the primary ethico-pedagogical virtue, meşk enabled the grafting of serious learners into the major trunks of artist lineages (*silsile*)—what Eickelman calls "quasi-genealogical chains of authority" (1978, 492). As Behar underlines, meşk was much more than just a pedagogy or method of instruction. In a context of oral musical transmission—up until the mid-nineteenth century, the Ottoman musicians showed little interest in notation—meşk was *the* means for the transmission of the repertoire itself,[21] playing a "mortar-like" (*harç*) function in the social organization of Ottoman music (Behar 2015, 19).

Although with the beginning of the twentieth century the use of notation gradually became a common practice in music education contexts, this apprenticeship-style learning practice retained its pillar-like function in lineages of ney musicians. In the critical years of absence of support for the teaching of Ottoman classical music, the ney tradition survived in the hands of individual masters, continuing through webs of hoca-talebe relationships. If we take a look at Salih Hoca's own lineage, Neyzen Emin Dede (1883–1945), who was the chief ney player of the Galata convent at the time the Sufi tekkes were closed down, continued his teaching service in his house in Istanbul's Tophane neighborhood.[22] His guiding of a new generation of neyzens at a time when tekkes were no longer in operation played a vital role in enabling the continuity of the neyzen lineages over the twentieth century.[23]

Other civil sites in which musical sociality and exchange among the aficionados of Ottoman classical music could continue involved *cemiyets* (music clubs), *gazinos* (a type of Turkish nightclub; see Beken 1998), and convivial house gatherings (see Poulos 2018; Yavaşça 1981). Poulos's (2018) observation concerning the vital pedagogical function of private musical assemblies (*meclis*) during the early Republican period is important. Through his study of the communal musical assemblies at the house of the late Ottoman intellectual and bureaucrat İbnülemin Mahmut Kemal (d. 1957), Poulos shows how participation in such convivial gatherings played a significant role in the ethical-musical formation of the "transitional generation of musicians, who lived through the gap of the absence of state-supported musical education for Ottoman/Turkish music to the establishment of the Turkish Classical Music Conservatory" (118).[24] The biographical narratives of the neyzen musicians examined in chapter 5 also attest to this point.

Over and beyond these civil initiatives, the state, too, paradoxically facilitated the public dissemination of this unwanted music through the new regime's primary propaganda tool, the radio. With the exception of the two-year period when the broadcasting of Ottoman music was banned (1936–38), the radio was in no position to exclude this music entirely from its airwaves. As a matter of fact, audiences' tuning into the Egyptian radio in those years to satisfy their taste was strong evidence that radio programming devoting its time to broadcasting a Western music repertoire would find little popularity among the majority of the population. In one way, then, radio was compelled to incorporate Ottoman classical music air time even if such broadcasting was relatively limited compared to Western music offerings until the 1950s.[25]

Yet despite these limitations, the pedagogical function of the radio programs was significant, even if the learning activity they facilitated through mediated listening lacked the broader ethical and affective dimensions of meşk. For instance, in his memoirs the kemençe artist Cüneyt Orhon recounts the crucial role that listening to Ruşen Kam play on Ankara Radio fulfilled in his own musical learning: "I would check the time, tune my kemençe and wait in front of the radio. . . . That way, I chose someone who didn't know me as my hoca" (Aksoy 2009, 22). Similarly, Poulos discusses how the prolific tanbur artist Necdet Yaşar was first "initiated" to the art of tanbur playing through the radio while a university student in the 1950s, especially through listening to Mesud Cemil's programs (2011, 173). The radio carried out its pedagogical function in more direct ways, too. The training of new generations of musicians according to certain aesthetic conventions was essential in order to ensure the quality and routine delivery of the radio programs. Yet at a time when the teaching of Ottoman art music was officially proscribed, this task could have been fulfilled by no institution other than radio itself. Hence, both the Istanbul and Ankara Radio fulfilled an educative function for many young musicians, offering training in music theory as well as vocal and instrumental Ottoman music performance.[26]

In the early 1950s one particular program of Istanbul Radio played a crucial role in re-enabling an appreciation of the ney sound by wider audiences. This was the weekly "Instrumental Pieces on the Ney" (*Neylerle Saz Eserleri*), programmed by Neyzen Süleyman Erguner (1902–1953), who was accompanied by his son Ulvi Erguner (1924–1974) and Neyzen Niyazi Sayın. A student of Emin Dede, Süleyman Erguner, with an artistic style distinguished by its nonbreathy sonority, was one of the most influential ney players of the early twentieth century. In his memoirs, Neyzen Doğan Özeke refers to Erguner as "the person who reminded the Turkish nation of the forgotten ney, and made it loved by them, after the banning of Turkish music on the radio" (2000, 66). In the words of Neyzen Burhaneddin Ökte, a well-acclaimed neyzen of the same era, "Every Monday night thousands of people would wait for the instrumental pieces arranged on Istanbul Radio and, in his [Süleyman Erguner] ney, they would encounter God" (S. Erguner 2005, 53). The repertoire of this program included not only instrumental works in the forms of *peşrev* (instrumental prelude) and *saz semai* (instrumental postlude), but also the vocal genres of Mevlevi *ayini* and *ilahis* (religious hymns) purposefully played without their lyrics. This "strategy," which allowed some agency to these ney artists to feature various examples of the religious repertoire in the program, illustrates the continuing pressures, and even censorship, on religious music at the time. As Nezih Uzel, a well-known performer of Ottoman classical music, notes in his biography, in the early 1950s "one had to have the heart in order to perform an ilahi or Mevlevi ayini on the state radio. This required struggle" (2006, 23).[27] The state's policing of the musical forms and repertoire to be disseminated continued in later years—the banning of *gazel* form is another example—as evident in the court investigation opened up against Neyzen Ulvi Erguner for the religious music programs (*The İftar Hour* and the *Ramadan Hymns*) he initiated on Istanbul Radio in the years 1968–69.[28]

New Forms of Revitalized "Sufi Music"

In 1952 the officials' granting of permission for the first public performance of the Mevlevi mukabele to be held in Konya nearly thirty years after the closing of the dervish lodges opened up a new route for the ney's public performances. The permission was given on the condition that it would be treated as a "cultural" and not religious event. Annual sema ceremonies continued to be staged thereafter in Konya, not at the dergâh but at various "non-religious" settings, such as a local cinema, library, and gymnasium hall.[29] As the ceremonies began to attract a growing international audience, the Tourism Association of Konya took over "ownership" of this now state-authorized ritual, assembling its own whirling dervish group in 1961. In his biography, Neyzen Kudsi Erguner describes the changing audiences of these sacred liturgies:

> At first, the audience consisted essentially of members of authentic Sufi brotherhoods, but from the 1970s, it became Westernized. Our first trips to the West prompted many Europeans, who wished to find the source of what they practised in London or Paris, to go to Konya. One could meet Sufis from California or New York, mystics from Paris, followers of Gurdjieff:

> and all sorts of people versed in various degrees in mysticism. They came in coach-loads, and watched the ceremonies with an interest that had been sharpened by their respective spiritual guides. (2005, 49)

The Mevlevi mukabele in Konya gave birth to a new wave of interest in Ottoman-Sufi music outside Turkey. In 1968, sema ceremonies were first held in Paris, followed by London and then in a series of U.S. cities in the following years, triggering "the most recent phase of the Mevlevi expansion" (Vicente 2007, 17) on the global scale. This revitalization of Sufism and of Mevlevi music outside Turkey provided ripe ground for the emergence of new artistic projects, live and recorded, that made extensive use of the ney. Paris-based Neyzen Kudsi Erguner (b. 1952) and his brother Neyzen Süleyman Erguner (b. 1957), grandsons of the first Süleyman Erguner, were prominent figures in this new phase. Under the title "Erguner Brothers" these ney musicians performed extensively throughout Europe in the 1980s and produced some of the first commercial recordings of ney and Mevlevi music.[30] Süleyman Erguner describes the 1980s and 1990s as the busiest time of his career. The performances he conducted together with his brother and other musicians from Turkey would feature examples of the classical repertoire played on the ney accompanied by other instruments such as kemençe and bendir. In my interview with him, he recounted his excitement in performing this repertoire in large concert halls to audiences intrigued by hearing the sound of the ney in an era when there were no equivalent performances in Turkey. This feeling of excitement would disappear upon their return to Turkey, where the sites for the ney were limited to music ensembles of the radio and recording studios:

> My first studio experience was in 1975 when Neyzen Aka Gündüz asked me to fill in [at] a recording session for him. In the 1970s, the ney used to be a part of large ensembles performing Turkish art music, an idea embraced by musicians like Yıldırım Gürses, Zeki Müren, Emel Sayın. This genre maintained its popularity in both live and recorded forms until the mid-1990s. Because of this demand after the 1970s something called studio ney playing (*stüdyo neyzenliği*) emerged. I remember how I would often find myself in a recording studio right after a concert in Europe. There [in Europe] we would play to curious people wanting just to hear the ney, but in Turkey, it was like any other instrument in a large multi-instrumental art music ensemble (Süleyman Erguner, personal conversation, 2012).

Erguner's account reveals the dual musical constituencies of the ney in the 1970s and 1980s and how the instrument's "Sufi" identity was firmly in place in its beyond-Turkey musical world (even if there is a historical genealogy to its associating with Sufism), marked by a global thriving of the New Age spirituality movement and its incorporation of Sufi practices. The rehabilitation of Mevlevi music—and of the Indo-Pakistani *qawwali* (Sufi devotional music in South Asia)—within New Age spirituality (see Qureshi 2013) generated the backdrop of the ney's exposure not only to larger audiences but also to emerging new musical styles via musical practices of cultural synthesis and fusion. Kudsi Erguner describes this shift as one from the traditional into a musical cosmopolitanism, leading to new artistic challenges in the process:

> We were moving further away from the purely traditional field, and were now in touch with artists from other cultures who were asking us to participate in some of their projects. . . . I was confronted with a new situation. I had a specific cultural heritage and an instrument, the *ney*, which was particularly well-suited to my tradition. To play another type of music was quite a challenge. . . . I made the *ney* follow melodic lines in a language which was not its own. I found myself in the situation of a Chinese poet obliged suddenly to express himself in a language other than his own. (K. Erguner 2005, 77)

According to Kudsi Erguner, one of the major international proponents of the ney today (and of "Sufi music"), it was the embrace in Europe of the "traditional" music he performed alongside his musical collaborations (with Peter Brook, Peter Gabriel, and Maurice Béjart, to name just a few) that later granted him increasing acclaim in his own country, while also enabling the ney to regain public interest: "Young people, who had until then refused to listen to this instrument, were at first intrigued and then seduced by the way in which certain Western musicians were using it" (K. Erguner 2005, 79). Although the claim here overlooks other musical developments taking place in Turkey around the same time (for example, the rise of instrumental music in the 1990s and the popularity of the duo *Yansımalar* [Reflections]),[31] it crudely underlines how the identifying of "Sufi" music in the global music industry and the popular musical performances appropriating Sufi themes stimulated similar trends in Turkey. The staging of a ney concert by the Erguner brothers as part of the Istanbul Festival in 1990 was an important sign of the changing sociomusical soundscape in Turkey, which now involved musical collaborations between neyzens and jazz musicians.[32]

Similar artistic practices sonically articulating the sound of the ney and Sufi music within new musical genres (in other words, jazz, rock, Western symphonic music) appeared in the period 2000–2010, a decade in which the "world music" phenomenon was already well established in most places. Stylized and marketed under this new label, "Sufi music" has become part of the popular music parlance in the international music industry and in Turkey, where it has a following among urban dwellers. Renowned as "Sufi-world music" artists with the greatest international fame, Montreal-based Arkın Ilıcalı, who performs under the stage name Mercan Dede, and New York-based ney player Omar Faruk Tekbilek created diverse musical forms through eclectic approaches to Sufi music. Take Mercan Dede for example, whose artistic work fuses Sufi musical elements with a wide array of genres, including jazz, ambient, techno, electronica, rap, and arabesk. While the artist's music does not share much with the Ottoman classical music repertoire discussed earlier—nor does it display the core musical and technical features of such repertoire, such as its makam structure—the "Sufi" associations in his music are effected by his prevalent use of the ney sound, alongside the use of Mevlevi imagery stylizing the promotional material of his work, as well as his adaptation of the sema into a new form of choreographic dance in his stage performances.[33]

One vital implication of these artistic developments has been their stimulation of the popular category of Sufi music to emerge as a genre in its own right within the Turkish music industry (Şenay 2015). While fusion and hybridization has been a defining element of the popular Sufi music albums promoted under the label of world music, the commercial examples of Sufi music in Turkey have manifested themselves in even more varied forms, adding to the kaleidoscopic diversity and ambiguity of the genre. Rather than corresponding with a particular musical form, the category functions as a continuum with disparate repertoires, aesthetic styles, and artistic and/or religious orientations, from more classically oriented expressions to pop. While the ney acoustically affirms such self-claimed "spiritual" status of this new "Sufi" music, the imagery of whirling dervishes is often used to grant them their "Sufi" cachet. Together they serve as the sonic/visual signifiers of a marketable "Sufi authenticity." These practices have generated intense debates among ney musicians concerning the very existence of a thing named "Sufi music" and the ney's place in it.[34]

The Turkish State, too, has been one important force participating in this revitalized "Sufi music" market. Despite the paradoxical continuing illegal status of the dervish tekkes, there is a complex coopting of "Sufism" by the State institutions, including their creation of urban places and events that resound with "Sufi music": the fabrication of art festivals with Sufi themes, the restoration of Mevlevi lodges as museums, the sponsoring of "Sufi music" ensembles, and, most evidently, the State's commissioning its own "dervishes" under the patronage of its Ministry of Culture and Tourism. As the ceremonies showcased under the title *International Mevlana Festival* (otherwise known as "Whirling Dervishes Festival" or "Mevlana celebrations") became a lucrative resource for

FIGURE 1.2. The album cover of Sufi Selections, Omar Faruk Tekbilek (Zet Müzik, 2011).

tourism and pilgrimage, they have also expanded over time from eight days in 2004 to eighteen days in 2007 (Vicente 2007, 321).[35] Additionally, since 2004 the ritual calendar of Konya also includes the *International Mystic Music Festival*, this time introduced in celebration of the anniversary of Rumi's birth. Ironically, the organizers claim that this festive event pays heed "not only to the presentation, but to the *authenticity* and *originality* of the mystical music traditions of the world" (emphasis added). These spatial strategies applied by the Ministry of Culture and Tourism and local officials are intended to create Konya's image as a "city ripe with mysticism," as they put it.[36] Yet clearly the State's touristification[37] and promotion of sema as the nation's folkloric ritual par excellence is not without political intent. The speeches delivered by government authorities every year, echoing in the sema hall of the Mevlana Cultural Center before state-employed dervishes begin to spin, give away the message. By claiming an ancestral ownership of Rumi as the great "Turkish mystic," and by trademarking "Turkish-Islam" as "humanistic," "inclusionary," and "tolerant," the official discourse appropriates the selected symbols of Mevlevi Sufism in creating its own ethnic Islam.

This increasing entanglement of Konya with faith tourism and of sema with cultural nationalism has corresponded with the explosion of whirling dervish troupes in urban Turkey. Today, "sema shows" are held—often in a modified form, excluding various components of a complete religious ceremony—in a multitude of sites: concert halls, restaurants, wedding locales, hotels, shopping malls, *hamams*, and even at Istanbul's Sirkeci railway station, once the terminal of the famous Orient Express. Fifty years after the re-instituting of the mukabele in Konya, the Mevlevi order has found itself in a position to run petitions in order to end the touristic display of sema because "it harms the tradition" (Hendrich 2011, 4).

Ney Pedagogies Today

The processes briefly delineated above, including the creation and consumption of new forms of "Sufi music," and the popularization of Sufism sponsored by both private and state actors in Turkey, have all contributed to the current revitalization of the ney, albeit in a way that confines its meaning merely to an "instrument of sema."[38] In the eyes of many ney masters, the instrument's widely circulating associations with spirituality no longer derive from an organic relationship with members of a Sufi order and their devotional places but rather are produced by the music industry or state institutions for commercial or political benefit. The impact of all of these processes on the economy of ney making is a further important matter. "In the 1970s and 1980s, the number of the neys that a neyzen used to own would not be more than three," Salih Hoca recounts. "We would have one mouthpiece only, made for our smallest ney. We would wrap it with paper and use it for our bigger neys. Now things have changed, the ney is everywhere."[39]

As the introduction has already noted, one significant dimension of this recent expansion of the public life of the ney has involved a striking interest in ney learning in Turkey's major cities. In Istanbul alone, ney lessons have expanded across a wide variety of urban sites, from private music schools, ney ateliers, and conservatoriums to religious associations and council-sponsored community education centers (known as İSMEK[40]). A whole cross-section of amateur learners—university students, middle-class professionals, and housewives, both pious and secular Muslims—have taken up the instrument, including a noticeable enrollment of young devout females. *Ney* lessons are also available at various associations sponsored by the Turkish State's supersized bureaucratic institution, the Directorate of Religious Affairs (*Diyanet İşleri Başkanlığı*), and are occasionally offered as part of the Qur'an courses provided at local mosque organizations.[41] The *Diyanet*'s sponsoring of *ney* education also extends beyond Turkey's borders, catering to willing learners in countries where sizeable Turkish-speaking migrant communities exist.

The ney pedagogies in play today are just as diverse as this new plethora of teaching sites. From traditional meşk to "interactive online ney lessons," we see a wide spectrum of teaching styles.[42] In order to survey the broader range of ney teaching activity in the city, I participated in and observed weekly classes offered at various lesson sites in Istanbul's socially diverse neighborhoods. Two of these sites were religious community organizations in the urban areas of Eyüp and Fatih, where lessons were held in a renovated tekke building and at an old library adjacent to a mosque building, respectively. In both places learning took a communal form—a common practice in many learning sites—catering to groups of roughly fifteen to twenty students, mostly university students. The mixed-lesson groups accommodated both males and females, although gender segregation was at place in the spatial configuration of the lesson rooms. Additionally, I visited a number of İSMEK centers in the areas of Bostancı, Fatih, and Kağıthane. The size of lesson groups was relatively larger at these communal spaces—accommodating as many as fifty students at one time—partly due to the free training provided at these institutions, which also meant that the number of enrolments fluctuated substantially over the teaching term. In all of these sites learning took more of a *kurs* form (teaching that follows a strict curriculum and restricts student-teacher interactions to the classroom) rather than meşk.

Although kurs-style teaching and learning was a common practice in many communal lesson settings, meşk also continues today. Unlike in the past, meşk is no longer an essentially oral-transmission method. Yet to restrict its definition to a nonliterate mode of musical transmission as some might argue would be to conceptualize it through the binary distinction of orality and literacy, while arbitrarily stopping the history of meşk in Ottoman-Turkey at the turn of the twentieth century. As Behar underlines in the updated edition of his book *Without Love There Is No Meşk*, meşk continued to be the preferred pedagogy among traditional masters even after notation made its way into music education in the early 1900s (2012, 161–93).[43] "Despite the prevalent use of notation in the twentieth century and the increasing tendency to apply 'modern' education methods," he writes, "*meşk* was not suddenly erased from or thrown out of the education system of traditional music" (185). Behar makes this point in the light of a revealing remark made by the composer and vocalist Alâeddin Yavasça (1927—), who was deeply involved in the educational life of the State Conservatory for Turkish Music in Istanbul from the day it opened in 1975: "Conservatoires are schools in this new order which have a certain curriculum. However, this order does not reject *meşk*" (Behar 2012, 185). This remark demonstrates that for skilled exponents of Ottoman music like Yavasça, musical literacy, and meşk—and conservatorium-based training and meşk—are not mutually exclusive. The artist biographies shared in chapter 5 also illustrate this point, revealing how Niyazi Sayın's meşk practice at the conservatory never followed a set curriculum or formalized teaching method.[44]

In sum, for the master musicians whose learning biographies and teaching practices informed this study, the key organizing element of meşk is not orality but *aurality*, realized in the unmediated co-presence of hoca-talebe. The primacy is always on sitting side by side with one's master and receiving the knowledge directly from him. For the talebe, to commit his loyalty to the master's interpretation of music (in other words, to the variant of a piece as performed by his master) constitutes the most essential musical-ethical principle in this learning practice.

To see how these sensibilities enable the crafting of a neyzen, we will now look at one particular site, Hazerfen Ney School in Üsküdar, a place both of intense musical instruction and deliberate ethical character formation.

CHAPTER TWO

Breath and Reed

Seventy-two nations listen to their secret from us
We are the reed-flute making hundreds of sounds
through a single note.
—Rumi

At the Ney Workshop

SALIH HOCA: Can you tell us why you've become interested in learning the ney?

NEW STUDENT (NECDET, A MEDICAL DOCTOR IN HIS FIFTIES): I read the *Mesnevi* and became curious about the ney. I think the sound of the ney most closely resembles the human voice. I mean, it seems to be closer to the human soul than any other instrument.

S: But you said you've been playing the *oud* (short-necked lute) for some time. Why have you given up the oud for the ney? Technically, they're very different instruments. First of all, there is the element of breath with the ney. The oud demands hands to play. But to this the ney adds breath. Look [pointing at me], she got nervous and couldn't control her breathing. Oud players can stuff themselves with food and can still manage to play, whereas neyzens would end up getting a heart attack if they played on a full stomach. The body is more involved when playing the ney. Have you taken any lessons before?

N: Yes, I have. A couple of years ago, I took lessons at the *Ayasoyfa Medresesi* for six months. But I had to quit. Last year, I attended ney lessons at İSMEK. And recently I had taken three months' lessons from a ney player in Üsküdar.

S: OK, then, can you give me a sound?
N: But I haven't brought any scores with me.
S: A sound is sufficient. Just play a note, a single note.

[Taking his ney (a kız ney) out of its case, the man prepares his body to play an ilahi (hymn) in the makam (mode) *Rast.* His tense fingers race over the ney's tone-holes, rushing from one note to another, with a whistle-like sound.]

S: [*interrupting him*] OK, I've got some advice for you. Watch us today. And when you get home ask yourself: "Can I learn anything from this hoca?" What matters is showing the commitment to stay with one hoca. If you show that commitment, he might be able to guide you. There is a ney-learning craze these days. Ney lessons have sprung up everywhere. But if my talebes leave me, I never accept them back. Because we can only move forward if we stay on one path. Musical instructions are available everywhere: method books, the internet—an explosion! But what really matters in this art is to imbibe a style, to go after one particular style. Now, if you decide to come back next week, forget about playing. Playing isn't just about melody, it's also about obtaining a good sound . . .

[The man never appeared again.]

For a newcomer, joining Salih Hoca's communal lessons for the first time is no easy task. You are asked to sustain a good ney sound before an acclaimed master—if any sound can be obtained from the reed—all under the watchful eyes of a group of "insiders." In these climactic moments, old-timers collectively hold their breath, awaiting an almost inevitable public embarrassment for the new student. If the person reveals with no shame that she or he has already changed a number of teachers, or if they insist on playing a melody rather than blowing the single sound requested of them, more experienced students anticipate how the exchange is about to unfold. After all, everyone had gone through a memorable "first-day" conversation!

My own experience still sticks in my mind. Salih Hoca asks me if I have managed to get any sound from the ney. "Yes," I reply. He asks me to give a sound, "*any* sound." I adjust my stiff body and start playing the piece that comes to mind: the first *hâne* (section) of the instrumental *peşrev* in the mode *Segâh* composed by Neyzen Yusuf Paşa. Cutting my playing off before I reach the *teslim* (repeated theme), he gives me my first lesson: "Never play anything in this mode. Segâh sounds like an easy makam on the ear, but you must wait until you can do justice to its pitch inflections." Unbeknown to me, I had immodestly transgressed one of the core ethico-musical conventions of ney learning: one must know when to attempt the soundscape of a particular makam. Segâh was not a makam to take lightly.

I began taking lessons from Salih Hoca not long before he opened the Hezarfen Ney School in Üsküdar. When we first met, he was giving lessons in another privately owned ney atelier in Beşiktaş across the other side of the Bosporus. When he announced that he would no longer continue teaching there, the whole group of students followed him to Üsküdar. The new place was designed both as an atelier and a teaching space. Although Salih Hoca never considered himself to be a manufacturer of neys, he was well skilled in their making, as well as in the craft of *başpare* (mouthpiece making).[1] While the upstairs area accommodated a large atelier section, the downstairs floor was reserved for lessons, music rehearsals (including the weekly Mevlevi ayin rehearsals), as well as for the monthly *sohbet* (conversation) events, which involved interactive conversation and listening sessions with a guest speaker (often a musician) from outside the ney school. Exquisite works of calligraphic art adorned the two long walls of this meşk room, a design preference that complemented its soundscape. "The walls of a *neyzen*'s room should not be bare. Otherwise the ney gives no sound," Salih Hoca used to say. To discipline the ear, the eye required training too. "If nothing stirs in you when you look at the [Arabic] letters *elif* or *lam*, you can't feel the depth of a pitch either." Among the calligraphic plates (*levha*) stood out a carefully placed portrait of Niyazi Sayın, capturing the great virtuoso's ney-playing posture: leaning forward, fingers on the ney's holes, the ney angled left to right across his body, right hand resting on the right knee, left elbow sitting on his left leg, his head tilted to the right, and eyes directed toward the lower part of the ney.

The ney school was home to a varied group of talebes. There were adult learners actively attending Salih Hoca's lessons. While the majority consisted of amateur learners, those taking up the challenge with professional intentions were not absent either. In fact, some talebes combined the formal music education they were receiving at various Istanbul conservatoires—the main pathway for gaining a recognized diploma potentially qualifying one for an occupation in music—with their continuing meşk with Salih Hoca. Alongside this constituency of novices, the regular presence of another cohort of talebes working with Salih Hoca when he was teaching at the conservatoire needs mentioning. Although some of these senior talebes were successful in establishing themselves as professional musicians in their own right, Salih Hoca's support of their careers continued in many ways. Minimally, the workshop also catered to their teaching activities. Close contact and exchange with this earlier generation of neyzens directly taught by Salih Hoca played a vital role in fostering the musical learning and ethical shaping of committed apprentices.

Salih Hoca only gave group lessons, each accommodating ten to fifteen students and held on different nights of the week. Groups were mixed rather than arranged according to members' proficiency, meaning that a newcomer and someone who had been exposed to lessons for more than five years could sit side by side (as often happened). These shared lessons were tailored to accommodate the individual needs of each person, even if other learners were present: Salih Hoca would attend to one student at a time, listen to his or her playing, comment, and demonstrate his instructions by playing on his own ney. Yet there was no expectation that each student would perform in every lesson. Indeed, this hardly ever happened. In a typical three-hour lesson (from 6 to 9 P.M.), the number of those playing their rehearsed piece rarely exceeded five. As there was no set time allocated to each student, sometimes a whole evening would be dedicated to analyzing a single compositional piece. The apprenticeship method at work here intended to facilitate students' enskillment through extensive engagement in collective listening. In fact, during the whole time I spent at the studio, some of my fellow learners stopped bringing their neys to class, yet they were diligent in not missing a single lesson, as they also attended the classes of other groups, held on other evenings of the week. "The best lesson is the one when hardly any playing happens," I was told by my fellow learners.

What was it like to be learning the ney in this meşk context? The next three chapters explore different aspects of this process. I begin with addressing the first and ultimately most esteemed action in ney playing: crafting a beautiful sound. Many factors must combine to achieve this. Developing a forceful sound on the ney is a whole-body experience. It requires particular kinds of corporeal, sensory, and kinesthetic modifications, providing serious learners, in turn, with "an expanding repertoire of powers, or 'I cans'" (Sheets-Johnstone 2011, 195). The first of these chapters analyzes the scaffolding process that lends itself to building an ideal tone in tandem with the question of what is "heard" as a desired sound in this apprenticeship context. To which particular sonic qualities must novices pay attention in their sound work? What new aural perceptions are at work here? Further, as we will see, to gain competence in "sound-ing well" also means to enter into the material world of the "willful" reed and to skillfully engage with it. As Tim Ingold puts it, "skilled practitioners do not impose preexistent forms on inert matter but intervene in the fields of forces and currents of material wherein forms are generated" (2011b, 9). This view, sensitive to the material life of things, helps us think about developing a skill—in other words, a good ney sound—as an attentive engagement with the substance one works with, and not merely as a mechanical performance of some preformulated rules and procedures.

"Listen to the Sound of the Ney"

Why do so many people want to learn the ney? The answer most probably lies in the ney's sound or, more precisely, in how its sound is "heard." Few instruments are endowed with such extraordinary abilities to create an ecstatic affect in listeners as the ney. The ney "enjoys special emotional powers," A. J. Racy (2003, 77) confirms. The widely circulating metaphors about the affective qualities of the ney sound and what it *does* to the listener exemplifies this point: a "mournful" (*hüzünlü*), "plaintive" (*ağlamaklı*), and "burning" (*yakıcı*) sound with "solemn tones" (*vakur tınılı*) and deep "melancholic" effect that is "enchanting" (*büyüleyici*) and "penetrates straight into the heart" (*kalbe nüfuz eden*). The ney's sound, some listeners say, is a direct expression of one's "inner voice," a sound that evokes "a sense of spirituality" and a state of devotional longing (*hasret*). For others, the deep tones of the reed-flute help one connect with the Divine or, as the seventeenth century Ottoman traveler Evliya Çelebi (d. 1682) heard it, "stimulates the heart to prayer and to tears of contrition" (Feldman 1996, 136).

As anthropological studies on sound and voice have shown, our ways of relating to sonic entities in the world are culturally and historically situated (Feld 1982; Schäfers 2017). The metaphorical connotations and "distinct" meanings that charge the acoustic character of musical sounds (sound objects, timbre, pitch, rhythm, melodic modes, and the like) are not created ex nihilo but are constituted through socially constructed perceptions. For example, in her work on the Indian sarangi, ethnomusicologist Regula Qureshi (2000) shows how sonic encounters with the sarangi and prevailing perceptions about it as "the expressive voice of feeling, loss, and longing" are powerfully "instituted and perpetuated by the Indian media" (2000, 815). As in the biography of the sarangi, the Turkish film industry has also played an effective role in creating the sound image of the ney as a voice of mourning and separation by recurrently associating it with funeral scenes.

Yet there is a much more efficacious perception-constituting force generating communal associations surrounding the ney: Islamic poetry. The ney's intimate relationship with Sufism is not confined to its vital performative function in Sufi musical contexts but extends also to the performative role that it fulfills as a *metaphor* in Sufi literature and poetry. In fact, according to Neyzen Halil Can (1966, 121), if the literary representations of the sound of the ney paramount in Sufi poetry and prose were "all pieced together a *divan* [a large collection of lyrical poems] would emerge." The metaphorical constitution of the ney is evoked nowhere more forcefully than in the eighteen introductory verses of the

Mesnevi, known as "The Song of the Reed." As I noted in the Introduction, the archetypal longing that the petitionary sound of the reed expresses in Rumi's poetic exposé is the voice of the "human-ney" yearning for reunification with the "Real-neyzen." Rumi asks:

> Who ever saw a poison and antidote like the reed? Who ever
> *saw a sympathizer and a longing lover like the reed?*[2]

Although the reed's revelations antedated the *Mesnevi*,[3] it is Mevlana's poetry that communicates and publicizes its powerful sonic image as the "soul in exile." In the current context of the reinvigoration of Mevlevi spirituality both in Turkey and globally (chapter 1), Mevlana's words circulate ever more widely. Indeed, my research showed that many enthusiasts were inspired to play the ney after their contact with Mevlana's writings or by following their interest in Sufism. In a questionnaire I handed out to students in one teaching site sponsored by Fatih Municipality (in Istanbul), nearly one-third of the students (out of thirty-eight members) reported an interest in attending *Mesnevi*-related activities run at various religious associations around the city. "The ney is different from other instruments," one female student claimed, adding that it is the only instrument of Ottoman-Turkish classical music that "carries a philosophy" (*felsefesi olan tek enstrüman*).[4]

Yet for those who take up the ney, musical apprenticeship itself also encourages new ways of aurally engaging with the instrument by fostering new forms of hearing and listening that are different to those acquired earlier in life. As anthropologist Alessandro Duranti (2009) shows in his work on jazz practitioners, any musical training involves the transformation of previous ways of hearing and listening (what he calls "pre-modificational ways of hearing") so that new aural sensibilities—a "hearing *as*"—can be developed. In other words, by modifying learners' pre-hearing and pre-sentiments, skilled learning guides novices into perceiving sonic entities in a new light, sponsoring a new capacity to be affected by them.

The quality of the sound one can obtain from the ney, a breath instrument, is the first essential element of its mastery. Not only should one develop a full sound from the reed, but a certain texture with just the right amount of breath in it is to be produced. Indeed, the first perceptual modification one has to go through in this skilled practice is to grasp that true adeptness in playing lies in crafting a beautiful tone. The learner needs to become attentive to sound articulation as something to be perfected in itself, rather than conceiving it as a means for executing a certain melody. That is, a shift needs to take place in the intended goal of the player in order to deliberately resist the urge to play a musical piece by steadfastly practicing a single tone over a period of time. Verbalized instructions endlessly foster a sense of perspective that reorients learners to prioritize tone over melody:

> "Find a good tone first. Playing can come later."
> "That desire to immediately get on to playing a melody is an egoist [*nefsi*] sentiment. It always pushes back good sound."
> "You should have a passion for achieving a good tone, not a passion for playing."
> "Music is not about melody. It is about sound.
> "Your playing doesn't have to be beautiful, but your sound has to be."
> "It is the sound that makes playing precious."
> "Play less [melody], but sound well."
> "Playing can be perfected later, but tone cannot."

On this occasion, the last instruction followed an unnecessary trill (*çarpma*) that I included while playing a melodic line:

> "You should develop a liking for a more simple life. Play one note but make sure it contains the sound of all other pitches in it."[5]

Building up a fuller-sounding ney tone is not an easy task, nor is it something to be achieved in haste. It requires great concentration and commitment to blow a single note repeatedly until each note making up the instrument's two-and-a-half octave range is executed smoothly. In other words, a novice must let go of the desire to play a melody in the initial stage and labor on each note by sustaining a steady long-tone practice. To encourage this, Salih Hoca would deliberately delay beginners' physical interaction with the ney by giving them a short piece of reed with no finger holes, and asking them to practice blowing on this pseudo-ney instead. Once the student gained a good sense of how to produce sound from the reed, then they could begin to work on a *mansur* ney[6] made specifically for them. The somatic infrastructure required to obtain a ney sound comprises a series of skilled actions that involve knowing how to angle lips on the ney's mouthpiece, how to position the head, how much force to exert on the embouchure hole, how to control the airstream as well as the diaphragm for efficient breathing, and how to coordinate movements between the head, lips, and hands in getting the right pitch.[7] Although acquiring this "knowing through the body" (Marchand 2008) can only be achieved after repeated trial, the master's voice intervening in critical moments helps learners to recalibrate their focus of attention when failing to get a movement right: "Don't lose your angle," "Push your lips more forward," "Lower your chin close to your chest,"

"Relax your shoulders," "Keep your fingers straight on the ney," and so on. In the following extract from my field notes, Salih Hoca addresses a new beginner on how to obtain sound from the instrument—a rare occasion in which his instructions are articulated in a detailed verbalized form—following his own demonstration of the prescribed choreography of movement first.[8] Speaking slowly, he paints an image:

> . . . the right elbow firmly sitting on your right leg, your left hand resting on your left knee.[9] The finger pads, not the finger tips, cover the ney's holes [a characteristic of the Turkish ney]. Make sure that your chest is open, shoulders down, and body upright, not slouching over the ney. Now create a forty-five degree angle between the ney and your body. Head should be slightly tilted to the left [in this case the ney is angled leftwards], jaw lowered towards the chest. Unlike some other instruments, there is no resonator [*ses kutusu*] in the ney; our chest performs this task. Now bring your lips up to the edge of the mouthpiece, make sure they are firm and pushed forward, and say a long "*Hû*" [an intensive added to *Allah* in Arabic to indicate "God himself"] . . .

In all of this, stillness and seriousness are essential to the ideal bodily posture to be displayed. As one master remarked to me, "A neyzen should play without attracting any attention to himself." Similarly, exaggerated body movements and facial gestures were to be strictly avoided while playing in our own lesson contexts. "A neyzen must play as if he or she is not playing when watched from five meters," instructed Salih Hoca. The corporeal disciplining at work here demands not only a still body, but also a body refined of emotional expression, including pleasure. The aesthetic criterion that characterizes the "choreography" of the neyzen-body is extremely subtle.[10]

As in all skilled learning activities, establishing appropriate posture is fundamental to developing the "techniques of the body" vital to that practice, which Mauss describes as "the physio-psycho-sociological assemblages of series of actions" that become more or less habitual (1979, 97). As Wacquant says, "the function of pedagogical work is to replace the savage body . . . with a body 'habituated,' that is, temporally structured and kinetically remodeled according to the specific demands of the field" (2004, 60). This inculcation of the "body habituated" is always a dramatic experience for a neophyte, even when the training process involves relatively subtle physical actions. Muscles once unknown to the body begin to make their presence felt as one proceeds on the right track. For example, in the beginning (the "pre-modificational way of being," as Duranti says) the muscles in and around a ney player's lips are

FIGURE 2.1. Salih Bilgin's playing position, 2016. Courtesy of Salih Bilgin.

so loose that only through the physical workout that goes into adjusting the embouchure technique do these once-unperceived tools become available to one's perception. The tension that builds up around the lips after a good couple of hours of blowing practice gives these miniature muscles a new sensually felt presence. In this sense, enskillment in the ney demands the novice work on his or her body in a way not that different to an athlete or a martial arts practitioner, even if the goal here is to train much smaller muscles. Through repetition and practice, those once-awkward corporeal movements become innate (or "second nature"), with no need to be "remembered" any more in the course of their minute execution. In *The Absent Body,* Drew Leder describes this vital transformation as "bring[ing] within a body": "A skill is finally and fully learned when something that once was extrinsic, grasped only through explicit rules or examples, now comes to pervade my own corporeality. My arms know how to swim, my mouth can at last speak the language" (1990, 31).

Once this somatic infrastructure is in place, what else is required to produce a skillful and desired ney sound?

A Single Note Enclosing "All" Notes in Itself

There is a story told about Neyzen Hakkı Dede (d. 1918), a dervish of the Galata Mevlevi convent, who became the chief ney player of this lodge following the death of Neyzen Aziz Dede. Known to be a devout man, Hakkı Dede would never play his ney outside the *mutrıb* (the Mevlevi ensemble accompanying the mukabele). One day his talebe Emin Dede and Neyzen Rauf Yekta (d. 1935) visit Hakkı Dede in his dervish cell. Begging his apology, they ask him if they could hear his ney. Not wishing to offend his visitors, nor to compromise his principle, Hakkı Dede takes his ney and blows a long, single *neva* (D). The resonance of that neva emanating from Dede's ney is sufficient to fill them with delight. "We have never heard a neva like that," his listeners declare.

The sound of a single note proves the artistry of Hakkı Dede.[11]

As the previous section has emphasized, cultivating a fine tone is fundamental to ney competency. Indeed, no other skilled action in this practice has primacy over shaping a sonorous and refined sound. The value attributed to an attractive ney sound is often foregrounded in anecdotal stories about acclaimed ney players where it is not the technical brilliance of a neyzen (in other words, to ability to execute complex melodies or modes with amazing dexterity) but rather the qualities of sound that are the explicit focus of appraisal. Likewise, when beloved masters are fondly remembered by their talebes, it is the virtues of their "voice" that becomes the immediate focus of attention. "I have never yet obtained a sound like his from my ney," pronounces *kutb-i nayi* Niyazi Sayın (see chapter 6), speaking about his teacher Halil Dikmen. Even if this statement is understood as an expression of gratitude and modesty, it simultaneously posits the attainment of a beautiful sound as a virtuous skill in its own sake. This primacy given to the aesthetics of a single sound should come as no surprise given the arduous nature of perfecting one's tone, a task that requires dedication and perseverance and is always in the making in this skilled practice. For the trained ear, a single note is enough to reveal the labor that has gone into it. Thus, an aesthetic sensitiveness to sound is continuously demanded in every stage of the apprenticeship process, as epitomized in Salih Hoca's primary instruction: "Play one note, but make sure that it contains all other notes."

But what is considered a desirable ney sound (for at least this community of ney artists)? Which aesthetic features do masters look for in the resonance of a fine tone? The first criterion is sonority. An ideal tone is voluminous and has intensity, a sound that is said to create an impression in listeners that the reed "trembles" (*zangırdamak*) or is about to "crack" (*çatlamak*). The following description from Ayvazoğlu's biographical book, *The Secret of the Ney* (Ney'*in Sırrı*), about the profound sonority and expressiveness of Aziz Dede's ney gives us a clue about the sonic qualities valued here. Ayvazoğlu notes that "according to those who had the fortune to hear Aziz Dede, he was worth ten neys together. When he began playing, the listeners would imagine that his ney would split off and break into pieces" (2008, 36–37). Ayvazoğlu reports that on one public occasion, Aziz Dede joined the military band to play a piece from Giuseppe Verdi's opera *La Traviata*. The story goes that not only did Dede play the piece from beginning to end without a single mistake, but that the sound of his ney stands out among all those much louder instruments of the marching band (37). On another occasion, the sound of the ney that Aziz Dede played in Dolmabahçe (following the call to prayer in the early morning) could be heard from Üsküdar, on the other shore of the Bosporus (37).

A second vital aspect of the aesthetics of tone quality concerns its sonic *texture*. The intensity of the airstream blown into the ney and the amount of breath that is maneuvered through the mouthpiece hole are essential in shaping the shades of color and tension that one expresses in sound. Generally speaking, an impure and slightly breathy sound aesthetic is a common feature of the Ottoman-Turkish style of ney playing. In other words, unlike in the Persian ney tradition, tonal clarity is not a sought-after quality in the Ottoman musical aesthetic (Tammer 1993). In the former, the embouchure technique is entirely different, as sound is produced by inserting the edge of the vertically held ney in between the two top front incisors (known as the tooth-and-lip technique). The result is a "cleaner" tone, refined from the impurities of breath. By contrast, many masters I spoke to in Istanbul pointed out that given the expected association between breath and reed, the ney sound should embody a certain breathy tone quality.

Yet while "Turkish" style considers "some" impurity (*fosurtu*) to be of unique aesthetic import, the question of how much breath an ideal timbre should retain is a topic of debate among contemporary ney players. Although aesthetic preferences vary between and within musical lineages, one place where this becomes a live issue is in the recording studio. There, the acoustic aesthetic demanded from ney musicians is a clean and pellucid sound, cleansed from the effect of *fosurtu*. Neyzen Eyüp Hamiş, who has played in some five thousand album recordings since he first began working in the recording industry in the early 1980s, is a renowned exponent of this particular ney sound. Describing himself as a "studio musician" (*stüdyo müzisyeni*), this is how he comments on the intricacies of performing the ney in the studio context:

> *Fosurtu* is a much-debated issue today. Most neyzens playing in tekke style prefer blowing with fosurtu, where you can hear overtones and some amount of breath, depending on the intensity of the person's blowing technique. When you play solo, whether on stage or in the studio, your tone may not be a problem, but when you play in an orchestra, the tone of the ney can change the whole sound. Generally, *tonmeisters* [engineers] don't like fosurtu: if someone plays like that, they amplify the sound differently. What they look for is a clean [*temiz*] and smooth [*pürüzsüz*] sound. That's what I have always strived to achieve during all these years of work in the studios, a clean sound and a good intonation, of course. Ney is a very sensitive [*hassas*] instrument. Its tone or even a tiny ornamentation you execute on the ney can change the whole style [*tavır*] of the music. Not every instrument can shape the overall sound so strongly. Thus, when you play with an orchestra, the eyes of the tonmeisters are always on ney players. We always play on a knife-edge [*diken üstünde*] (personal conversation with the artist, June 2014).

Yet not everyone accepts the production aesthetics demanded from ney players in the studio context. In fact, many ney artists self-identifying with the "classical style" (*klasik tavır*) are concerned that the preferences of sound engineers are changing the whole character of ney music. One eminent ney player (a student of Sayın's) said to me that he had had to walk out of the recording room several times when pressured by the sound mixer to play without any fosurtu. "Neyzens like us, playing in the classical style, are no longer desirable; the fashion [*moda*] today is to play the ney like the *kaval* [shepherd's pipe]," he asserted, suggesting that a softer flute tone associated with folk-style playing is more in demand. What these insights echo is that the acoustic character of tone also constitutes a vital sonic marker, demarcating different artistic styles of playing. This is reminiscent of the prevailing juxtapositions associating a breathy timbre with the "tekke style," and a clean, pure tone with "kaval style" or, worse, with the "arabesk style."

A key aspect of the skilled practice here involves becoming attentive to different shades and intensities of tonal expression, as well as to how the desired sound is produced through extensive listening and watching. The training of lips carries most weight in crafting the "right" sound, which for those of us learning from Salih Hoca meant apprenticing a sonorous tone with just enough texture of breath. The relative strength and texture of the tone is influenced by the speed and angle of the air stream, the placement of the head and the jaw, as well as the position of the lips, and how much tension they exert on the mouthpiece. Coordination between all these somatic elements is also essential for octave jumps. As the diagram from the method book by Neyzen Ahmet

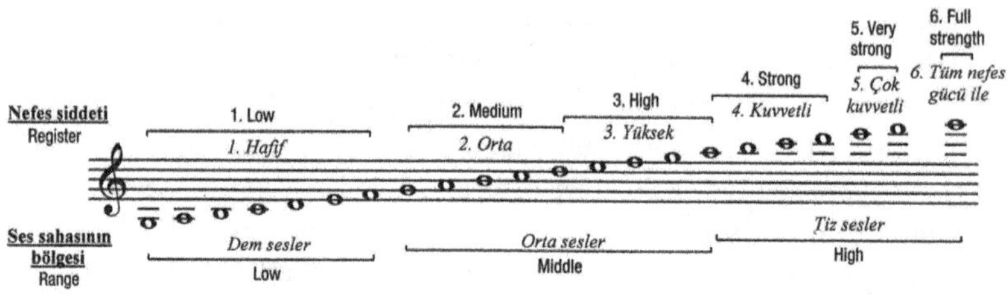

FIGURE 2.2. Tonal range of the ney. (Toz 2013, 9)

Toz illustrates (figure 2.2), in theory the tonal range of the ney extends from the low G (*kaba rast*[12]) to high G (*tiz gerdaniye*), comprising three octaves. However, in practice, most players can only play two-and-a-half octaves (from low G to high D). The higher the register, the more air stream is needed. These sudden break attacks one needs to hit high pitches make it difficult to obtain a satisfying tone color in this tonal area while keeping the volume steady and the intonation flawless. To strike a high note is one thing; to play a high note with a mature (*olgun*) tone is another. Of course, the ney, too, must cooperate with the player in executing these notes smoothly, for not every reed has the perfect proportions to afford those sounds higher than high D (*tiz neva*).

Further, the ney demands from lips not only firmness—the tighter and more puckered/pursed the lips are, the more fosurtu can be attained—but also elasticity. As Neyzen Ulvi Erguner (d. 1974) likens it, "Lips must move on the mouthpiece like a peg top [*topaç gibi*]." The aim is to allow them maximum freedom and flexibility of execution over the embouchure hole. As chapter 3 reveals in more detail, this element is particularly vital for calibrating the right pitch, a skilled action that a player must constantly deal with in interacting with a "fretless" instrument like the ney. To encourage this proficiency early on, Salih Hoca assigned novices—once a full sound was obtained from the middle octave—a peşrev composition in the makam Rast, the mode with which melodic and modal training always began.

As a common practice, beginners would be asked to play the peşrev written by Neyzen Raşid Dede in the makam Rast. The choice of this piece in the ocean of repertoire was not arbitrary. The piece dives straight into the tones of the first register, making abundant use of the tonal range between the notes *yegâh* (D) and *rast (G)—especially* the pitches *hüseyniaşiran* (E) and *ırak* (F-sharp)—which are challenging, if not daunting, notes on the ney. Their skillful articulation requires a fine coordination between the angling of the lips and the head position. While E demands an almost fully vertical blowing position,

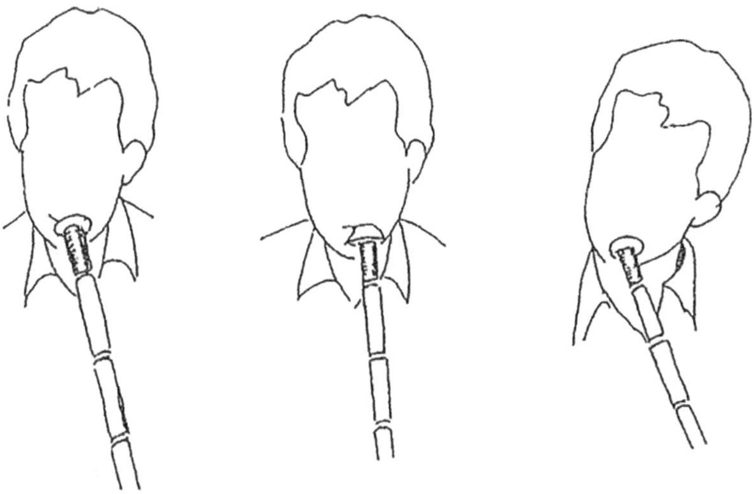

FIGURE 2.3. (from left to right) Standard—vertical—tilted head position. (Source: Salih Bilgin's teaching manuals)

F-sharp requires the largest angle with which any note can be obtained on the ney! To move from one to another, the lips must move too, assisting in fine-tuning the correct pitch.

Let me continue with the notes of the lowest octave—otherwise known as *dem sesler*—a topic that deserves discussing in its own right.

"Three Hundred *Dem*"

Under the entry *dem*—in Persian, "breath"—in the "Turkish (!) Religious Music Dictionary," Neyzen Halil Can (d. 1973) provides the following description:

> "*Dem*: An expression used to refer to the sounds of the ney from kaba rast [low G] to yegâh [D].[13] The person who wants to learn the ney is instructed to produce these dem sounds first. The more tuneful [*ahenkli*] and powerful [*kuvvetli*] a neyzen's dem is, the more successful she or he is in managing other notes and in performance [*icra*]" (Can 1966, 56).

Why a separate entry dedicated to dem sounds in a dictionary on religious music? What is it about this particular tonal area of the ney that makes it receive special attention? Halil Can gives the answer in an autobiographical account of his own initiation into musical apprenticeship under Emin Dede (Yazıcı) at a time when Sufi lodges had not yet been closed down. He recounts:

> The next Friday, I began my first lesson at the Galata *Mevlevihanesi*. My *Hoca*, Emin Efendi gave me a ney and I began learning by blowing dem first. In those days, at the *dergâh* novices learning the ney would be asked to blow "three hundred *dem*" [*üç yüz dem*]. That means [that] lessons would begin only when the person's dem sounds gained their consistency after having being played for three hundred days for four to five hours each day. With me, this sound came in less than three hundred days. Having obtained the sound in probably three and a half months, I would imitate in one of the [dervish] rooms the improvisation [*taksim*] that *Hoca* played upstairs [during the Mevlevi mukabele]. One day *Hoca* hears me play and asks, "Who is the person playing in the next room?" "My lord, it is the young Halil from Üsküdar," they said. He then invited me to come to his house the following week, and that's how we began lessons. (Cited in Üngör 1973)

As Can's memory reveals, there is a long history of the importance given to dem sounds in ney artistry, at least among those neyzens connected to the lineages of the Mevlevi musicians. The skilled action of gaining competence over the ney's low notes has a vital pedagogical and symbolic substance. In apprenticeship contexts, producing a rich dem sound fulfilled a "rite of passage" role, a sonic confirmation that the initiate had earned the right to receive meşk. Anecdotal stories manifesting the gravity that these notes carry in ney practice are not rare. For example, İbnülemin Kemal (1958, 238) recounts an interesting exchange between two well-known nineteenth-century Ottoman neyzen figures, the Armenian Oskiyam and Raşit. Raşit asks Oskiyam to comment on his playing, yet the response he receives is not something he expects. "You are blowing a whistle" (*Düdük üflüyorsun*), Oskiyam replies dismissively. Seeing Raşit's frustration, Oskiyam invites him to his house, assuring him that he will "prove" his words. Some days later, Raşit visits Oskiyam's Samatya home where he finds him at a *rakı* table. Oskiyam takes his ney out of the cupboard and draws out "a dem like the horn of the Odessa steamer" (*Odesa vapuru gibi bir dem*). Thereafter, Raşit submits himself to Oskiyam, mastering dem sounds under his guidance, and that's how he earns his reputation as "Baba" Raşit.

Unlike in the past, the ritual of beginning ney instruction with dem sounds hardly survives today, yet the value credited to dem sounds is still paramount in ney artistry. Why was there an aural attentiveness to dem sounds? At least three technical, ethical, and musical points can be put forward. First of all, technically, obtaining an appealing sound on the ney is most difficult in this lowest register. Body skills include an embouchure position where lips are pursed most firmly and there is a subtler control of the intensity of breath, since with the slightest increase of the air stream, the pitch easily slides into the middle register. Dem sounds are inherently breathier, a material quality that gives them their unique sonic character. The only way to achieve this is long-tone practice—that is, playing each dem note repeatedly, engaging with one at a time until different shades of tone color become discernible. Yet as arduous as they are, competent dem sounds have great effect on the maturity of the tone obtained in higher registers.

Second, what better trial than commencing the learning activity with dem sounds if the intention and seriousness of a novice is to be put to the test? Beyond its pedagogical function, this musical task has an ethical import. To commit oneself to the monotonous activity of long-tone practice for an extended time—as emblematic in the old Mevlevi ritual of "three hundred dem"—demands an ethical modification from the learner. In a conversation I had with him in 2012, Neyzen Yılmaz Kale articulates this point by referring to his own teaching activity in the city of Gaziantep, which continues to retain the production of dem sounds as the first step of meşk. He states:

> When you look at how *dedegân* [the plural of the Mevlevi title *dede*] taught, dem sounds always came first. They began [teaching] with this most arduous part of the ney, so that if the novice [*müptedi*] was not really up for learning this music, they would give up and leave. Nowadays things are even more complicated, given so many people want to learn the ney. So that's what I do in my own teaching. If the talebe shows the steadfastness to stay, we begin.

According to Kale, there is something else to this appreciation of the sonic affect of dem notes. He argued in the remainder of our conversation that this is in keeping with the broader musical aesthetics of tekke music, suggesting that it is in the middle and lowest registers that the character of pitches (*perde*) is best captured. For him, the fact that the şah ney was the primary ney preferred by the Mevlevi neyzens proved this aesthetic perception. A technical note is necessary here. Neys come in a number of standard lengths based on their tuning (*akort*): from the lowest to highest register, *bolahenk* (D), *davud* (C), *şah* (B), *mansur* (A), *kız* ney (G), *müstahsen* (F), and *süpürde* (E).[14] The timbre of the ney varies substantially according to its size. The longer the reed is, the deeper is the tone. Smaller neys—considered to be those smaller than mansur—have a much brighter tone color and are relatively easier to play. Where the musical context of the Mevlevi dervishes is concerned, there was a clear preference for longer neys, in particular for the şah ney (858–884 mm).

My informant's comment here concerning the compatibility of deeper tones with the musical aesthetics valued in this tradition is not merely a personal reflection, but given his lineage affiliation, there is a clear genealogy to his understanding. Kale is conveying what he received from his late master (and father), Emin Kılıç Kale, who witnessed firsthand the lifeworld of the Mevlevi music, in particular of the ney just prior to the closing down of the Sufi tekkes. Thus, E. K. Kale's insights about the pride of place given to the şah ney in the Mevlevi tekkes are worthy of quote, given his biography. Kale recounts:

> The fundamental aim in our music is this: the melodies will be expressed through deep tones, and in a slow pace. Even though Mevlevi dedes did have mansur ney, I never saw a single one playing it. They wouldn't. It was always şah, always deep tones, an inclination toward lower tones and slow execution. . . . Hacı Emin Dede never taught me with mansur. Indeed, he gave me a mansur as a gift, but that was his blessing to me. Now things have changed! Kız ney and so on. They would never play those [shorter] neys, never take them in their hands. This would be considered shameful [*ayıp*]. (Kale 1983)[15]

Over the twentieth century, the tonal use of the ney took on a much more heterogeneous form with the entanglement of the instrument with a wide range of new music genres, artistic forms, and performance places. The preference given to the şah ney continued for a while, albeit mostly in some select meşk contexts. For example, where the artist lineage central to this study is concerned, masters' fidelity to şah ney persists until Niyazi Sayın, who, in a conversation I had with him, confirmed that şah was the only key that he played during his fifteen years of meşk with Neyzen Halil Dikmen. In the second half of the twentieth century, especially following the opening of the "Turkish Music" Conservatorium in 1975, mansur (tuning: A, around 78 cm) and kız ney (B, around 70 cm) become the standard keys in ney pedagogy with the increasing preference for the latter in the present.

The Reed Matters

Until here, this chapter has examined the somatic infrastructure and particular kinds of aural sensibilities (skilled hearing) that go into the crafting of a forceful ney sound. Yet there is another vital process involved in acquiring ney competency: governing the embodied relationship to the material with which practitioners engage. Producing good sound requires a skillful engagement with the reed. And as Ingold urges, to engage with things, one has to "join with them in the processes of their formation" (2011b, 14). What does this mean for the ney? Is there another, a better way of thinking about its sound-making? Hearing firsthand from an experienced, skilled practitioner describing what happens in the practice of "sounding out" is helpful here. As one well-known neyzen remarked to me during a visit to his studio in Istanbul's Kadiköy neighborhood:

> First the ney makes you resemble itself [Ney seni evvela kendine benzetir]. You must hold it in the way that it demands. You must place your lips on its mouthpiece according to what it wants. And you must blow into it with the angle, intensity, and texture that it wants so that it will sound out. It is all about what it wants. See how it begins to make you resemble itself. You learn to show patience to its demands. You fail, but you keep going; you fail but you don't give up. Hah, at last you're reconciled [*gönlünü aldın*]. The connection [*irtibat*] is established. The ney begins to sound.

The implication of this description is that sound or desired ney tone is not a result that the serious learner achieves by following a series of preformulated instructions as demanded by one's master. It—sound-in-the-making—is the form that unfolds through working *with* the reed and through learning *from* it (in other words, a dialogical encounter). Ingold is again instructive here: "The role of the artist—as that of any skilled practitioner—is not to give effect to a preconceived idea, novel or not, but to join with and follow the forces and flows of material that bring the form of the work into being" (2011b, 13). The metaphor of becoming like a ney, "to resemble it," captures this dynamic process of aligning one's movements with the trajectories of the reed, to use Ingold's terminology, so that the reed resounds. Learning, as the metaphor illustrates, is becoming.

How do the material qualities of the reed [*kamış*] shape the sonic engagement and embodied dialogue between the player and the instrument? What particular attributes of the reed must one become attentive to in crafting a good sound? I will highlight two features here, although more can be said about the reed's materiality. The first is its organic nature. Indigenous to the ecological areas surrounding the Mediterranean Sea, reed cane (scientifically, *Arundo donax L.*) belongs to a grass family that likes warm temperatures and flourishes in moist areas, especially alongside ditches and riverbanks. Its variations with tight vascular bundles and a light golden yellow color are most ideal for mutation into a ney. The stalk, if to be used in ney making, is cut when it is three or four years old (Tammer 1993). For the best result, this harvesting must be done during autumn, although in the current context of the bourgeoning demand for ney production as well as intense competition over reed collection, "pre-mature harvesting" is not uncommon either (Introduction). Once cut off, the stalks are left in a shady place so as to slowly lose their moisture, a process that often takes one to two years on average. The care with which all these steps are undertaken directly shapes the instrument's sonic quality and form. For instance, if harvested before the right season or if processed before completely drying up, the reed easily becomes deformed, gets wrinkles on its body and loses its straight shape. The reed is in a state of constant transformation and regeneration even after its metamorphosis into a ney. Once in sustained contact with breath, its inner flesh continues to mature, gradually contributing to a richer sonority. This transformation is more easily discernable in a newly made ney. Not only does it demand more breath work to gain the tonal character distinctive of the instrument, but it also comes across as relatively lower in overall pitch. The longer the reed interacts with breath, the more intimate is the connection (*irtibat*) between these two "tools," as the sound begins to attain its desired consistency (*kıvama gelmek*) and the intonation of the ney settles down. Or, in the opposite scenario, the reed starts to go deaf (*sağırlaşmak*) or, worse, becomes "sulky" (*küsmek*) with its player.

Given this dynamism characterizing the life cycle of the reed as an organic substance, for those who work with it (players, makers), reed is an animated and living material.[16] The reed is not a static entity: it "breathes," "weeps," and "sings." Or, in the words of Schimmel, it "suffers": "its head has been cut, exactly like that of the reed pen—hence both instruments are media to convey information about the Beloved, one by singing, the other by writing" (1980, 211). Note here how the material properties of the reed invite projection of particular kinds of human qualities that are imputed to the ney and its voice—what Sennett calls "anthropomorphisis" (2009, 136). Metaphoric associations of reed and the musical virtues of "simplicity" (*sadelik*) and "naturalness" (*doğallık*) abound, evoking the imagining of its voice as "pure" (*saf*), a sound from "within," a sound that resonates closest to the human voice.[17] The ney is also said to be "modest" (*mütevazi*), requiring—unlike, say, the Western flute or the oud—minimum technological interference in its assembling. Its "modesty" and straight body-form induces, in turn, another powerful imagining: the reed-flute resembles alif, which, for Rumi, "was honored by being the first letter of the [Arabic] alphabet because of its *unity* and *sincerity*" (Schimmel 1990: 95, emphasis added). *Alif* appears in special places in the Qur'an, calling attention to itself: "The lover who emulates it by becoming endowed with Divine attributes will be first in line as well" (95). In the famous lines of Hafiz:

> There is on the tablet of my heart nothing but the *alif* of my
> Beloved's stature—What shall I do? My teacher gave me no other letter to memorize! (95)

If *alif* is recited as the letter of Unity (94), the ney is "heard" as its sound. Both correspond to the human being created in God's likeness.

The second material dimension of the reed to highlight here follows from the first point. Given its organic form, no two reeds are ever the same. Each reed exhibits its own character, developing its specific strengths and fault lines. For example, there are always certain variations that might relate to the diameter of the cane, the thickness of its flesh inside, the texture of its outer skin (*sır*), the proportions of each nine-node segments on the body, the contraction of the reed, and so on. All of these directly affect the tuning of a ney. Reed, in this sense, is far from being a homogeneous material that can be treated in a standard manner.

This material particularity lends itself to creative problem solving in the first instance, for the craftsman who, always striving to produce better neys, is "engaged in a continual dialogue" with the reed (Sennett 2009, 125). To work well with this material, one must explore its inherent idiosyncrasies and thus get to know its possibilities. As in the tuning of any instrument, nuanced adjustments are essential in the tuning of a ney, in particular in the placement of its tone holes. This skill requires both manual dexterity and "aural acuity" (Roda 2014, 363).

The technique—known as *müstakil açkı*, nonstandardized tuning—employed by expert makers involves making millimetric shifts (*kaydırma*) in the placement of the finger holes by paying attention to the peculiarities of the reed and by performing what Roda calls "diagnostic listening" (2014, 361).[18] For example, the structure of nodes and the balance with which the reed contracts toward its root are critical in shaping the adjustments that one must perform. Diagnostic listening entails also the fine-tuning of the ney with respect to the player, once a ney maker obtains an embodied familiarity with the instrument. Through long-time tactile and sonic interaction with the reed, a good craftsman comes to anticipate the behaviors of the material and knows how to tailor each ney according to the character of the reed. Respecting the capacity of the material is the principal virtue in good craftsmanship. As Salih Hoca says:

> A good craftsman takes the reed in his or her hands and asks: "What would you like to become?" If the reed says "I want to become a half-tone ney [*mabeyn ney*]," then the maker turns it into that. In this atelier, we obey the reed [*biz kamışa tabiyiz*]. If it says, "Nothing will come out of me," then we leave that reed aside.

Just like the ney maker, the player, too, must deal with the perversity of the reed. A good player knows how to take the reed seriously, especially when it comes

FIGURE 2.4. Neys and mouthpieces crafted by Salih Bilgin. Courtesy of Salih Bilgin.

to getting the right pitch (see chapter 3). Indeed, masters always say that there is no perfect ney, but the player has to become perfect by becoming attentive to the reed's imprecisions while also taking advantage of its affordances. In all of this, the player is the one who is made to submit his or her will to the authority of the ney, not the other way around. As one player remarked to me, "The ney does not accept any ego: you must submit yourself to its will" (Ney ego kabul etmez, sen onun isteğine tabi olmalısın). Similarly, in one lesson context Salih Hoca put it like this:

> When we play the ney we become subject to it [*biz ona tabi oluyoruz*]. A competent player finds the right pitch even in a badly tuned ney. This is why neyzens know music well. Because the ney educates them [*Çünkü ney onları eğitir*].

This perception of the ney's being a "law unto itself" reverberates with the call in anthropological studies to take material substances seriously. Materials are not some inert or inanimate things as typically envisioned by modern thought; they are "the active constituents of a world-in-formation" (Ingold 2011a, 28). As the foregoing comments reveal, what is being formed for these neyzens is not only their sensory world but, at the same time, their perceiving of being. Submitting one's will to the ney, skillful engagement with its substance—in short, learning *from* it—modifies both the aural and ethical perceptions of the player.

The ney is said to discipline the player through other means as well. The rich metaphorical language that informs how skilled practitioners talk about building up a good ney sound reflects this. The late Neyzen Emin Kılıç Kale remarks: "The ney [nây] does not wail [*inlemek*] by itself. Who makes it wail? The master of breath [*sahib-i nefes*], a person who has matured, one in charge of his or her breath" (1983, 29). Similarly, an analogy is often drawn between the ney's disciplining—the commonly used expression here is *terbiye*—of the player's breath (*nefes*) and its disciplining of one's *nefs*, a term which is defined in Sufi writings as "the lower self, the base instincts, what we might render in the biblical sense as "the flesh." The renunciation of nefs, a constant struggle with it, has been called by the Sufis "the greater Holy War" (Schimmel 1975, 112).

Breath segues into other immediate metaphoric meanings. Consider, for example, how the act of blowing cultivates a deeply intimate contact between the reed and the body, so much so that the ney is felt like an extension of the lips. In his book *The Neyzens' Coffeehouse*, Neyzen Doğan Özeke expresses this imagery evocatively: "As a matter of fact, the ney should not be seen as an instrument," he writes. "It should be considered as an extension of the body. Not even as a prosthetic, but an extension of the neyzen's lips" (2000, 44). Consider also how the breath of neyzen becomes the archetypal metaphoric image for Creation. Just as the reed-flute wants to be blown into in order to "sound," the human-ney seeks the breath of its Divine.[19] The body is an empty flute. Salih Hoca's instruction quoted earlier, inviting the student to think of her blowing posture as reciting *Hû* (God himself) only makes sense in relation to this intended analogy. In the Sufi cosmology, *Hû* stands for that which is in every breath taken in, the One beyond all being. Thus instructing imaginatively, his words evoke an imagery of blowing as a means for remembering (*tevekkül*) its "Real" source.[20]

What can we learn from paying attention to the material qualities of the reed, real or imagined, that I have outlined here? Skilled learning is a mutually transforming event that facilitates an intimate intersubjective relationship between the participant human and nonhuman actors.[21] Anthropologist Alison Leitch's fascinating work on marble and the ways in which workers relate to it in the quarries of Carrara gives us a clue here. What Leitch shows is that work is experienced "not as a relationship between an acting subject (workers) and an inert field (marble), but rather as an inter-subjective, reciprocal and, indeed, dynamic relationship" (2010, 67). The skilled "labor" that goes into cultivating a good sound can also be understood in this light. It is quite literally a process of cooperation between the reed and the neyzen.

Finally, as Sennett tells us, the ways in which we engage with materials and go about making things (in other words, a good ney sound) matters for at least one other important reason. As he expresses by way of analogy: "Learning from things requires us to care about the qualities of cloth or the right way to poach fish; fine cloth or food cooked well enables us to imagine larger categories of 'good'" (2009, 8). Ethics is inherent to such imaginative processes. For the skilled practitioner, working toward a good ney sound too (*to do the best one can*), we might say, lends itself as an animated metaphor for other practices that he or she labors on in life. Let us, then, hear the final analogy from Salih Hoca:

> We should aim to get a good sound from this ney [the instrument-ney]
> so that this ney [the human-ney] also sounds well.

CHAPTER THREE

Mode and Mood

Music is the spiritual relationship between any two tones.
—Niyazi Sayın

HAVING DISCUSSED WHAT PRODUCES an exemplary ney sound-in-the-making, we can now turn our attention to another core pillar of the art of ney playing. As much as crafting a desired ney tone is paramount to good playing, a high premium is also placed on the competence of the player to bring pitches (*perde*[1]) into intimate relationships that are appealing to the ear. In keeping with my own teacher's language, I refer to this overarching skill in ney playing and more generally in Ottoman classical music-making as "pitch sensitivity" (*perde hassasiyeti*). The aural task of giving each note its rightful place in a melodic line is not a matter of replicating it by faithfully following the "footsteps" of notation. It is a skilled act that rather requires maneuvering each note so as to bring it into the desired alignment with other notes and thus is akin to form giving. While all players are encouraged to discover for themselves the best dialogical relationship between notes according to their own aesthetic sense, this musical election is by no means randomly performed. Given that Ottoman classical music is always set in a mode (hereafter, makam) or in a modal system, the novice must learn how to bring forth the sonic "place" of a pitch effectively while satisfying the musical expectations of a larger form, the mode in which the melody is dressed. In what follows, I explore the aural perceptual modifications that one goes through so as to cultivate this capacity, a topic that engages with broader questions of discretion, intuition, and individuality in performance.

Hearing the "Right" Pitch

I have been rehearsing this piece (set in makam *Neva*) for nearly two months. Today I will play it for the fourth time in front of the class. While making my way to the workshop, I could hear myself silently singing the melody in my head. Will my pitches come out as I am hearing them now? Will my breathing allow me to play them smoothly?

My breathing stumbles and I am overly conscious of getting the *acem* [F] right. After I finish playing (I only reach the second page), Salih Hoca says: "Your pitches are not stable yet. You are playing the *nota* [score], not the *perde*. If you want to evoke the *Neva* and bring out its character, you must think about the makam as a whole and give its feeling." He then plays the first four lines, telling me to pay closer attention to how his F sounds.

I realize that the pitch is in constant flux. The same pitch appears more than twenty times just on the first page, and hardly any of them are identical. Some are slightly flatter, some sharper, depending on the melodic movement. It constantly oscillates between *acem* (F) and *ırak* (F#) even if it looks the same on paper. Hoca says: "You must do justice to this pitch. You must calculate its value with your ear, not according to the notation." He then gives me a description of *Neva*: "*Neva* gives one the impression of an easy makam, its accidentals, its general look appear not so complex. But it is a makam that we can never quite pin down. You might know its scale, but if they ask you to do a *taksim* [improvisation] in *Neva*, to bring it to life is no easy task. You must listen to *Neva* a lot to make sure that makam sinks in [*otursun*]."

The foregoing extract from my fieldwork notes illuminates the kind of feedback we often received from Hoca when rehearsing a piece before him. How one executed the pitch subtleties in their playing and whether or not they had successfully brought out the character of the makam in question was always the archetypical focus of his musical instructions. After all, these two interrelated skilled actions reign supreme in all performance contexts of Ottoman classical music. Consider the artistry displayed by the best exponents of this music over the twentieth century, among them great vocalists such as Bekir Sıtkı Sezgin (1936–1996) and Kani Karaca (1930–2004) and instrument virtuosos such as Niyazi Sayın and Necdet Yaşar (1930–2017). All of them share one musical feature: an exceptional ability to create finely distinct relationships between pitches. "The path to know this music goes through working out its pitch relationships [*perde münasebetleri*]," remarks Sayın.

I first met Niyazi Sayın almost by chance, at his old workplace, the Conservatory of Turkish Music in Maçka, where he had taught for more than twenty years following its founding in 1975. Although Sayın retired long ago, he continued to visit the place every now and again, and he was humble enough to listen to and comment on the playing of willing students during these occasional visits. I accosted him, crossing the quadrangle; we went inside. Half way through our conversation, which was about everything but the ney, a student with a ney case under his arm knocked on the door to the tutorial room, where we were sitting. Upon finding out that he had come from France to spend a semester at the conservatory, Sayın agreed to his request to listen to him play. The young man took out the scores of an instrumental peşrev composed in the makam *Şehnaz* by Kemani Ali Ağa, carefully arranging the sheets on the coffee table. Sayın listened politely to his rather long performance. Without commenting on the playing, he simply said: "Music is the spiritual [*manevi*] relationship between any two pitches. At least, that's how I describe it. To obtain those spiritual relationships, the pitches should come from the inside [*pointing at his heart*], not from the written score."

This brief exchange illuminates, among other things, how players must approach notation as a mediator of musical meaning. I will have more to say about this later. But as Sayın's comments show, learners are explicitly instructed not to take the score for granted or to strive to reproduce it faithfully. The reason is not because any musical piece is always created anew each time it is performed. Or at least, over and beyond this, there is a more technical reason at play here. The notation system in use (the Western staff notation) provides only limited guidance when it comes to dealing with the microtonal pitch inflections that are characteristic of Ottoman classical music. Thus the experience of learning demands a particular kind of engagement with the score.

While the precise expression of pitch subtleties is a well-respected skill in Ottoman classical music, the stress given to discerning the "right" pitch is especially manifest in the art of ney playing. The ney is said to be played by the ear (*Ney kulakla çalınır*), and the right pitch is said to be not on the ney but in the neyzen's ear. As Alâeddin Yavaşça (1926—), an acclaimed composer and vocalist of Ottoman classical music, remarked to me during our interview: "The pitches of a neyzen must be precise [*kâti*] and extremely reliable [*güvenilir*]. The ney is not for everyone to play."[2] Why is there this additional emphasis on aural acuity when the ney is concerned? As I discussed in chapter 2, the material qualities of the reed play a key role in sound expression. The reed's nonstatic nature and its fretless design demand that the ear do more work in calibrating the right pitch. The ney has no "machine-like accuracy," unlike, say, the piano (Machover 2007, 16). Nor does it have a standardized form that allows precision in pitch expression unlike the *bağlama* (the long-necked lute), an instrument that literally takes its name from the frets tied on its body. Stokes notes that "an important element of the rhetoric which surrounds the playing of the *bağlama* is its logical and systematic organization as a musical instrument. . . . Teaching upon the instrument stresses logic (*mantık*) at every turn. The fingering . . . is not left to chance or individual whim but systematized according to precise rules" (Stokes 1992, 71).

Perhaps the physical differences between these two instruments partly contributed to their remarkably different trajectory in the foundational years of the Turkish Republic. The high esteem attributed to the "logical" and "rational" organization of the bağlama earned it in the eyes of the Kemalist rulers the status of a "national" sonic icon in the project of their radical cultural engineering (see chapter 1). By contrast, the material features of the ney connected it with a very different set of musical meanings. Unlike the bağlama, the ney does not serve as "a model of logical thinking" about music, nor does its teaching lay down a concept of music which can be talked about as though it is systematic and rational. While "a good [bağlama] player is often said to play with the precision of a machine" (Stokes 1992, 98), what most credits a ney player is his or her ability to assure certain intonational effectiveness. Here the emphasis is not on correct fingering but on skilled hearing in the first place, for there is no direct march from a tone-hole to the correct pitch.

In the eyes of its practitioners, it is precisely these ambiguities and tensions embedded in the ney's material substance that endow the instrument with its unique character. Musicians take pride in the "unsystematic" and "peculiar" nature of the ney, and how it leaves so much room for the discretion of the ear. They also take pride in the fact that its fretless design makes it especially well suited for microtonal inflections that allow the player, if well trained, to render the most minute shades of intonation. Thus an intimate connection is often made between the affordances of the ney and the tonal character of Ottoman music, as one revealing statement suggests: "The one who cannot hear the peculiar tones of Turkish music cannot give this instrument [the ney] its due" (Halıcı 1998, 29).

Let me return to the fundamental questions driving this chapter. How does one learn to discern the "right" note on the ney? What kind of sonic and melodic elements does skilled practice foreground for learners? And, following Duranti, what does it mean for ney students to cultivate an "Ottoman classical music" way of hearing? The phenomenological perspective urges us to think of sonic properties of music (in other words, pitch relationships, chords, rhythm, timbre, and so on) as not ontologically inherent in what is being heard. Nor is the ability to hear them a mere product of "enculturation" as cognitive psychologists claim (Krumhansl 1990). Instead, listeners actively constitute such sensory perceptions through making them the subject of their active attentiveness. Duranti's work with jazz musicians is again instructive here. As he shows, learning to improvise entails in the first place "developing a 'jazz way' of listening to music" (2009, 210). Competency in this skill requires that the alert musician be able to "respond on the spot to any change in rhythm, tempo, harmonic structure, or melodic lines" initiated by another band member during a performance (210). Becoming responsive to each of these musical components is only possible if certain kinds of perceptive modifications take place in how skilled practitioners hear. Thereafter one may not be able to "remember" their prior modes of hearing.[3] In the same way, to become attentive to melodic modes, to "feel" them, and to be emotionally transformed by them, novices must experience a series of aural modifications. We shall investigate the secrets of the trade by first analyzing the ways in which the spoken language at play in musical apprenticeship makes musical modes "knowable" for learners, by setting forth certain aspects of their sonic, aesthetic, and affective forms.

Tasting, Feeling, Becoming a Makam

What is a musical mode (makam in Turkish, *maqām* in Arabic)? In this section I show that there are two very different ways of speaking about makam. One explains them in the discourse of musicological theory. The other focuses on what makams do, expressed in a phenomenological language that explores musical experience and perception.[4]

Briefly, how does musicological discourse describe makam? In a pioneering treatment on this topic in English first published in 1977, Karl Signell provides us a detailed analysis of the makam theory. He explains: "The makam system is a set of compositional rules by which the melodic component of a piece of music is realized. The closest counterpart in Western music would be the medieval mode. There are approximately 60–70 makams recognized today, each with its own name (RAST, BEYATİ, etc.) and its own distinctive structure" (2004, 16). The book's analysis is organized around five themes, which Signell identifies as the organizing musical elements of a makam: scale intervals, stereotyped melodies, melodic direction, characteristic modulations, and tessitura.

In another definition, Reinhard, Stokes, and Reinhard (2001) underline a similar set of characteristic features in delineating what makes a makam:

> The Turkish modal system is based on the term makam, which might be usefully described as composition rules. Today makams consist of scales

> comprising defined tetrachords (*dörtlü*) and pentachords (*beşli*) governed by explicit rules concerning predominant melodic direction (*seyir*, "path"). The *seyir* indicates prescribed modulations and the general shape of phrases, understood as either predominantly upwards (*inici*), predominantly downwards (*çıkıcı*) or a combination of both (*inici-çıkıcı*). There are terms for the "opening note" (*giriş*), "tonic note" (*karar*), a significant tonal center other than the tonic (*güçlü*, "dominant"), and a note lower than the tonic (*yeden*).[5]

A similar systematizing musicological discourse pervades most music theory books and teaching manuals on Ottoman-Turkish classical music published in the Turkish language (Karadeniz 1984; Özkan 1984).[6] The standard method of teaching is to outline the structure of makams by mapping out their scales, their accidental notes, and their constituent tetrachords and pentachords (figure 3.1). These are groups of four and five notes respectively—what we might call "mini-scales"—that make up the main scale of a mode. Once a breakdown of the standard constituent elements of the mode is provided, the written language then prescribes to the reader how to generate the makam in question. To give just one example, Karadağ's ney-learning manual prescribes that:

> "The makam *Uşşak* is formed by adding the *Buselik* pentachord to the *Uşşak* tetrachord on *neva* [D]" (2013, 20).
>
> The makam *Rast* is formed by adding the *Rast* tetrachord on *neva* [D] to the *Rast* pentachord on *rast* [G]" (2013, 21).

Here, the formulaic language that goes into explaining how a makam is brought to life can be likened to the systematizing language that typically organizes a recipe.

Back in the studio, I prepare myself to play an instrumental composition in the makam *Hicazkâr* written by Kemal Niyazi Seyhun (1885–1967).

> Hoca gives his permission to play and says: "Now take us to old Istanbul. To which era? Let's say to the early 1900s. I reckon this makam belongs, in spirit, to that age. We didn't experience those years ourselves, but we spent time with people who knew what it was like to live in Istanbul back then, we listened to their stories. To me, some makams, like *Hicazkâr*, like *Suzinâk*, have the *hâl* [affective state] of that period. That is my feeling."
>
> I start playing. When I reach the end of the first section, I am told to go back to the beginning. This time I am more warmed up, I can hear my pitches coming out with more control. After last week's lesson, I know that I have to be careful about *şehnaz* [A♭—A four comma flat], one of the unstable pitches in this mode. *Segâh* [B𝄳] is another one. The score is showing "B one-comma

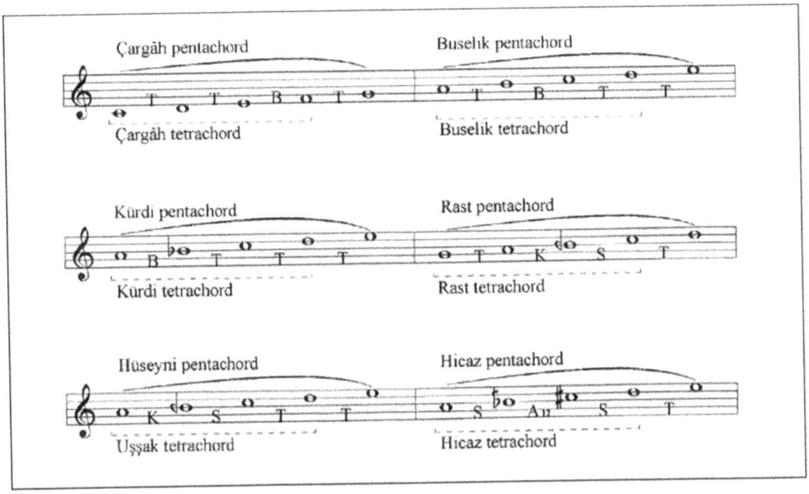

FIGURE 3.1. The tetrachords and pentachords used in "basic modes." (Aydemir 2010, 25)

> flat," but in the audio recording Hoca is playing that pitch a little sharper, in some places as high as *buselik* [B]. I am trying to replicate his pitch inflections in my own rendering.
>
> When I finish, he comments, saying: "Some of your *segâh* came out well. But you must warm it up [*ısındırmak*] more when you come on to it from *şehnaz*. Niyazi Hoca would always want us to play that *segâh* [B♭] like a *buselik* [B] to strengthen the feeling of *Hicazkâr*. This is essential for bringing out the character of the makam and to distinguish it from *Zirgüleli Suzinak* [another mode]. For example, *Hicazkâr* doesn't like strolling around the lower area, it doesn't stress the *hicaz* flavor between *rast* [G] and *neva* [D] unlike the latter. If you emphasize this flavor too much when improvising in *Hicazkâr*, then you end up playing *Suzinak*. Because *Hicazkâr* doesn't make much use of that tonal area, we take the liberty [*tasarruf*] to play that pitch like *buselik*. That's how Niyazi Hoca taught it to us. Without these nuances, we cannot create the atmosphere of *Hicazkâr*. (Field notes)

Here is a different definition of makam for us. What this account draws attention to is the sonic-affective form of a makam as an organic whole, rather than the individual parts that compose it (in other words, tetrachordal organization, the succession of pitches, and so on). To create the "atmosphere" of the makam I must grasp *Hicazkâr* as a whole, hearing not its "note-for-noteness" but how it behaves as an aural form, and pursue that form by being attentive to its family resemblances. In other words, I must make sure to retain the makam's peculiar character and not mix it up with its allied modes. Indeed, even two different modes with an identical scale have their own distinct character. Take, for example, *Beyati* and *Uşşak*, two modes with an identical skeleton, which share the same tonic (A), the same dominant (D), and the same leading tone (G). Yet their melodic inclinations and sonic possibilities impart them distinct personalities. Makam is larger than the sum of its individual notes, which in some cases are the same.

In this sense, what Fox-Strangways observes about raga also applies to a makam: each "gets its special flavor not so much from its being just what it is, as from its being something else, closely allied to it, which is present all the time in the musician's consciousness" (1914, 170). My knowing of a makam emerges precisely out of this aural relationality: that is, out of my fostered intuitions concerning how a certain makam relates to others—how it interacts *with* or *against* them. Thus the musical situation here begets intersubjectivity. If makams have their own intersubjective relations as the master's spoken words above foreground for us, this intersubjective dialogue contributes to and shapes how we constitute the meaning and force of each makam *for ourselves*.

This subjective knowledge is cumulative; it builds up in time through extensive listening and mastering one makam at a time. In all of this, proceeding (literally) at a snail's pace is a virtue, as one acquires credibility by mastering the intricacies of a single mode over an extended period. The time dimension of this learning experience is carefully designed. At Hezarfen, the assignment of makams to students followed a certain order, although this always varied slightly according to the immediate needs of the player. Yet as a norm, each student began modal learning with the makam *Rast*[7] first, which would be followed by the makams *Beyati*, *Hüseyni* and *Uşşak* in the first two years of training. There was no generic order that determined the order of makams to be mastered by each student.

Importantly, the temporality of this skilled practice is charged with an ethical import. Mastering modal techniques is not just a matter of gaining technical dexterity and aural acuity. In the process, one also gradually learns when and where it is appropriate to play in a certain makam. Failing to display this knowledge is often interpreted as breaching *adab* (appropriate manners), an indexing of the player's immodesty. In one revealing incident Salih Hoca asked a new student, who had already worked with another teacher for a few years, to play. The young man began playing an instrumental composition in the makam *Suzidil*. Cutting his playing short, Salih Hoca commented: "To do justice to *Suzidil*, one has to wait. When you set your eye on a makam, you should also consider its consequences. Making an early transition to certain makams is like a child dying her hair. Everything has its time." One has to achieve a certain maturity to move on to a particular makam. In all of this, one must also learn to display a commitment to proceeding slowly, taking one step at a time. As Sennett reminds us, the craftsman's working time is slow: "mature means long, one takes lasting ownership of the skill" (2009, 295).

Consider also the language and imagery organizing Salih Hoca's verbal delivery of technical instructions. Here, spoken words encourage a way of thinking about the aural intimacy between pitches as something that is said to be "absorbed" by one's body. Likewise, a makam is said to "penetrate" into and "sediment" in one's body. This is not a knowledge that is "taught" or "learned" in the technical sense. Rather, through sensory disciplining, the body gradually becomes receptive enough to "take in" the right pitch or to "digest" a makam.

Moreover, a makam is known through its "feeling," through the "atmosphere" it creates, and through the "affective state" it induces in the listener. It also becomes a sonic marker of a particular place at a particular time ("Now take us to old Istanbul. To which era? Let's say to the early 1900s."). To generate the intended affect of the makam, I must imagine the historic city, contemplating the way of life of its residents. In the process of giving shape and meaning to the makam, I reconstruct it by bringing to bear a great deal of what I already know, not just about music but about the world. What I invoke is perceptual and experiential, mediated by my past horizons. Musical apprenticeship exposes learners to other ways of knowing/imagining makam as well. As Salih Hoca remarked on another occasion, "[Makam] *Segâh* has a certain scale: you learn the series of notes that comprise it. But to produce *Segâh* means something else. You must generate its *feeling*, you must create its *taste*" (emphasis added). Thus, learners are encouraged to cultivate an embodied familiarity with the emotional charge of a makam, developing a sense of how it "tastes." Or a makam is said to appear to the player in a particular "mood" and is regarded as capable of inducing distinct emotional responses in cultivated listeners. At other times it is perceived as having a particular "scent" (*koku*) or is identified as possessing a particular shade of "color." What these metaphors tell us is that learning a makam attunes practitioners to its sensual-affective powers. As Tala Jarjour puts it, "the aesthetic system here, or the economy of aesthetics, is at once musical and emotional" (2015, 52). We see this clearly in the following anecdote recounted by the late neyzen Emin Kılıç Kale:

> One day I went to Hacı Emin Dede's house for a lesson. Apparently, a beggar had turned up at his door just before I arrived. Hacı Emin Dede said: "My

> son, if only you had come five minutes earlier. I've never heard a [makam] *Gerdaniye* like that in my whole life." Imagine the great Hacı Emin Dede. He has so many *taksims* of his own, yet he can't forget one sung by a beggar. This goes to show that makam in the way that we know it is not about *do diyez* [C#] or this and that. Those are just a story. Every makam is a world unto itself [Her makam bir alemdir]. Each has its own bearing [*tavır*]. The beggar had brought forth a new world. (Kale 1983, 12)

Kale adds as an afterthought:

> No matter which makam you play, if you haven't become that makam yourself, it doesn't surrender itself to you. (33)

In the lesson context, it is not only modes that are spoken about as if they possess a "character" (subjectivity) of their own, but *perde* (notes) are also imbued with such. Ottoman classical music has a highly intricate microtonal structure. According to the established music theory (*nazariyat*), an octave consists of twenty-four unevenly positioned tones, made up of not only whole tones and half tones but also of microtones. Whereas Western music theory divides the interval between C and D into half, here there are smaller, nontempered intervals to be discerned between two tones. The mathematical value of these smaller intervals is measured with the Pythagorean-based comma (*koma*[8]). The music theory suggests that a note is flattened or sharpened by the use of one, four, five, or eight commas. The accidental signs (flats and sharps) used to represent each of these unevenly divided intervals are shown in table 3.1.

Yet back in the lesson room, a different kind of language permeated Salih Hoca's instructions guiding our attention toward working out the intricacies of pitch relationships (music theory calls it "interval" or "ratio"). A pitch was identified not according to its mathematical value but according to its attributes. We were meant to refer to each pitch with its own name (these are often originally Persian and Arabic words), rather than with Western solfege names (i.e., do, re, mi, etc.), the standard practice in music education in Turkey. Further, these pitch names simultaneously indicate both the value of a pitch and its place in the octave. For instance, while both the terms *dügah* and *muhayyer* stand for the note A, the former refers to A in the middle octave, whereas the latter points at A in the upper octave. According to Salih Hoca, the solfege name is what a perde becomes when stripped of its character. Perde transcends fixed notes indicated on the five-line staff, shape-shifting according to its particular place in the melodic development and in accordance with the particular makam being played. Thus, rather than corresponding to a single note, it is to

TABLE 3.1. Alteration signs used in Arel-Ezgi System

Number of Commas	Lowered	Raised
1	𝄳	𝄲
4	♭̸	♯
5	♭	♯̸
8	♭̸̸	♯̸̸

be imagined as a sonic "zone" (*bölge*), or as a "color" with many shades. There is, for example, no one pitch *segâh* (B flattened by one comma), but many. According to the makam being played, the player must continuously calibrate the right segâh each time it appears in a melodic line.[9] Far from being couched in precise language, Salih Hoca's instructions always came in a non-numerical form: "play that pitch a little flatter," "raise that pitch a little bit" (*bir miktar*), and so on. Primacy was always placed on listening and hearing the right pitch directly from his playing.

What these insights show is that, even if modes do indeed possess an internal order, their mastery entails a kind of knowing that cannot be attained by following a set of predetermined rules. The analogy of a recipe is again instructive here. According to Oakeshott, because a recipe does not "exist in advance of the activity," it "cannot be properly said to govern it" or to "provide the impetus of the activity" (cited in Jackson 1996, 35). As Michael Jackson writes: "Our gestures, acts and modes of comportment do not invariably depend on *a priori* cognitive understanding. Practical skills, know-how, a sense of what to do, are irreducible. The meaning of practical knowledge is in what is accomplished through it, not in what conceptual order may be said to underlie or precede it" (1996, 34). Theoretical knowledge, in this sense, can be best understood as more "a *post facto* rationalization of what is said and done than an explanation of it" (35).

To Give "Flavor" to the Makam

Let us now move from the discussion on how the musical pedagogy subjectively constitutes the concept of makams for the learners to analyzing what its skilled playing involves. How does one go about creating the taste of a makam or bringing out its character?[10] One key perceptual modification that learners must experience in gaining proficiency in makam music involves cultivation of an aural sensitivity to discern, literally, the "flavors" (*çeşni*) of a makam. This is a core aspect of acquiring an "Ottoman classical music" way of hearing. *Çeşni* (meaning taste, flavor, spice) is a particular combination of a series of notes in a certain ascending or descending order. In the established musicological language, çeşni corresponds to a tetrachord and/or pentachord making up the scale of a makam. For example, the *Rast* flavor on *neva* (D) means the Rast tetrachord on the note neva. Music theory directs one's attention to the scale organization of a mode.

By contrast, the skilled learning process at work in the studio trains the ear to hear the flavors embroidered in the melodic texture, rather than the eye to scan the notated tetrachord. According to tanbur artist Murat Aydemir (1971—), "the tetrachords and pentachords create the skeleton of the makam. The notes of this skeleton (pitches and *çeşnis*) reflect the spirit of the makam" (2010, 8). Aydemir further articulates the difference between these two modes of attention:

> I describe the *çeşnis* to my students in this way: think about spices. Every spice has its own particular taste, aroma and color. What if we were to read all about a spice, learn its composition and examine its color but never tasted it? We might gain some ideas about it but would never recognize its flavor. Only after learning its flavor would we be able to decide ourselves where to use it, and in what quantity. This is precisely the case with the *çeşnis* of Turkish music. It is not sufficient to calculate the intervals, memorize the tetrachords and pentachords and learn the content of the scales theoretically. Only when we hear these pitches from a reliable source will we have "tasted" the *çeşnis*, and only by listening to and imitating them time and time again may we internalize them. After this process the musician will be able to use the *çeşnis* wherever and however he wants, and identify the makam of a piece that he hears. (2010, 8)

In the same vein, in the actual practice of experience of learning a makam, primacy is always placed upon discerning a sense of the effect of each "flavor" so that one can learn to recognize it when it occurs in a particular melodic line. This is a skill that affords greater freedom to the player. Once familiarity with the particular character of a flavor is attained, one can also freely reconfigure its sonic-sensual effect from the desired pitch. This kind of mastery lends itself to grasping the "personality" or "attributes" of a mode. Through exposure to listening to a certain mode for an extended period and through many painstaking attempts to reproduce its flavors in my own playing, I began to build up a good sense of which particular flavors the mode has an inclination for, and where in the melodic development it is indispensable to create those flavors.[11] As I start to feel the mode, my attention is no longer on chasing individual notes—what novices typically do—but on imagining how the melodic progression behaves as a whole. Flavors lend flesh to the texture of the melody, continuously imbuing its idiosyncratic movements with new meanings.

Flavors, in this sense, are sonic signatures of a mode, yet not in a rigid fashion. Indeed, musicians are often willing to improvise subtle changes in the sonic form of a flavor so as to make it more pleasant on the ear—without sacrificing the integrity of the flavor, of course. Salih Hoca's teaching method foregrounded this skilled action strongly, encouraging a reflexive engagement with microtonal relationships. Let me proceed with an example. *Hicaz,* often described as a "potent" (*tesirli*) makam, is one of the beloved modes of Ottoman classical music (and of other makam traditions throughout the Middle East as well). A large repertoire of compositions exists in *Hicaz*—and it is one of the five modes in which the call to prayer (the evening prayer) is recited, at least in Turkey. In Salih Hoca's teaching practice, most students would move on to learning this makam after two or three years of lessons and would spend a great deal of time mastering the intricacies of the mode as well as of its allied modes. One of these intricacies pertains to the *Hicaz* flavor on *dügah* (A, B♭, C#, D), a characteristic "motif" of the makam. Salih Hoca would want us to raise the second step (*dik kürdi,* B♭) a little—that is, playing that note sharper than what the notation signposts, so as to enhance the affect of the flavor. According to him, this slight intervention in the intonation of the flavor helped create the desired feeling of *Hicaz,* giving the "Ottoman-Turkish" version of *Hicaz,* in turn, its distinct aesthetic-emotional character. This microtonal adjustment to be made was not restricted to the makam *Hicaz.* But each time the same flavor came up when playing in another mode, the same skilled action was to be executed. As a matter of fact, a significant number of modes in Ottoman classical music use this particular flavor. *Sabâ* is one of them, a makam that is said to resonate well, especially on the ney. Here the *Hicaz* flavor appears in another tonal area, this time on C (C, D♭, E, F, G). Yet the same adjustment is required to create the taste of the flavor—and of the whole makam—through raising the second step (D♭, *hicaz*) a little and creating a slightly new kind of bond between that pitch and the succeeding pitch. In these situations, which skilled practitioners must continuously negotiate, the intentional modification of pitch relationships operates on a fine intonational level. Yet without such subtle adjustments the mood of the mode cannot be created. As Racy notes, the manipulation of microtonal relationships "can raise the musical expression to a higher ecstatic level" (2003, 107).

In brief, these musical examples foreground for us the dialogical and mutually affecting relationship (*münasebet*) between the three building blocks of this music: the pitches create the flavors, and the flavors are bonded together to create the whole form (makam). By keeping the taste of the flavor and the makam in mind, one must constantly calibrate the right pitch. This entire process can be likened to form-giving, which is dynamic, requiring a continuous modification of individual parts for the sake of accommodating the sonic-affective unity of the larger form. To engage skillfully with each of these musical elements, the novice must learn to constantly negotiate the internal tensions and interactions between them as they unfold in the actual process of performance.

The intricacy of this skilled action can be suggested by the intricacy of another artistic practice. Anthropologist Yuehping Yen has said much the same about understanding visual composition in Chinese calligraphy. Just like the notes in a melodic line, "No character or stroke stands alone on paper. Each is situated in a web of calls and responses, actions and reactions" (2005, 97). As Yen explains, the practice of creating intracharacter bonds between parts in calligraphic composition requires the skilled practitioner to constantly modify the size, shape, and density of individual characters (perde) so as to integrate them into the whole character (makam) (93). In this sense, "the writing of a whole piece of work becomes a continual judging and adjusting process, striving for the wholeness of impression and graphic effect" (95). This point provides us with a good visual analogy for imagining what it means to give each note and each flavor its rightful place in a melodic line.

Notation, Discretion, and Intuition

In this final section, I discuss more explicitly a vital topic that has been only obliquely discussed in this chapter until now: How do skilled practitioners (whose hearing has been modified through the learning process) approach notation as a mediator of musical meaning? What do they do with the "text"? As we have seen, the skillful reckoning with makam involves negotiation with pitches, as well as working out how best to bring them into a state of "flavorsome" interdependency. This creates a situation in which the player must constantly assess how much to abide by the instructions of the score in the real time of making music. The questions, then, are how much amendment is allowed, and how much liberty can one take?

In "raw" form of course, this is a question that concerns all practitioners of music, regardless of the genre. A reflexive dialogue with the score is fundamental to all creative performance, which can be usefully understood as a guided act of improvisation. As the pianist and conductor Daniel Barenboim remarks during a conversation with Edward Said on this topic, "the score is not the truth.

The score is not the piece. The piece is when you actually bring it into sound" (Barenboim and Said 2004, 33). For Barenboim there is no absolute object called the piece or such thing as faithfully reproducing a piece. Every time a piece is brought to life, it is given a new meaning, it becomes a new event, a new creation. This "essential unrepeatability of music," as Barenboim describes it (122), lies in the fact that improvisation and modification are already intrinsic to the acts of interpreting and performing a written piece.

Over and beyond this performance-generated ontological status of notation, in the musical experience analyzed here, there is also a more technical reason shaping the engagement that one develops with the written score. This pertains to the limited guidance that the notation system in use provides when it comes to dealing with the microtonal pitch inflections that are characteristic of Ottoman classical music. Known as the Arel-Ezgi System,[12] the established music theory uses an adapted version of Western staff notation to symbiotically represent/communicate a twenty-four uneven tone-scale. Yet as we have seen above, in the actual practice of playing in a makam there are more pitches, many of which cannot be fully captured by the accidentals of the notation system. There are pitches (for example, *hüzzam, uşşak,* and others) that cannot be pinned down to symbols. In this sense, the score only provides partial guidance when it comes to microtonal pitch inflections, instituting at most a bare outline of a makam.

How do musicians respond to this incongruity between the notation system and practical knowledge? The topic has generated much heated debate among music theorists and skilled practitioners of Ottoman classical music during the twentieth century. Even today, new theoretical systems proposing an alternative understanding of pitch intervals and new notation methods are not rare.[13] While for some experts the solution lies in inventing a notation system that is more precise and fully aligned with the "real" pitch intervals of the music, others are more content with this discrepancy. In fact, some ney musicians argue that if a new notation system were to be introduced, it should be nothing other than the old *Hamparsum* notation. Developed by the Armenian cantor and composer Hamparsum Limoncian (1768–1839), this notation method was widely used in the second half of the nineteenth century to score both Armenian Church music and numerous Ottoman compositions. It was also invariably used in ney education up until the late 1960s. What causes this particular symbiotic device to be seen as more appropriate for capturing the soundscape of Ottoman classical music, at least for some masters?[14] The answer lies in the inherently imprecise nature of this notation method. Its logic assumes that the player is already conversant with the characteristic pitches of each makam and leaves it to the discretion of the person to work out the intonational relationships conducive to creating the atmosphere congenial to the makam.

From this perspective, the absence of a full uniformity between the standard musicological system and the performance aesthetics offers infinite possibilities for the expression of individuality. The malleability of the score creates an extra space for putting one's own discretion into work or for exercising what Racy refers to as "interpretive liberties" (2003, 92). Musical apprenticeship values and valorizes these explorative capacities, just as it fosters them. The following instruction by Salih Hoca would suffice to illuminate this point. On this occasion I am rehearsing the instrumental prelude composed by the great tanbur player Cemil Bey in the makam *Muhayyer*. Salih Hoca says:

> The score tells you to play this note as segâh [B one comma flat]. But the makam gives you the freedom to raise that note as high as buselik [B] in some parts of the melody. Music theory [*nazariyat*] would never tell you this. You will play it intuitively [*insiyaki çalacaksın*]. One could look at this in two ways. One is to say it is a problem; one is to say it is richness [*zenginlik*]. For me, it is the latter. Because it leaves it to your discretion [*tasarruf*] to work out the right pitch. You play it according to how you heard it from your own hoca. Or sometimes it is your mood that affects how you shape a pitch. That gives us pleasure [*keyif*].

These words draw attention to two significant points about the creative process at work here. First, while music theory objectifies makam by systematizing a corpus of rules and principles to generate it, the practice of skilled learning does exactly the opposite: it subjectifies the makam by setting up a context in which every novice discovers its taste for herself or himself through their own *intersubjective encounter* with its constituent components. For musicians, the objectivity of these musical elements is constituted out of this subjectivity (in other words, the makam Hicaz *according to* Salih Bilgin). This intersubjective encounter is not without a past horizon. To be able to intuit the right pitch, to use one's own discretion to bring out the feeling of a flavor, and to be able to render one's own interpretation of a mode—in short, the art of *tasarruf*—all require a high degree of learned skill. Above all, it requires the talebe to sit side by side with their hoca and to hear the right pitch from him. Here we come back full circle to meşk. Only by becoming grafted into an artistic lineage and through disciplining in its "ways of doing things," skilled learners acquire the institutive discretion to use that capacity freely. Lineages, in this sense, are not abstract kinship groups; they have an ongoing existence. As mediators, lineages mobilize both the perception of the student and the objective skeleton of the makam to bring these two actors together in an intersubjective encounter. The lineage creates people who hear the world in a particular way, even as it creates the musical world by shaping pitch relationships (in other words, makams) in a particular way.

A second point of interest that Salih Hoca's words highlight for us concerns the mood of skilled learning, inspired by becoming better at doing things. This is a practice of exploration (*keşif*). Successful striving to obtain a better sound from the ney or to craft better musical relationships between the pitches produces *keyif* (pleasure). As we will see in the following chapters, keyif is both an important mood and an essential motivation in becoming a neyzen. According to Salih Hoca, discovering the city's affordances and limits—where to eat the best *kurufasulye* (baked beans) or to drink the best coffee—is also part of becoming a neyzen. Such knowledge is not separate from musical knowledge.

Let me step back here and reflect on ney learning as encountered in the ethnographic material analyzed so far. As the rich language constituting Salih Hoca's teachings demonstrates, talebes are not only mastering technical skills. The metaphoric language that guides bodily skill instructs by way of suggesting interrelationships and analogies between music and other spheres of daily life. This fostered mode of knowing invites new insights and ways of thinking about such relationships (in other words, one thing comes in the image of another thing) while recognizing the key role of imagination in configuring students' learning by more intuitive means. As Sennett writes, the language that directs bodily skill "works best when it shows imaginatively how to do something. . . . [W]e can understand those imaginative processes that enable us to become better at doing things" (2009, 10). As will unfold more clearly in later chapters, this music pedagogy sees no fault lines between the development of musical craft and of an ethical self. Both are required for conducting music/life with skill.

CHAPTER FOUR

Improvisation and Journey

Taksim is the sound of how
one lives his or her life.
—Niyazi Sayın

IN CHAPTER 3 I EXAMINED the ways in which ney pedagogy guides learners to cultivate a sensitivity to the subtleties of tonal relationships as demanded by the aesthetic canon of makam music. I discussed in particular how teaching the instrument emphasizes discernment of the right or "better" pitch at every turn, a skilled action conducive to bringing out the character of a piece of music. As indicated earlier, playing composed music is deeply improvisatory, given that skilled practitioners must constantly calibrate the pitch intervals during performance. In this chapter I examine another core skilled action in which a much more explicit relationship to improvisation emerges: the art of *taksim* (*taqsim* in Arabic).[1]

Generated in performance, the meterless and "free-flowing" (*serbest*) improvised melody of a taksim intends to embed a certain makam in listeners or, more precisely, to prepare the ears of the listeners to the mood and affect of the makam. The melody can be created in a single makam, or it can wander through more than one in the course of its performance. In the first instance, then, modal improvisation demonstrates at once both the practitioner's subtle depth of knowledge of the makam's aesthetic and emotional character, as well as their skill in enlarging its aural possibilities: as Racy says, an evocative taksim combines "what *is* with the realization of what *can be*" (2003, 96).

In his probing analysis of the historical origins of the taksim in Ottoman Turkey, Feldman (1996, 282) notes that the taksim as nonmetrical improvisation had already emerged as a distinctive genre or musical form by the seventeenth century, practiced "within both the courtly and dervish musical spheres." The category encompassed vocal and instrumental improvisation alike, although it has gradually come to be associated primarily with the latter. Feldman's discussion of one of the key historical texts written on Ottoman music by the seventeenth-century composer and music theorist Dimitrie Cantemir (1673–1723) gives us important clues about the high premium held by the art of taksim at the time. Cantemir's text "present[ed] *taksim* as the highest form of performance," describing its melody as illuminating "the power of the musician" (Feldman 1996, 279).[2]

Today, taksim continues to be considered the pinnacle of the classical repertoire of Ottoman-Turkish classical music. The reasons are many. First, because improvisation affords (and gives permission to) the player the greatest freedom to show his or her wares, it is considered to be the most sublime sonic statement of one's artistry. Skillful improvisation requires deep musical knowledge, a great deal of technical prowess, and an ability to formulate in the moment modally "convincing" yet also "tasty" (*lezzetli*) melodies. As a matter of fact, when a player's artistic abilities are judged, it is the creative skills displayed in his or her taksim performances that are assessed, alongside the emotions (*hissiyat*) that the player's melodies are capable of creating in listeners. Although there is no rule that every player must be expert in the art of improvisation, ultimately one must demonstrate proficiency in rendering his or her own taksim in order to be recognized as a competent musician in his or her own right. As I was explicitly told by one of my informants, "to be regarded as a neyzen, one must have proven an ability to perform a taksim in some kind of musical gathering, formal or informal."

Needless to say, there is more to this skilled action than its revelation of the musical or artistic capabilities of the player. Alongside the player's musical self, the social/moral persona, too, is understood to be expressed in the course of a taksim performance. The virtues that the taksim reveals are said to attest not only to the breadth of one's musical knowledge, artistic style, and technical competency, but they are heard also as a reflection of the self. The art of improvising connects in many ways to the art of living, sounding out an aural revelation of how one lives his or her life.

On Not-teaching How to Perform a Taksim

If modal improvisation carries such a premium in Ottoman-Turkish classical music, then how is it taught and learned? What place does it occupy in musical pedagogy? An immediate answer would simply make the point that taksim cannot be taught: it is the student who must self-learn how to perform it. As a matter of fact, despite its highly praised status, the teaching of modal improvisation receives very little attention in musical pedagogy. This absence of an explicit attention to its practical mastery contrasts with the ways in which improvisation is taught in some other musical traditions. Take jazz music, for example, a genre in which improvisation is said to be its *chief* virtue. As the literature on jazz and jazz improvisation reveals, in that musical genre one can find a variety of methods, strategies, and even specifically designed practice sessions intended to guide novices in improvising their own jazz renditions (see Berliner 1994; Duranti and Burrell 2004; Wilf 2010). For instance, Duranti's (2009) work on the significant role performed by language in music education shows us how jazz instructors' spoken instructions during jazz combo classes help modify students' ways of listening to the recorded improvisations of famous jazz musicians. By contrast, even when formal education contexts are concerned, there are no specific programs or explicit instructions devoted to teach ney students how to become competent in taksim performance. Autobiographical reflections by musicians on their own experiences of learning to perform taksim reinforce this point. For instance, Salih Hoca explained that taksim was always a part of his conservatorium-based lessons with Niyazi Sayın but that it was never taught as such. "Sometimes Hoca would ask one of us to hold the drone for him while he would be performing a taksim, that was it," he recounted. The learning trajectories of Salih Hoca's own students were also predicated on the same principle of "not-teaching" taksim. As one neyzen who had become a talebe to him at age twelve while a student at the conservatorium confirmed: "We did not explicitly learn how to perform taksim, but Hoca used to tell us strictly whom to listen to and whom to turn a deaf ear to. Our ears were totally disciplined [*terbiye edildi*] in line with his listening instructions."

Similarly, in our own learning context, modal improvisation constituted a vital component of the lessons' musical content. Yet again, instead of being explicitly "taught" by Salih Hoca, doing taksim was something that each person had to discover for themselves once a sound knowledge of a certain makam had been attained. On one occasion, however, one competent talebe took on himself to perform an improvisatory piece, not of his own rendering, but a "copy" of a well-known Hüzzam *taksim* performed by Niyazi Sayın. Upon receiving Salih Hoca's permission, the student took out a piece of paper displaying a handwritten transcription of the taksim's melody and began playing it before everyone. Salih Hoca listened and, appearing uneasy with the student's reproducing of the sketched notes of the melody, commented briefly: "You should listen to a taksim many times and try to imitate what it does, but only to play what remains in your ear. What matters is not whether you can fully replicate that melody or not, but what you can do with those components of the melody which you were able to memorize. After all, the same taksim never comes twice."

The importance of listening to recorded musical performances as a first major step to developing improvisational skills has been underlined in the anthropological and ethnomusicological literatures. Paul Berliner discusses this point at length in his seminal book *Thinking in Jazz* (1994), showing how jazz students devote hours every day listening to the recorded improvisations of prominent jazz figures. Eventually, through memorizing chunks of musical material aurally "captured" from those performances (melodic lines, chord progressions, and the like), practitioners form a "store of ideas" (221) and can begin to generate their own renditions. Thus, recordings are extremely important tools in learning to improvise. Similarly, even if the art of taksim is not taught as such, ney masters repeatedly tell their students that they must attend to the taksim performances of renowned artists in order to train their ears to pick up the compositional techniques in model taksim melodies. Salih Hoca's statement above not only hints at the core mechanisms of how one learns to fashion his or her own improvised melodies—repeated listening and copying—but it also recognizes the fact that creativity can only come via repetition.

No doubt, Niyazi Sayın's large body of recorded taksim repertoire constitutes a primary listening reference for most ney students today. This repertoire involves Sayın's solo taksims as well as his joint improvisations with two other highly acclaimed exponents of the taksim genre in Turkey: the tanbur player Necdet Yaşar (1930–2017) and the *kemençe* (pear-shaped bowed fiddle) player İhsan Özgen (1942—). These master musicians elevated the art of modal improvisation to new heights over the second half of the twentieth century, developing together the most complex examples of a particular improvisatory form known as "joint taksim" (*beraber taksim*).

Niyazi Sayın's musical companionship with Necdet Yaşar dates back to the 1950s, when they played together in the Ensemble of the Istanbul Radio led by Mesut Cemil (1902–1963) and in the Istanbul Conservatory Performance Ensemble (*İstanbul Belediye Konservatuvarı İcra Heyeti*) directed by Münir Nurettin Selçuk (1900–1981). Over the next three decades, Sayın and Yaşar performed extensively as a duo, with taksim occupying a vital place in their performance repertoire. Their joint improvisations broadcast on Istanbul Radio became an admired feature of their musical partnership, listened to with great anticipation by Turkish audiences. "We chose to display our compositional skills, our talent in the form of taksim performances" (Biz bestecilik yeteneğimizi, tüm hünerimizi taksimlerde göstermeyi tercih ettik), recalled Yaşar.[3] A significant aesthetic feature of these musicians' joint improvisations is their polyphonic sonic effect. Rather than following a typical question-answer format, their melodies utilize a much more intricate design whereby their sentences occasionally weave into each other, creating startling contrapuntal and harmonic effects. Needless to say, this form of improvisation requires a deeply shared sensibility among players over the techniques of creating an effective modal identity.

What kinds of listening practices were formative, then, in shaping the artistic horizons of these musicians? As Sayın and Yaşar acknowledge at every opportunity, a major part of their intensive aural disciplining and artistic training involved listening to the recorded instrumental works of the late legendary Ottoman composer-virtuoso Cemil Bey (1871–1916).[4] Following their release in the early 1910s on 78 RPM records (*taş plaklar*), Cemil Bey's taksims performed on a number of stringed and bowed instruments, including tanbur, kemençe, *lavta* (a long-necked plucked lute), and cello, have remained the benchmark for generations of musicians following him. As ethnomusicologist Frederick Stubbs (1994, 15) notes, Cemil Bey "is said to have gone in search for sounds to use in his music; utilizing a variety of extra-urban borrowings audible in his *taksims*," a creative element that has immensely inspired artists following in his footsteps, such as Niyazi Sayın. "Even though I am a neyzen, Cemil Bey is my model," remarked Sayın during one of our conversations (March 26, 2014). "What pitches come out of his tanbur, his kemençe, his viola! Only a [perfect] human, a human being like Cemil Bey can play those pitches" (Ancak insan o perdeleri basabilir, Cemil Bey gibi bir insan), he commented, recognizing how Cemil Bey's pitch articulations set an exemplary model for him.[5] Sayın's long companionship with, and musical learning from, Cemil Bey's son, Mesut Cemil (also a renowned tanbur and cello player) also influenced his artistic style significantly. Similarly, Necdet Yaşar underlines the enormous pedagogical role that listening to and analyzing the recorded performances of Cemil Bey and other great masters played in his and Sayın's musical socialization:

> We used to compete with each other to find Tanburi Cemil's recordings from secondhand booksellers, from Kapalıçarşı. We would then listen to these recordings at the Doğancılar house [referring to Niyazi Sayın's Üsküdar house] for days and analyze them. We would try to work out how, alongside his virtuosity, Tanburi Cemil was able to fit so many melodies and makams into three-and-a-half minutes, how he was able to retain that lyricism in his melodies. I never forget, one day I introduced Niyazi to a recording, he got

FIGURE 4.1. Niyazi Sayın (on the left) and Necdet Yaşar, Toronto, 1980.

so excited that he began whirling around the gramophone like a dervish. We would repeatedly listen to all *sazendes* (players), *hafızs* (reciters of Quran) of the past and talk about their performances. This analyzing went on for years. (Author's translation)[6]

In "Rethinking Orality in Turkish Classical Music," Panagiotis Poulos (2011) discusses the vital role that mediated listening practices play in the enskillment of classical musicians by presenting as its case study the musical biography of Necdet Yaşar. Once preserved in sound, performances of renowned artists function as vital "aural texts" instrumental for the musical training of the following generations of musicians, best illuminated in the dissemination of Cemil Bey's work. As Poulos discusses, following the emergence of the Turkish recording industry around the first quarter of the twentieth century, aspiring music practitioners, alongside their meşk practices, had the benefit of using performances from gramophone records as learning supplements. The practices of studying and memorizing recorded performances later "extended to joint listening-practicing sessions by musicians" (172), best exemplified in the musical companionships of Sayın, Yaşar, and İhsan Özgen, who joined Sayın and Yaşar in the late 1970s.[7] In the following excerpt cited in Poulos, Sayın and Özgen reflect upon how they made great use of Cemil Bey's recordings in developing their own skills in the taksim genre:

> *Niyazi Sayın*: We developed it (the *beraber taksim*) by listening together with İhsan to Tanburi Cemil Bey's *taksims* and by *copying his melodies* [emphasis added].
>
> *İhsan Özgen*: To achieve that, one needs to have the same music understanding, and the same listening references with his fellow musician. In our case that was Tanburi Cemil Bey. (180)[8]

What these autobiographical reflections show us is that the skilled acts of copying and imitation are integral to the process of creating one's own distinct melodies. At no stage in the enskillment process are these actions intended to reproduce a blueprint of an already crafted piece—after all, the ultimate aim in the art of taksim performance is to prove musical originality. Yet as Sayın's and Özgen's words clarify for us, the path to create original melodies goes through the royal road of copying, of modeling one's own movements on existing sound events, at least in the beginning. For Ingold, copying is already improvisatory:

> The process of copying . . . is one not of information transmission but of guided rediscovery. As such, it involves a mixture of imitation and improvisation: indeed these might better be understood as two sides of the same coin. Copying is imitative, insofar as it takes place under guidance; it is improvisatory, insofar as the knowledge it generates is knowledge that novices discover for themselves. [. . .] Both are aspects of the situated and attentive engagement that is fundamental to becoming a skilled practitioner. (2001, 143)

The skilled practice of Islamic calligraphy provides us with a good visual analogy of what Ingold describes here. In the weekly lessons that calligrapher (*hattat*) Efdaluddin Kılıç (b. 1968) taught at our workshop, which I took great pleasure in sitting in on, students would be asked to copy a series of characters, or expressions, either from the teacher's own writing or from an old calligrapher's (figure 4.2). The lesson format was highly routinized. Each student would take turns to sit next to the master and watch him go through the student's copy, which had been rehearsed at home. The master would mark one by one which letters looked exactly like the model work and those characters that did not, repeating the correct hand movement on the same paper one more time under the alert gaze of the student. The novice would repeat this act of copying the assigned piece over the following couple of days or weeks until his or her "copy" satisfied the master's taste.

FIGURE 4.2. Master calligrapher Efdaluddin Kılıç. Courtesy of the artist.

What exactly is it, then, that the novice copies by watching the master's hand? Yen (2005) answers this question succinctly in her study of Chinese calligraphy. "Reproducing" the model composition as closely as possible, she notes, "is not so much to reproduce rigidly the spatial layout of strokes in the model work as to acquire the motorial pattern required to write them" (119). As such, in each repeated act of copying individual characters and the lines connecting them, the hand comes to know better how to mobilize the brush/pen and paper: how much pressure to bring to bear on the paper, how tightly to grip the brush/pen, in what exact angle to contact the paper, and so on. "Through copying the outward appearance of a past master's writing the apprentice is in fact copying the master's bodily propensities of movement, therefore his body techniques" (120). Eventually, the student can bring his or her writing body into a deep alignment with the master's body, and thereafter fluidity in writing emerges.

Some of the same processes are involved in learning to copy the improvisations of master musicians. Copying and memorizing equip skilled practitioners with a supply of musical resources, enabling them to develop the tools and techniques necessary for crafting their own renditions. Here, too, copying model performances is done not so much to reproduce in a strict sense how melodic sentences were woven together in others' previous actions but to acquire, by doing so, an embodied knowledge of the general procedures, patterns, and gestures that go into the sonic design of a taksim. These may pertain to the structure of the melodic content (melodic progression, ways of establishing modal substance, modulation into other modes, and so on) or may concern micro-actions that can enhance the emotional efficacy of the performance (in other words, the use of cadential motifs, the alteration of a certain note, melodic repetition, the creative use of silences, sustaining long notes, ornamentation, and the like). After all, taksim is not the sounding out of some arbitrary melody. Even though there is a spontaneous element to it, that spontaneity has to be executed within "a rigorous and tightly knit system of structural principles" (Nettl and Riddle 1998, 391), the learning of which requires long years of apprenticeship. What Duranti and Black argue for verbal improvisation applies also to musical improvisation, that "in addition to being oriented toward the accomplishment of something new or at least partly different from what was previously done by themselves or others, verbal [or musical] improvisation is guided by practical, aesthetic, and moral canons that are specific to the cultural tradition that gives meaning to the ongoing activity" (2011, 459). On that note, the perceived similarities between verbal and musical improvisation is another point to underline, as one of my informants discussed:

> We should think of the art of taksim as an art of oratory. When you make a taksim, you also construct sentences [*cümleler*] and try to order them fluently. Just as one needs to build up a rich vocabulary to speak well, the player also needs to create for themselves a rich vocabulary of expressions and sentences to choose from when making a taksim. This will only come with listening to a lot of taksims and copying what others did in their own melodies. Gradually, you build your own vocabulary and your own way of phrasing. For instance, we know how much Niyazi Hoca admired Cemil Bey and dedicated himself to listening to Cemil Bey's taksims. We know also that

> he was very familiar with Western classical music. Now when you listen to Niyazi Hoca's taksims, you hear straightway the richness of his listening experiences, the richness of his musical imagination.

Note here how the music–language analogy is evident in the metaphors that musicians use to talk about taksim melodies (in other words, "musical vocabulary" or "musical sentences"). Similarly, Stubbs draws an analogy between making a taksim and speaking, describing "*makam* as language and *taksim* as oratory" (1994, 134; see also Nooshin 1998, 112; Berliner 1994, 492–93). According to Stubbs, at the core of learning taksim lies the cultivation of two essential skills: "the grammar of the modes and the rhetoric of *makam* oratory" (231). The former concerns the musical knowledge necessary for establishing in sound the makam in question, whereas the latter entails learning the modes of declamation that stylizes a taksim performance. (In my interviews with ney musicians, the rhetoric of taksim was often likened to the oratory of Quranic recitation.) The following two sections in this chapter will discuss in more detail a series of skilled actions that feed into mastering what is glossed by Stubbs as the "grammar and rhetoric of *makam* oratory." What modes of attention does the art of taksim demand from the player? What kinds of compositional strategies can be mobilized to create masterful sonic journeys? Engagement with these questions must bear in mind the two inseparable "functions" of modal improvisation, both musical and emotional—that is, to manipulate the sonic potentialities of the makam so as to enhance the change in the collective mood of the listeners.

Establishing "Modal Presence"

In the classical tradition, taksim primarily serves as a means through which the modal substance of a piece of music can be established. To use the musicians' jargon, a good taksim must show an ability to "warm up the ear" (*makamı kulağa ısındırmak*) to the makam to be introduced in the course of a performance, making the audience's listening susceptible to the musical effect of that mode. Thus, to warrant credibility, the taksim melody must, in the first instance, effectively create the sonic individuality (*hüviyet*) of the mode in question by revealing its essential features that are "at least to a degree obligatory" (Nettl 1974, 13). Expert musicians utilize a wide range of creative actions to generate a strong "modal presence" (Racy 2003, 100). For those students who are embarking upon the task of mastering this skill, the learning process always begins with familiarization with the melodic progression peculiar to each makam.

The intricacies of melodic progression are well described through the use of the term *seyir*, literally "path" or "journey." Seyir is associated with the morphology of a given makam, accounting for the conventional ways in which melodic progression unfolds in that mode. It involves knowing which tonal area to begin the melody from, where to rest, which particular notes to emphasize, how to expand the tonal possibilities of the melody before bringing it to a conclusion. The realization of seyir comprises, in this sense, a series of movements purposefully enacted between a set of destinations that are peculiar to each makam, though such movements should not be thought of as a set of "rules" that dictate a certain melody. Seyir contours the "rest" points that the player should stop at along the path, but nevertheless it leaves it up to the person to configure his or her own route. What forms these "rest" or "destination" points then?

As chapter 3 discussed, the melodic structure of each makam consists of a set of characteristic notes such as the "tonic note" (*karar* or *durak*, first degree of a scale), which creates in listeners' ears a sense of ending, and the "leading note" (*yeden*, the note just below the tonic, the seventh degree of a scale), which confirms the musical effect of the final cadence on the tonic, creating a more powerful finale. The "dominant" (*güçlü*, either the fourth or the fifth degree) is another "backbone" note of a makam's tonal center. Temporary rests (*muvakkat kalışlar*) on this note play a key role in giving further direction to the voyage. For instance, when playing in the makam *Hüseyni*, dwelling on and circling around the makam's dominant note *hüseyni* (E) is highly crucial for evoking the musical character of this mode. The makam *Beyati*, on the other hand, typically relies on amplifying the note *neva* (D) in order to affirm its modal affect, and unlike its "kin" mode *Uşşak*, it rarely descends below the tonic. In another example, Signell cautions us that "the makam *Pençgâh* should emphasize the fifth degree, but if one lingers just a bit too long around the third degree, the *seyir* resembles *Sazkâr*, a different makam" (2004, 46). These examples affirm once again that the makam is not a scale. It is the seyir that enfleshes the scale, bringing the makam to life. The scale is "form," the seyir is "form-giving." And as Ingold says, following Klee, "[form is] death; form-giving is life" (Ingold 2010, 92).

The art of taksim, then, is the art of form-giving whereby the player executes skillful knowledge of how to move—in other words, knowing where to begin the melody, which tonal areas to dwell upon, which notes to give due weight to, where to rest and where to stop so that the makam can be efficaciously brought to presence. Improvising, in this sense, is akin to journeying through a tonal landscape. As Neyzen Bülent Özbek said to me, "to do taksim is like to take a journey to somewhere." The metaphors that musicians use to describe each one of these movements also give this meaning away: "to move" (*hareket etmek*), "to stroll" (*dolaşmak*), and "to repose" (*istirahat etmek*), for instance. Each time the player performs a new taksim in the same makam, a new sense of temporality, too, is potentially enabled. The course through which the makam takes its shape during the melodic excursion is shaped not only by the player's musical knowledge but also by his or her emotional state in the moment. "How I construct the melody of the taksim is bound to how I feel [*hissiyatımla alakâlı*] in that moment. There is always pleasure [*keyfiyet*] in taksim performance," explained one ney player. Sometimes an unforeseen mistake is also part of the course of how the seyir unfolds, in the same way that a "clam" is in jazz music. As one of Salih Hoca's senior talebes explained to me: "Musical competence [*ustalık*] lies also in converting an unintended mistake into a correct action. Let's say you hit a wrong note during the seyir. You must create the following sentences in such a way that even that wrong note becomes nicely embroidered in the melody." As Ingold says, skilled action is "not so much imposing form on matter as bringing together diverse materials and combining or redirecting their flow in the anticipation of what might emerge" (2010, 94).

The musical context of the taksim configures the creative decisions of the player about what shape to give to a melody. The intention of the improvisation, when exactly the taksim comes during a musical event, and, most important, who constitutes its audience all determine a range of choices from how long/short to keep the taksim to how much artistry to display through the melodic journey. Depending on such contextual elements, seyir can be realized very differently. In the pedagogical sense, a taksim can intend to merely demonstrate the pure melodic progression of a given mode—in other words, the seyir. This type of composition avoids any surprising elements such as modulation, while weaving its melody by adhering to the conventional melodic contour of the mode in question: the opening statement begins around either the tonic or the dominant note, continuing with a series of sentences amplifying the key notes in the makam's scale before a rest on the dominant note is made. On its way to the final destination, the melody imparts an affect of tension and incompletion by making suspended cadences (*asma karar*) on the notes leading toward the tonic and by emphasizing the leading note before an affirming stop is made on the tonic. Although, generally, a taksim designed to render modal progression only would lack artistic appeal, it does, however, serve as a crucial learning device for mastering the makams as well as the skill of improvisation. Stubbs's work provides this pedagogical value of *seyir*, describing it as "the only explicit instructional tool offered to the student who wants to learn to improvise" (1994, 126). His musicological analysis covers seyir examples performed by Niyazi Sayın and İhsan Özgen in the years 1984 and 1986, respectively, in seventeen

EXAMPLE 4.1. Taksim by Niyazi Sayın in the mode *Uşşak*

different modes. In example 4.1 I refer to one of the seyir examples Sayın created in the makam *Uşşak*.[9] Yet we must note that "translating" the aural text of the taksim into a written form is not a straightforward process. The transcription of the taksim should be read only as a limited outline, or skeleton, of the original melody.

The melodic progression in this taksim (example 4.1) begins in the lower tonal area. The makam likes to extend over *yegâh* (low D with the *Rast* flavor) and makes a long emphasis on the tonic *dügâh* (A). To accentuate the tonic, the melody strolls around the A–D tonal area (first two lines) and makes a series of trills on the pitch *rast* (G) to further reinforce the effect of the tonic. The first sentence of the taksim comes to an end by giving an impression that a suspended cadence will be made on *segâh*, but Sayın completes his sentence by coming on to A. The second phrase (third line) begins to explore the area around the dominant by quickly stressing the note *acem* (F), typical of this makam. The seyir makes abundant use of the pitch *segâh* (lines three and four) and comes back on to the tonic A by accentuating the taste of *Uşşak* flavor, which gives the mode its character. In his third sentence, Sayın begins to establish a new rhythmic movement by using the tonal relationships between "E, F, G (high), E" and "D, E, F, D," respectively. He then goes higher up to *muhayyer* (high A) and strolls back to the tonic by strongly emphasizing F and the *Uşşak* flavor. The fourth melodic section of the taksim is constructed on the tonal area between D and the tonic A, with a long rest made on the A (line 8). He then quickly drops down to *yegâh* (low D) to make a skillful transition on to *neva* (D). Thereafter he brings the melody to a complete end, preparing the final cadence on A by strongly emphasizing the *Uşşak* flavor. In all of this, the *seyir* presents us with a pure *Uşşak* melody, bringing out the taste of the mode in the simplest manner.

By contrast, the following taksim by Salih Bilgin played in the same mode during a stage performance follows a slightly different path (example 4.2). The opening sentence begins around *çargâh* (C). Following a rest on *dügâh* (A), a suspended cadence is made on *segâh* (B one comma flat) (bars 1–2). The second sentence moves from D to A by accentuating the *Uşşak* flavor (D-C-B-A), and continues by showing the mode's leading note, *rast* (G), and by making a suspended cadence on F# (the beginning of bar 4). The following phrase extends from *yegâh* (low D) to D by giving us a taste of the *Rast* flavor first, and then makes a rest on the tonic A by accentuating the *Uşşak* flavor (bar 5). The seyir, then, goes on to explore the possibilities of the makam further, by way of constructing the melodic progression on D. Here Bilgin emphasizes the pitch *hüseyni* (E) strongly so as to reinforce the hearing of the makam's dominant tone, a typical movement that the artist often uses in his improvisations in this makam. The new sentence introduces new flavors by going up to *gerdaniye* (high G) and using a *Kürdi* flavor on E. Here an alteration is made on the note F (the sudden return from F# to F) to create an effect of de-temporalization, another strategy often used in Bilgin's taksims (bar 8). Following this, the melody first takes a rest on D, then begins to stroll down to G by using a *Rast* flavor, and moves the melodic construction once again around the tonal area of "E, F, G." The melody modifies our hearing by introducing the *Hicaz* flavor (G, F#, E, D) (bars 12–14). A strong ornamentation is made on F (bar 15), an aesthetic element of Niyazi Sayın's artistic style. Following this, we hear the *buselik* flavor on D (D, E, F, G) and a suspended cadence on *çargah* (C) with a *çargah* flavor, a movement that this makam likes. This short rest on C reinforces the feeling that the melody is fully in tune with the makam *Uşşak*, preparing the melodic flow for conclusion. *Uşşak* flavor is emphasized again on A, and the extension towards *yegâh* (low D) is made with a *Rast* flavor (bar 19). Finally, the final cadence on A is made with the *Uşşak* flavor. To strengthen the cadence, *rast* (G) is used as a *yeden* (the note below the tonic).

Both of these taksims create the affect of *Uşşak* by following relatively "familiar" modal tracks. In each of these melodic constructions, the seyir unfolds in accordance with the basic conventions of the mode *Uşşak*, without making any modulations into another mode or incorporating surprising elements that temporarily obscure the mode. One major difference between the two melodic paths is the creation of the *Uşşak* effect through persistent rests on E in the melody composed by Bilgin. Their renderings generate the modal efficacy of *Uşşak* through intonational inflections (for instance, B flat [*segâh*] is flattened in descent more than indicated in the score), through giving emphasis to the central notes of the mode and through the use of cadences. Cadences are important devices in establishing modal presence, as they help the scale of a mode to be heard as a makam. A full cadence (*tam karar*) played on the tonic inspires a strong sense of conclusion, whereas suspended cadences enrich the seyir by mobilizing additional flavors and by creating various degrees of tension and resolution. As Racy elucidates, the artistic and emotional efficacy of a cadence "depends significantly upon its timing, the precision with which it is executed, and the novel ways in which it is rendered" (2003, 104). Especially when modal improvisation is concerned, a short pause (silence) following an elaborately executed cadence can enhance the emotional power of the performance considerably, charging the melodic phrase with an extra capacity to resonate in a listener's mind.

Although taksim is often said to be a "spontaneous" event, skilled practitioners often do have a more or less clear idea about the melodic seyir that their composition will take. For instance, one time, when he was asked to perform a joint taksim with tanbur player Murat Aydemir at an upcoming concert of the Presidential Ensemble of Classical Turkish Music, Salih Hoca began to rehearse possible forms of seyir in the makam *Gül'izar* in which the improvisation was

UŞŞAK TAKSİM

Salih BİLGİN

EXAMPLE 4.2. Taksim by Salih Bilgin in the mode *Uşşak*

to be set in. The actual taksim melody eventually emerged in the moment of playing together with his companion, yet the destinations were somewhat prefigured. Similarly, Stubbs reports İhsan Özgen mentioning that in his joint improvisations with Niyazi Sayın certain of the modulations (see next section) "would be planned ahead of time, and that this pre-arrangement could, to a certain extent, be rehearsed" (1994, 246). This goes to show that the popular conception of taksim as "impromptu" composition that emerges "on the spur of the moment" is only a half-truth.[10]

Finally, stereotyped phrases or motivic patterns (*beylik melodi*) are other vital tools that musicians use to affirm in listeners' ears a familiarity with the mode being evoked. These phrases, which often appear at cadential points or function as opening or closing sequences, contain important structural notes, and upon hearing them, a knowledgeable ear can easily identify the makam of the melody.[11]

Taken together, all of these skilled actions, temporal or structural, from scaffolding the seyir and making fine pitch inflections to effective cadencing and the use of elaborate stereotyped motives, allow the player to bring the listener to a familiar sonic terrain whereby they can make sense of what is going on during the improvisation. This is the trademark of an effective improvisation. Competent players signpost for competent listeners how the mode unfolds and is brought into existence. Indeed, performance requires a skilled listener. The world of the listeners and musicians is a joint world where the musician needs the listener to complete his or her work/improvisation. They dwell in a shared sound world whereby the improviser relies on the creative listening of his or her audience or "persuades understanding from the listener" (Stubbs 1994, 23). Accordingly, each skilled action that establishes modal presence places the listener on a familiar pathway by affording a certain degree of familiarity with the musical event and a pleasurable capacity to anticipate what is to unfold.

A skillful improvisation must achieve these and more. In the words of Necdet Yaşar, "To qualify as a taksim the melody must generate various discoveries [*buluş*] which move the listener and provoke contemplation in him or her. Only when artistic creativity is executed does a true taksim unfold." What affords credibility to a taksim transcends its ability to successfully create the musical affect of a given mode; the performance must also impress its listener emotionally by creating instances of surprise, incomprehension, or even tension before a sense of resolution is achieved again. As Racy puts it for the Arabic taksim, "Improvisation constitutes a merger between the familiar and the novel . . . an appropriate balance between satisfying the musical norm and departing from it, perhaps an intermediary between compliance and defiance" (2000, 305–6). Expert listeners can take delight in encountering something they were not waiting for—in other words, in being taken momentarily to a new sound terrain.

The Emotional Power of Taksim

Among musical circles the phenomenon of improvising is spoken about not merely in musical terms. The shared language surrounding this skilled act is at the same time a language of affect in which attention is also directed at the abilities of a given taksim to create certain emotions in listeners or to generate in them a certain affective state (*hâl*). The genre of taksim is in itself conceived to be conducive to affect. Being fully unbounded by the conventions of rhythmic cycle, the player is given ultimate freedom to produce the mood of a given mode or, more precisely, to make the listener become susceptible to the emotional influence of that mode.[12] The widespread discourse on improvisation often associates the distinct emotional substance of this musical event with freedom as well as with the imagination of the performer.

In what idiosyncratic ways does an impressive taksim heighten the hâl of listeners then? Before delineating some of the key micro-actions that enable this, we should note one useful way of understanding the emotional impact of improvisation as suggested by Jonathan Shannon, who describes it as the altering of the listener's perception of time. In his view, listening to a taksim "brings listeners out of the normal flow of time into a state of detemporalization" (2003, 85) whereby time is experienced as "suspended or transformed" (87). It is such perceived transformations in time that elicit a heightened emotional response in listeners. Following this through, those creative elements that help create the modal efficacy of a makam (seyir, cadences, stereotyped phrases, melodic repetition, and so on) during the auditory journey also serve to establish a "temporal space" for the listener (86).

Modulation is another skilled action that plays an extremely crucial role in altering listeners' perception of temporality. Modulation occurs either when the flavor resonating strongly with another mode is integrated into the melodic flow or when a transition from the original mode to another mode is made, resulting in a full swing in tonal centers. Thus, in the case of the latter strategy, the player intentionally "cancel[s] out the path of the *seyir*" (Feldman 1996, 272) or transforms the course of the movement in some unanticipated way, which, according to Shannon, generates "a momentary re-temporalization of the aesthetic experience" (2003, 86). A skillfully executed departure from the path of the original mode and a smooth return back to it—"recapitulation" in Signell's words (2004, 67)—is an efficacious device for avoiding monotony and has, therefore, great potential to enhance the artistic power and emotional effect of the performance. Modulation constitutes also another highly effective strategy for creating an unfolding affect of tension and resolution or, to borrow

Cantemir's words, an effect of "agreement" and "consonance" in and through the taksim melody. Feldman notes: "To Cantemir, the major significance of the *taksim* lays in its ability to create musical 'agreement' or 'consonance' by uniting the separate modal entities of the makam system through modulation" (1996, 298). In fact, Cantemir assigns a great value to the genre of taksim, especially because it "allows the musician the greatest freedom in modulating between the modal entities" (279). When he claims that modal improvisation demonstrates the "powers of the musician," he particularly has modulation in mind.[13]

Aesthetic questions about how modulation is executed form a significant issue when judging the artistry displayed in an improvisation. No "rules" govern what series of modulatory actions to undertake (there are no rules about how many times modulation can occur in a single improvisation, either). Based on their knowledge of modal theory and on how they feel in the moment of performance, a player might opt for either a more predictable modulation, whereby a switch is made to a related mode, or, alternatively, a less standard modulation. For instance, based on their tonal makeup, the modes *Hüzzam* and *Segâh* or *Suzinâk* and *Hicazkâr* can be considered as neighboring makams. Modulating between these modes requires less-complex movements (in other words, shifting the dominant note of the original makam to a different degree of the scale would potentially allow a smooth modulation) compared to a modulation that takes place between two relatively more unrelated modes (from the makam *Mahur* to *Segâh*, for instance). If executed with artistry, modulation made into a dissimilar mode can produce a much more dramatic effect on the listener's ear. In all modulatory scenarios, competence lies in executing the modulatory act without causing a sense of abruptness for the listener by way of "warming up the melody" (*melodiyi ısıtarak*), to use the vernacular language. An expert listener should be able to recognize—and take pleasure from—the transformation made in the modal texture, enabled by a smooth shift.

The timing of the modulation and for how long the player stays on the makam to which the modulation is made are also considered to be revealing of one's musical artistry. As a general norm, modulation should come not in haste but only after a solid modal presence of the original makam is first established. A rushed modulation can be heard as a sign of ineptness or as revealing an egoist sentiment to "show off" one's artistry. The player must also ensure that the presence of the mode revealed during modulation does not override the presence of the original mode, which the taksim is meant to evoke. The former serves to illuminate and reconfirm the modal efficacy of the latter, not to dispel it. As Racy states, "The artist needs to safeguard the modal creation against the adverse extremes of both understating and overstating" (2003, 101).

Niyazi Sayın's improvisations on the ney provide some of the most elegantly executed examples of this complex skilled action. Among his well-known improvisations, his fifteen-minute rendering of a taksim in the makam *Pençgâh* is a specimen of his brilliant command over modulation. This taksim continuously alters the listener's perception of passing time by making a series of novel modulations, all rendered with rare ease. The melody also impresses listeners with its unusual expressions and motifs, its remarkable intonational precision, and its impressive technique. Further, despite the nonmetric feature of the taksim form, Sayın's taksims often manipulate the element of rhythm through his careful pacing and pausing, as well as skillful use of syncopations and legatos, which make his artistic style depart considerably from the established artistic canon before him. Another taksim by Sayın in the makam *Uşşak* (example 4.3) illustrates his unparalleled articulation of the legato technique (as well as his tremendous control of breathing).[14] Despite being performed at a live Radio program under substantial time pressure—it is an eighty-one-second performance—Sayın manages to create momentum by his brilliant contrapuntal traversing of octaves. The melody begins around low *çargâh* (C) and wanders around the makam's notes in the low-pitched area. After the thirty-eighth second, the melody begins to progress in the middle octave and shows the makam's scale through a twenty-five-second legato movement, making repeated suspended cadences on a series of notes (D, C, B, A). The final cadence is played on A with the *Uşşak* flavor. The taksim expresses the flavors of *Uşşak* in a rather simple manner, but unlike Sayın's other *Uşşak* taksim analyzed earlier, here the melody demonstrates unpredictable movements and striking virtuosity.[15]

Yet it is not only the artistic creativity of a taksim that generates its emotional power. To be perceived as effective, an improvisation also needs to fit into its immediate musical context. For instance, if the taksim serves as a prelude to a following piece, its melodic articulation must be in tune with, and effectively engender, the "spirit" or "atmosphere" (*hava*) of that music. An emotionally impressive taksim bears a capacity to skillfully prefigure the mood of the musical piece to come after it. On one occasion, when Salih Hoca assigned me a piece in the makam *Mahur* by Abdülkadir Maragalı, he suddenly remembered a taksim by his hoca, Niyazi Sayın, performed before this piece during one old radio program. He said:

> Once Hoca made this unforgettable taksim during a radio program to introduce this piece [*Mahur Kâr*] by Meragalı. What a magnificent taksim it was! This is where the greatness of a player [*sazende*] lies. It lies in their ability to render the taksim in such a manner that when you listen to it, you

EXAMPLE 4.3. Taksim by Niyazi Sayın in the mode *Uşşak*. Transcription belongs to Ahmet Toz (2013, 117–18).

EXAMPLE 4.3. *Continued.*

> can feel the hava of the piece that will come next. When you listen to that taksim in [makam] *Mahur,* you know that only a grandiose [*görkemli*] piece like Meragalı's can be played next.

The skillful artist not only efficaciously brings into existence a given mode while exhibiting fine artistry on the spur of the moment, he or she also brings the listener to the right temporal space. Such prefiguring of the musical and emotional character of what is to come next must consider also the intention or function of the taksim performance. A taksim might serve as an introduction to a concert program, a *fasıl* (a suite of compositions arranged by makam) or a Mevlevi ayin, or it might serve to introduce a new mode (*geçiş taksimi*) so as to attune the listeners' ears and affective states (*hâl*) in line with the new modal atmosphere. Some taksims are rendered in the original makam of a fasıl or a concert repertoire in order to forestall any monotony in the flow of the overall performance. Aesthetic judgments about how to design the melodic path, how much artistry to display, and which strategies to utilize in order to prefigure the mood of the following piece need to reflect an adequate understanding/awareness of the demands of the immediate musical context. Some classical ney musicians criticize publicly aired taksim performances today for failing to take on this musical sensibility. One well-respected neyzen made the following criticism in relation to what he perceives to be a recurring flaw in the rendering of the introductory taksim (*baş taksim*) always performed on the ney at the beginning of the Mevlevi ayin ceremonies annually held in Konya:

> Now, the ayin always begins with the recitation of Itri's *naat* in the makam *Rast*. Let's say the ayin repertoire chosen for the ceremony is set in the makam *Hicaz*. The chief ney player begins his taksim by creating *Rast*. He goes on wandering around *Rast* for some time and finally gets hold of a note somewhere in the upper register and concludes the taksim with a quick *Hicaz* melody. What kind of taksim is this? A modulating taksim from *Rast* to *Hicaz*. But that's not what the introductory taksim is set out to do. You may begin the melody in *Rast* but the aim is not to create the atmosphere of *Rast*. If the ayin to be recited is in the makam *Hicaz*, you must satiate the listeners' ears with *Hicaz*. . . . Another issue is that baş taksim is not meant to be a "show off" taksim. This is not the place to overwhelm the listener with too much virtuosity. The task is to prepare the listener to the atmosphere of the piece to follow. The hâl your taksim creates should make the listener proclaim "Allah" [My God], making them feel the urge to get up and do *sema*. What type of taksims can achieve this? Taksims like those by Niyazi Sayın, and taksims we heard from Neyzen Aka Gündüz.

Note here how this narrative uses the expressions *havaya sokmak* (to set the mood) and *kulağı doyurmak* (to nourish the ear) to illuminate what skillful improvisation *does* to the listener. While a competent taksim performance is required to accomplish these tasks, some modes are perceived as charged with extra emotive power, as performers and astute listeners speak about them as "autonomous ecstatic packages" (Racy 2003, 99). For instance, according to some ney artists, the affective state aroused by makams *Segâh, Sabâ, Uşşak, Evcara,* and *Ferahfeza* is especially strong when such modes are performed appropriately on the ney. "A neyzen takes great pleasure in playing *Evcara,* because the makam fits well [*oturur*] on the instrument," explained one ney master, "Neyzens are generally attracted to the makam *Sabâ*," remarked another, adding that if a taksim in this mode is to take place in a group performance, it is invariably taken by a ney player. Salih Hoca, too, expressed special fondness for a cohort of modes, including *Hicazkâr, Suzinâk, Ferahnâk,* and *Nişaburek,* describing their expression to be extraordinarily potent (*ifadesi tesirli makamlar*). His feeling of affection for these modes stemmed from a perceived compatibility that defined the aesthetic character of these modes and that of the ney sound. Over and beyond this, he heard in them a sentiment that was revealing of an "Ottoman-Turkish" self: these are "Makams that express us well" (Bizi iyi ifade eden makamlar). Take the makam *Suzinâk* for instance. As he explained on one occasion:

> If I were asked to describe our music, my response would be that it is very much like the makam *Suzinâk.* To me, the essential manner [*eda*] of this music is retained in the spirit of this makam. There is no equivalence of *Suzinâk* in other music. The character, the hâl of this makam, is exclusive to itself. But *Nihavent,* for instance, is not like that. It recalls scales used in other musical traditions. Thus we must know *Suzinâk* well. Nobody would get tired to listening to a skillful taksim in *Suzinâk.*

In another lesson, he distinguished between the makam *Ferahfeza* and its close relative *Sultaniyegâh*:

> There are certain makams that better express Turkish music. For instance, *Ferahfeza* and *Sultaniyegâh* are made up of the same notes, but the feeling [*hissiyat*] of *Ferahfeza* is much closer to Turkish music. By contrast, *Sultaniyegâh* turns its face more toward the West. Even if both makams share the same scale, their emphases [*vurgu*] create very different feelings.

Michael Herzfeld (1997) might call these understandings examples of cultural intimacy; narratives that, in appreciating the emotional qualities of particular makams, both express and reveal a Turkish-Ottoman self and subjectivity. Here is a theory of makam (based on an experimental and empirical science) that intuits their varied affective power. For example, for Salih Hoca (and indeed for the musical lineage in which he trained) the makam *Suzinâk* reverberates or vibrates with a powerful charge that for a socialized Turkish listener "burns one's inside" (*içini sızlatıyor*). Many writers have discerned similar comprehensive understandings of the emotional efficacy of particular makams in other places. For example, Racy discusses how for Arab musicians the makams *Hicaz, Sikah-Huzam* and *Saba* generate "an extraordinary level of *saltanah,* or modal-ecstatic domination over the performer and the listener" (2003, 99). Similarly, Jarjour (2015) analyses the emotional power of the *hasho* or makam *Rahawi* used in Passion Week chants by Surjani (Syrian) Christians to produce *huzn* (sadness). In all of these cases, sentimental response to the special affect of a makam reveals and expresses collective identity, which may also be explained in a more or less ideological discourse as "how makam affects *us* (and not them)."

We see something of these debates concerning makam and relational identity in ney musicians' anxieties about the increasingly limited number of modes in which improvisations are rendered. In my interviews with lineage musicians, nearly all remarked on the fact that a diminishing range of makam dominates the contemporary ney taksimi, among them modes such as *Kürdi* and *Hicaz*. The makam *Kürdi*, a popular mode in Arabic music, is often the target of such critical comments. Many classical musicians express a worry about the increasing appeal of this supposedly "light" (*hafif*) and essentially "Arab" makam, especially among those disparagingly referred to as "market neyzens" (*piyasa neyzenleri*) or (more recently) as "*Kürdi neyzenler*." Such a "trend" is interpreted as a creeping *Araplaşma* (Arabization) in Turkish music.

Another criticism is directed at a more technical issue. It concerns the manipulation of difficult modes with intricate pitch intervals (in other words, those using "neutral steps" such as *Hicazkâr, Suzinâk, Şedaraban*) by way of the technique of transposition. Some ney masters, however, make the point that, once transposed, a scale does not resonate exactly the same as it does in its original tonal place in ney playing. Even if the same pitch intervals are retained, the resonance and the feeling of the given mode are not quite the same, they explain. In one musical gathering I attended, upon hearing one young competent ney player perform a taksim in the makam *Şedaraban* on the mansur ney by transposing the mode's scale into *dügâh* (A) (rather than playing it on *yegâh* [low D]), a senior neyzen commented that his ear heard the melody not as *Şedaraban* but as *Hicaz*. The modal effect of the original makam had been lost for him. Similarly, during one interview, my informant criticized a tendency in young players toward transposing as a shortcut "solution" to rendering microtones more easily. This, he reckoned, "destroys the pitch sensibility in Turkish music," leading to a homogenization of tonal flavor. He said:

> When you listen to ney improvisations circulating in the music market today, most of them are transposed into *dügâh* (A) regardless of the makam being played. Hardly one hears a taksim these days, which does not conclude on *dügâh*. Today only five to ten makams are being played anyway, and even then they play all of those makams from the same tonal area by way of changing the ney [neys come in twelve different sizes] and using the technique of transposition. This destroys the pitch sensibility in Turkish music. It feels like you are listening to the same makam all the time.

Improvisation as Revelation of Self

What emerges from the analysis so far can be summarized in two ways. First, good improvisational skills are acquired, not given, and the actions of copying and memorizing are fundamental to developing such skills. Skilled practitioners can improvise on the ney only when their hearing has been thoroughly socialized within the conventions of the art of taksim and when they have acquired a "vocabulary" or a repertoire of "improvisational building blocks" (Berliner 1994, 101) that they can spontaneously pick from when composing their own melodies. These conventions that facilitate a shared understanding between the performer and the listener may pertain to compositional strategies, techniques of seyir construction and phrase building, stylistic elements, ways of ornamenting, as well as the tonal and intervallic features of the makam music that help establish modal presence.

Second, the art of improvisation also mandates that the player execute novelty and inventiveness to impress the listener emotionally. Accomplished performers of the taksim form are celebrated not only for their great knowledge of makams and instrumental versatility but also for their unique artistry. Capable of avoiding cliché musical ideas, skilled improvisers have something new to say in their self-generated melodies, even when rendered in a single makam. Their improvisations convey imaginative components, exhibit originality, and express a musical self.[16] These creative elements are best collectively captured in the expression *tavır*.

In the vernacular language of Ottoman-Turkish classical music, tavır denotes "style," although the broader meanings it is charged with include manner, attitude, and demeanor. Tavır is one of the two key expressions that classical musicians use to identify artistic style: the other one is *üslub*, which communicates the meaning of an artistic style characteristic of a group (in other words, a lineage), whereas tavır stands for the individual style of an artist (for example, the tavır of Niyazi Sayın). That is, ideally, two members of the same meşk lineage would share the same üslub, but their individual tavır would be different. To take its own shape and to emerge as a recognizable style, tavır must be grounded and disciplined in an established üslub. One ney master explained their complementarity by using the following analogy:

> In arts, one must first belong to a certain üslub and then develop his or her own tavır. I liken the relationship between üslub and tavır to the two feet of a dervish performing sema. One foot anchored, the other revolves 360 degrees. Only when both actions are carried out together can the dervish

> whirl. Now in music, that anchored foot is the üslub of the artist. Without that anchoring, that firmness, tavır cannot emerge.

As the analogy here illustrates, tavır epitomizes open-endedness, freedom, and individuality, which are only allowed when one is sufficiently disciplined in the conventions of a certain üslub. Ney masters constantly remind their students that the cultivation of one's own personal tavır—a distinct musical self—is one of the ultimate aims of the skilled learning experience, but, nevertheless, they never talk about it as something that is only attainable through rigorous bodily practice. Neither do they disengage it from other activities of social life or from other domains of experience that shape one's social persona. Tavır is an individual creative expression that is understood to be carved out by a whole range of personal and impersonal qualities that contribute to the making of the person. It takes its shape not merely from practical mastery and musical knowledge but is influenced also from where one was born, the city one inhabits, what one eats, how one dresses, and so on. For instance, in one of our lessons with Salih Hoca, after we listened to a taksim performed by Niyazi Sayın in the makam *Şedaraban,* he made the point that what made his hoca so versed in this particular mode was not his musical genius only but also the fact that Sayın was truly *İstanbullu* (literally, "from Istanbul"). For him, this was a core element in his master's biography that contributed to the shaping of his distinct tavır. In the same vein, Salih Hoca reflected upon his own experience of having been born and lived in Afyon for some time and having had an *Anadolulu* (from Anatolia) side to his personal identity as elements formative of his own musical tavır. He then added: "To have full faith in your *hoca,* to surrender to that person allows üslub to emerge. But tavır is made up of many other things related to one's way of living [*yaşantı*]."

What this example hints at is that the entire being of the subject is understood to be constitutive of one's musical self. "Being İstanbullu" signifies much more than being born in that place; it also encompasses a certain urban sensitivity that organizes a whole range of embodied habits, from eating and musical taste to how one speaks the language. According to Sayın, the expression that best describes what Ottoman-Turkish music is *İstanbul musikisi.* How could one strive to master this music without crafting a skilled knowledge of the city? As we will discuss in more detail in chapter 6, Sayın's own relationship with Istanbul shaped his teaching practice in fundamental ways. His lessons with his talebes were never confined to his conservatorium room or his Üsküdar house but extended to the whole city, making abundant use of a select range of places, from historical sites, old bookbindery shops and bead-makers' studios to coffee shops to secondhand markets. These embodied activities intended not to create flâneurs sauntering around the city but to teach skilled practitioners how to craft an experience of living in that city. This endeavor also involved Sayın's training of his talebes to become experts in a range of skilled practices, from growing roses to practicing photography, from caring for pigeons to binding books, from marbling paper to carving wood, from inlaying pearl shells to making prayer beads (*tesbih*). His fine craftsmanship in such a huge range of activities earned him the reputation of *hezarfen*—literally, a person who demonstrates deep knowledge and brilliant abilities in a thousand fields of practice. For Sayın, tavır is not limited by musical knowledge and talent. It is "nourished" (*beslenmek*) by skilled knowledge gained through participation in a wealth of practices of extramusical kind too. "To get a beautiful sound from the ney, first a beautiful sound must come from us," he remarked during our conversation.

This brings us to another important "function" of the taksim. In its musical statement, we hear the player's tavır in its fullest sense. The musical assembly and artistic execution of a taksim's melody illuminate not only "the power of the musician" but also disclose "how they have lived their life," to use Sayın's words. It is an act of revelation of the self. For Sayın, this creative self reflected in the art of improvisation is a product of all the bits and pieces that form the subject's biography, constituted through perceptual modifications cumulatively experienced over time. In other words, it is not an ahistorical self born creative, capable of drawing out from himself or herself the hidden qualities of the world or the expressive depths of his or her being, as the Romantic notion of creativity suggests.

Eitan Wilf's work on jazz education helps us sort out differences between these two conceptions of self. Drawing on anthropological fieldwork at a postsecondary jazz school in the United States, Wilf examines how artistic pursuit of invention and originality and a searching for a unique self are deeply entangled in jazz pedagogy as they resonate with the Romantic ethos of creativity. According to Wilf, jazz educators constantly emphasize the uniqueness of each individual yet to be discovered, as illuminated in pedagogical imperatives such as "Find your voice" or "Be yourself." The ideal of self-realization demanded of the student suggests, first, "the idea of discovery of something that pre-exists such discovery, and second, the notion of something personal and unique that pertains to the prospective student and that is the subject of discovery ('your voice' and 'you')." A third point is that the only way for the skilled practitioner of jazz to achieve the mission of discovery is to strip away all those layers put upon them so that they can get down to their essential self, hidden in there almost from birth. As one jazz musician quoted by Wilf prescribes, one must "cut away the extra fat to get to the heart of the meat" to develop what he or she does well (2010, 569).[17]

By contrast, the ney pedagogy presents us a very different conception of the creative self. It assumes that the uniqueness or distinctiveness of each person—and each tavır—derives precisely from those accretions of experience that contribute to the making of the subject. Unlike in the case of jazz ethics, its model of self-realization is not one of subtraction ("cutting away the extra fat") but of appreciation, the addition of all the influences that one has been subject to in life. The two pedagogical practices therefore have different imaginations concerning time and temporality. Jazz pedagogy imagines a timeless self, a self always there, to be discovered through finding one's zero point, a reassertion of one's core. In the ney pedagogy, on the other hand, musicians' selves are built up through time, in particular through their slow mastery of a whole range of skilled practices, including via familiarity with the city. Here a temporally crafted and fashioned self is a core source of taksim; without this history of perception modification through time, a unique style of improvisation is not possible.

CHAPTER FIVE

Master Speakers, Master Listeners

He who has ears to hear, let him hear.

—Mark 4:9

This musical endeavor cannot be done without sohbet.
Without sohbet, the shell can be learned but not the essence.

—Salih Bilgin

THIS CHAPTER CONTINUES the theme of the previous chapter. However, it concentrates not on musical improvisation but on verbal improvisation. A key idea running through the chapter is that the technical skills and artistic knowledge fostered by education in the ney do not emerge only in the conduct of musical practice through watching, copying and imitating masters' playing bodies, but are also powerfully cultivated by listening to their words, communicated through the skillful practice of *sohbet* (in the first instance, conversation). As an essentially Islamic practice, which has a rich history especially in Sufism, sohbet constitutes the prime method of musical pedagogy. In the learning environment analyzed here, sohbet forms much more than an intersubjective activity through which musical instructions are disseminated by word of mouth. Sohbet is *the* practice: the musical teaching and learning happens in sohbet.

As those of us learning from Salih Hoca discovered, he was not only a musician acclaimed for his artistic talent, he was also astonishingly well versed in the art of speechmaking. As a standard norm, at least one-third of a two- or three-hour lesson would take a speech mode, throughout which Salih Hoca talked and we listened, occasionally sharing our own ideas or asking questions. These were not planned or formalized sessions separate from the lesson's technical content but rather arose spontaneously in the flow of the lesson. Salih Hoca improvised his words just like music: sometimes a comment about breathing would escalate into a sohbet about living in "chaotic" Istanbul; at other times, an anecdotal story of a Sufi master would foreground a certain dimension of the skilled knowledge for those who had ears to hear. In brief, musical teachings are inseparable from sohbet.

In addition, the essential place of another kind of sohbet event in the social life of the ney school should be mentioned (figure 5.1). These were listening sessions held periodically with a respected musician, who would be invited to engage in an interactive conversation about a certain aspect of his or her artistic work or biography.

Because sohbet is highly improvisatory (just like taksim), certain similarities can be discerned between these two performative events. First of all, the ability to perform sohbet effectively requires significant creative skill. As in the process of becoming a good taksim player, this skillfulness is not something one gains overnight; it takes years of experience to attain competency in speech. Second, the elements of immediacy and spontaneity are integral to both of these improvisational practices in the sense that they are never—at least entirely—planned. Sohbet is not only performed on the spot, but it also erupts when the mood of the moment is right. Its spontaneity also lies in the immediacy in which the speaker picks the rhetorical devices to convey his or her words. The same topic or a piece of instruction might come up again and again in different occasions of sohbet, yet each time a new speech event is enacted, the same "message" might appear in a new form, as in the shape of a new metaphor, analogy, or *hikaye* (narrative telling of accounts). Such rhetorical devices at the disposal of the speaker resemble "stock patterns" (Berliner 1994; see chapter 4) that musicians accumulate over a lifetime of listening and playing, and can, thereafter, be intuitively incorporated into their own composed melodies. Not only the choice of words and narrative devices but other improvisatory features such as the ways in which speakers mobilize the qualities of their voice (loudness, pacing, stressing, and the like), the modes of their bodily comportment (such as gaze or the bearing of the body) and how they artfully make use of silences during the talk are all integral to how the verbal performance unfolds.[1] Third, just as musical improvisation requires a skilled listener to complete the performer's work, sohbet relies on the listening skills of its audience. "Even the most silent of listeners is an author of an emergent narrative" (Ochs and Capps 1996, 21). Listeners are "co-authors" of

FIGURE 5.1. Sohbet by kemençe master İhsan Özgen, Hezarfen, 2018. Courtesy of Salih Bilgin.

the performance because they actively make sense of what is being said (Duranti 1986) and assign their own meanings to it (Goodwin 1986). Over time, however, as listeners expose themselves to the devices, detours, and conclusions of conversation, a synchronicity of meaning emerges between speaker and hearer. Fourth, in this always-emerging alignment of meanings between speaker and hearer, an efficacious sohbet relies on the mood of its listeners in order to work. This sense of shared presence between the performer and the listener is a crucial aspect of the temporality of each sohbet event, situated in a particular time and space.

Before discussing the vital tasks that sohbet plays here, we should note also that the significance attributed to listening and the recourse to "talk" in this pedagogical practice is exceptional when compared with many other forms of skilled learning that anthropological literature has examined. In many of these studies, the attainment of skill is associated with a mode of gradual learning in which spoken language is shown to play a minimal role in communicating knowledge between masters and apprentices. Here the execution of the task of teaching or learning is said to be silent, implicit, devoid of overt instruction and reflection. That is, verbal instruction, discourse, even speech are often seen as less significant in the learning endeavor than learners' practices of observation, imitation, and mimicry, performance of physical movements and the manipulation of the body. For instance, Marchand argues that "[c]rafts—like sport, dance and other skilled physical activities—are largely communicated, understood and negotiated between practitioners without words, and learning is achieved through observation, mimesis and repeated exercise" (2008, 245). Learning through "unobtrusive observation" emerges as a common practice in a series of anthropological studies focusing on a range of skilled practice from capoeira training (Downey 2005) to shipbuilding (Simpson 2006), from learning to sew (Prentice 2012) to masonry (Marchand 2009). In these accounts, the transmission of knowledge is claimed to be "non-reflexive," unfolding through physical and visual exposure to practice with minimal explicit didactic or analytical instruction (Simpson 2006, 161).

Why the emphasis in this literature on the significance of nonpropositional instruction? Or, to put it differently, why is verbal demonstration strictly demarcated from mimetic learning and imitation in this conceptualization of skills acquisition? A common epistemological premise these studies share is that spoken words are not constitutive of practice but are merely instrumental in describing it. Take, for example, the assertion by Keller and Keller, who note in their studies of North American blacksmiths that "speech is an instrument designed for talking about production, for reflecting on the doing of artist-blacksmithing, but it is not an instrument of the doing itself" (1999, 27). This premise has parallels with the silent learning practice that Marchand describes for apprentice masons in Mali and Yemen, most of whom are initiated in the work as children and gradually accumulate the skill through exposure to physical experimentation, "effectively 'steal[ing]' trade knowledge through careful observation, listening and mimesis" (2008, 252). Although Marchand acknowledges the regular use of words in such skilled learning practices, he explicates their function as means to "direct focus, coordinate activities and communicate conceptual ideas or values related to the enterprise" (2008, 247). Verbal communication seems to carry merely a deictic purpose in these learning contexts where skilled production often constitutes either a daily routine or a professional trade for apprentices.

Unlike these studies' discovery of the insignificance of speech or overt instruction in the process of skill acquisition, words perform vital tasks in the teaching practice of the ney. In fact, the transformative—artistic, affective, and ethical—potential of this learning experience is understood to be grounded in learning to play the ney in a certain way, through participating in sohbet. As we shall encounter in the rest of the present chapter, sohbet has a vital pedagogical substance, as it facilitates, through myriad rhetorical devices, new ways of hearing and musical understanding in learners. Second, speech allows the teaching activity to be situated in a discourse comprising both artistic and ethical discussion in which, through reflecting upon what constitutes good musical practice, listeners can examine also how they relate to the surrounding world. Participation in the listening act generates, in this sense, a reflexive dialogue with varied dimensions of social life, as in the serendipitous moment of sohbet a whole range of musical and extramusical issues are woven together, from spirituality to the "temper" of the age. Third, there is much more to the act of listening than interpreting the contextual message of the speech. The efficacy of a successful speech is not confined only to what it says and conveys—ideas, terminology, concepts, and so on—but, over and beyond this, masterful words can generate certain emotional states in listeners, which is something significant in its own right. Efficacious sohbet produces an affect of intimacy, best expressed as "companionship" (Silverstein 2008), between those participating in the listening act. I will visit each of these points in turn.

Learning the Ney through Not Playing

As mentioned above, sohbet (*suhba* in Arabic) is a key and long-standing disciplinary practice in Islam, with a rich presence in the social worlds of Sufi orders. Broadly speaking, this practice involves keeping company with a *mürşid* in order to absorb his blessing (Chittick 1989, 271; Algar 1992). In a more specific sense, the idioms "to do sohbet" (*sohbet yapmak*) or "to convey sohbet" (*sohbet vermek*) are used to denote a spiritual conversation between a *mürşid* and *talibs* (disciples). This verbal practice carries a number of vital roles in Islamic teaching and learning contexts. As Brian Silverstein's anthropological study on the sohbets of the İskenderpaşa Community—a branch of the Naqshbandi Sufi order—in Turkey shows, sohbet minimally sets up a context in which religious knowledge can be aurally passed down from the spiritual guide to his disciples. The sohbet events that Silverstein is writing about are structured around the reading and interpretation of Islamic canonical sources. He underlines that the kinds of sociability enabled by the act of listening are just as important, for they are considered "liable to constitute a morally structured disposition in the practitioner" (2008, 143). Writing also on the Naqshbandi sohbets, Algar, too, emphasizes the potential efficacy of this Islamic practice to cultivate an ethical self in Muslim seekers. "Keeping the company of the *shaykh*, sitting down near him and receiving his words," Algar says, "are all valued as a key medium for the spiritual development and moral transformation of the disciple" (1992, 214).

The firsthand accounts of those ney masters who had been exposed to learning through sohbet give us the best clues about the varied ways in which this discursive practice is performed in meşk context. For instance, Neyzen Sadrettin Özçimi's (b. 1955) recounting of how his master Niyazi Sayın taught suggests that sohbet constituted a significant field of talk in which the lesson unfolded. In our conversation at his ney atelier in Üsküdar in 2012, Özçimi says:

> We used to gather once a week on Wednesdays around eight o'clock and we would continue way into 4 or 5 A.M. of the following day. We were there to play the ney with our Hoca, right? But believe me, the time spent for playing the ney in that six- to seven-hour lesson would hardly make half an hour. Apart from that, there was always sohbet. There was sohbet about Sufism, about our music. Hoca passed on many things to us about his own hoca, about the great musicians of his time, and about the Sufi elders that he knew from his own years of growing up in Üsküdar. We obtained a lot of criteria from those sohbets, humanistic criteria [*insani ölçüler*]. Of course, everything in the end would come back to Prophet Muhammed. This is how our lessons passed. I mean, meşk was not just about playing. A talebe should try to learn not only the actual art from their hoca, but the spiritual [*manevi*] and ethical [*ahlâki*] dimensions of that art as well. Then meşk happens.

This narrative illustrates how "talk" constitutes an important pedagogical means of "scaffolding" (Wood et al., 1976), enabling over time a modification of the talebe's artistic and extramusical sensibilities. Sitting side by side with one's hoca and being exposed to sohbet on a wide range of topics—and not just on music—are understood to be significant in their own right. In chapter 6 I discuss in more detail how such embodied actions are conducive for skilled practitioners' ethical character formation. In another autobiographical insight, Neyzen Bülent Özbek, who also studied under Sayın, comments during our conversation in 2013:

> It was the end of the 1970s when I started taking lessons from Niyazi Hoca. I used to go to his Üsküdar home once a week. In the first six months of lessons, I can't remember taking my ney out of its bag even once. We were always busy doing other things. He would teach me about photography, how to make *ebru*, or how to use the lathe. We would cook together and repair old objects he would collect from secondhand markets. We used to have sohbets. . . . Much later I understood that I was learning the ney all that time. I wasn't actually having a ney lesson, but I was learning the ney. I learned it by listening to my hoca, not by playing. This is what I tell my own students now, that the ney is not like other instruments. You teach it through words.

Just like Sayın, Neyzen Halil Can (1905–1973), an acclaimed master of an earlier generation, is also well known for his skillful teaching through sohbet. Can, who had been initiated into the Mevlevi order and a talebe of Emin Dede's, played a vital role in the continuation of neyzen lineages in Turkey over the twentieth century at a time when the teaching of Ottoman music still received no support from the State. Neyzen Ömer Erdoğdular (1949—) recounts below how in the 1960s Halil Can's house in Istanbul's Erenköy neighborhood was like a "school of sohbet," open to any willing talebe who wanted to come and participate in listening:

> *Meşk* gatherings at Halil Hoca's house would be on Saturdays and Sundays. We used to go through the vocal repertoire only. Halil Hoca was a highly knowledgeable man. He would tell us a great deal about recent history. He had an exceptional memory. It was like he knew a whole book by heart. He would recount couplets from famous Sufi poets like Rumi, Nesimi, Nâbi, and Fuzuli. Later, when I was introduced to Niyazi Hoca and began going to his house for lessons, it was the same. He, too, has an exceptional memory, and did great sohbets. Whatever we learned, we owe it all to a few hocas like them.[2] (Personal conversation with the artist, 2013)

Note here how in this skilled practice the actual time spent with one's teacher does not consist of playing the ney only. To put it differently, the hoca teaches through companionable speech, and not just through the acts of demonstrating, instructing on the technique, and through correcting the talebes' playing. This contrasts with many other examples of skilled learning that the anthropological literature presents to us where a repetitive attendance to a given practice often seems to make up the entire content of lessons. For instance, Amanda Weidman reports on an absence of any verbal explanation in the teaching practice of South Indian music, indicating that "the guru shows by singing or playing and the disciple repeats it, and this cycle is repeated" (2012, 220). Weidman claims that the time spent by the student constantly practicing a certain musical passage in the company of his or her teacher is not considered a problem, "in contrast to Western classical musical pedagogy in which the student is not supposed to 'waste time' practicing in the company of her teacher" (2012, 220–21). If Weidman had compared Indian music with anything other than the classic colonial/postcolonial Western binary, she would have noticed an equally relevant comparative difference—that is, the peculiarity of the lack of talk in Indian music.

By contrast, in the skilled practice analyzed here, lessons are deliberately structured around the design element of "not playing." Repetition, in other words, is in students' listening rather than in their repetitive playing. This importance attributed to "not playing" in the actual lesson time was itself a common theme of Salih Hoca's sohbets, whose creative use of improvised speech as part of his teaching practice had been largely shaped by his own musical disciplining through years of exposure to Niyazi Sayın's sohbets. Salih Hoca's long attendance at the sohbet gatherings of the Cerrahi and Şabani orders in the earlier years of his life had also been formative in his learning to become a skillful listener and, later, speaker. For him, the best ney lesson was the one in which the talebe listened and, indeed, hardly any playing happened! In his own sohbets, Salih Hoca, too, would often remind students how his lessons with Niyazi Hoca were not all about blowing the ney, as was the case not only with their learning at their master's home but also with their conservatory-based meşk activity, which he would liken to a Sufi tekke:

> Sohbet was never absent from our lessons. The topics were of a huge variety, ranging from how to grow flowers to how to cut and sew cloth to make your own trousers. These were also part of becoming a neyzen. In addition to these, there was also the ney, of course. But the key thing in a lesson is not students' playing, it is their listening. That's how we did our lessons with Niyazi Hoca. He played, he talked, and we listened. I grasp the value of that "not playing" better today. You learn this music by listening, by being in the company of your hoca. Guidance [*İrşâd*] happens through the ear.

Here the explicit value assigned to listening is inseparable from the virtues that are understood to lie in sohbet's setting up of an unmediated co-presence, and ideally a relationship of affection, between the hoca and talebe, which inclines the latter to become a diligent skilled practitioner. More fundamentally, this appreciation of the task of listening is in keeping with the great authority that the oral (and aural) transmission of knowledge occupies in methods of Islamic instruction (Eickelman 1978; Hirschkind 2006). As Brinkley Messick states, "It is in the 'heard' texts mode that instruction most closely approximates the ideals of the legitimate transmission of knowledge" (1993, 92). According to Messick, this privileging of the oral transmission of knowledge "finds a model both in the initial transmission of the Qur'an and in its subsequent recitational use in ritual" (92). "The Qur'an is not the Qur'an unless it is heard" (Nelson 2001, xiv). In addition, Al-Ghazali emphasizes the affective potential or efficacy of receiving the knowledge through the ear: "There is no access to hearts except by the anteroom of auditory stimuli; . . . *samā* [audition] is the true touchstone for the heart," he says (Avery 2004, 81–82).[3] Salih Hoca's pronouncement that it is through the ear that guidance happens is, too, predicated on this point, which recognizes the affective and transformative potential of the task of listening. As I explore later in this chapter, listening establishes the conditions through which the listener/learner can learn to experience certain affective states conducive for his or her moral cultivation.

In line with this sensibility, the talebes were explicitly discouraged from attending to other modes of acquiring skilled knowledge. While the use of audio recording devices was allowed in the actual lesson time, visual recording was strictly discouraged. Even if reliance on written scores seemed to be in one way a breaching of the oral dimension of the instruction, the limited efficacy of scores was a constant topic of discussion in the lessons. And if a newly joined student made the fatal mistake of taking notes, they would be told to write down the knowledge not on a piece of paper but "in their ear" (*kulağa yazmak*). As noted earlier in this book, in this skilled practice, learning is understood as an orientation "produced" by the talebe—the talebe must demand to learn. And that demand for learning is essentially proven by the talebe by cultivating a disposition to listen. A good talebe is the one who listens well.

The Tools of Sohbet

If sohbet carries vital pedagogical tasks in the skilled practice analyzed here, what constitutes its narrative mechanisms? What kind of language does Salih Hoca engage with in order to give meanings to and communicate his musical instructions to his audience? In other words, what creative devices give force to the semantic capacity and emotional affect of his verbal improvisations? The rich figurative language and metaphoricity constituting his discourses is one essential characteristic of Salih Hoca's mode of speaking in a sohbet way. His spoken language utilizes a wide range of metaphors (*mecaz*) and analogies (*teşbih*), communicative devices by means of which a way of knowing about one thing can be facilitated through its similarity or difference to another thing. Lakoff and Johnson note in their foundational work, *Metaphors We Live By*, "*The essence of metaphor is understanding and experiencing one kind of thing in terms of another*" (1980, 5, original emphasis). Building on this, Shahab Ahmed points out that "in metaphor, a word or action projects and assimilates semantically to another thing to which it stands in a semantic relationship of *simultaneous sameness and difference; from which thing and meaning it is differentiated at the very same time as with which it is identified*" (2016, 394, original emphasis). In this sense, metaphors are not mere devices of embellishment; by way of implicating one thing as another, they facilitate new meanings or insights and enlarge our understanding of things.

The metaphoric language organizing Salih Hoca's utterances established a semantic field in which the complexities inherent in the skilled knowledge—

say, an intricacy of the melodic progression of a certain makam or the changing character of a note in a melody line—could be retained and communicated. Sometimes an analogy would come in the form of an entire story. As is well known, storytelling and the use of parables as narrative devices to "instruct, guide, or influence listeners" (Kirkwood 1983, 60) have been a central part of the teaching practices of a great many faith traditions. Christ taught in parables. Buddha conveyed his messages by word of mouth. Sufis and Jewish rabbis instructed through stories. Stories, of a biographical or fictional kind, also occupied an important place in the rich tapestry of Salih Hoca's sohbets, weaving certain resemblances between correct musical practice and ways of life. To give just one example, the sohbet narrative that follows takes its analogy from the devotional practice of Ibn ʿArabi (d. 1240), one of Islamic history's most well-known Sufi teachers, in order to convey its "message" on the importance of repetition in practice. Salih Hoca says:

> I played this piece [instrumental prelude by Salih Dede in the makam *Uşşak*] to you last week. Today I played it again, this time a little bit differently. Certain things in life cannot be comprehended immediately. You need to listen repeatedly. Likewise, I need to play it over and over again. Just prior to his death Muhammad Ibn ʿArabi said: "If I hadn't performed my *namaz* [formal prayer in Islam] over the last year, what state would I be in!" Saintly Arabi died at the age of ninety-five and had made his prayers since he was seven. Yet he still said: "What state would I be in!" Now, you know how they say, "*Namaz* is a Muslim's *miraç* [the Prophet Muhammed's ascent to heaven]" and that *miraç* can only happen once in a lifetime. Yet to experience that one moment, you might need to spend ninety years doing *namaz*. This is what lies behind its repetition.[4]

The sohbet then continued with a biographical anecdote about the late Ottoman calligrapher and *ebru* master Necmettin Okyay (1883–1976), developing the analogy further between the importance of repetition in the attainment of musical skill and in the mastery of writing God's words. By bringing these apparently separate practices—namaz, ney playing, and calligraphy—into a mutually informing relationship, the words draw out a shared fundamental similarity that inheres in their perfecting: each place faith in rigorous practice. Only by practicing the skill a million times over one can achieve an excellent taksim or a fulfilling namaz. It is repetition that leads to perfection, which is, in this sohbet excerpt, skillfully brought to our imagination through the use of the metaphor of "miraç." The spoken words allude to the complexity that inheres in the perfecting of these practices, yet without simplifying it.

In another example, the subject of the sohbet is the virtue of the skillful articulation of a full sound from a single note, the first and foremost element of ney playing. Here the speech is organized around the metaphors of *vahdet* (unity) and *kesret* (multiplicity) borrowed from Sufi terminology, which help us think about the relationship between sound and melody.

> There is a saying by Imam Ali: "Knowledge is singular, only the ignorant make it manifold." Just as with knowledge, music too can be conceived of as a unified sound. All sounds exit in one pitch. But we never go after a single sound. We strive for multiplicity, we seek melody. Melody is an enterprise of this world, the oneness of sound is a feature of the other. Melody is like multiplicity [*kesret*], a single sound is like unity [*vahdet*]. But don't forget that there is unity in diversity [*vahdetin içinde kesret*]. Let's think about the makam *Acemaşiran*. [*He plays a short melody in this mode.*] This melody is the *kesret* of this makam. [*He blows into his ney again but only to play a long, sustained note in* acemaşiran *pitch.*] This one sound, on the other hand, is the *vahdet* of makam *Acemaşiran*. Modes are built upon key pitches. So is life. If *Acemaşiran* were to be the universe, what sound would give it its specificity? Without the pitch *acemaşiran*, without this long ending on it, this mode would not exist. This is how multiplicity is melded into unity. What falls on us is to imagine that pitch *Acemaşiran* as "unity" and to obtain a sustained sound from that pitch to discover the spirituality embedded in that unity. Once you obtain that sound, the rest, *kesret*, is just verbiage [*laf kalabalığı*]. And here is a definition of makam for you.

The unity between humanity and God, or the notion of the "unity of being" (*vahdet-i vücud*), has been central to the teachings of many Sufis from Attar to Ibn Arabi. "The divine reality is utterly transcendent, yet everything that exists [*kesret*] is a manifestation of that reality [*vahdet*] and is embraced by or encompassed within the divine," says Ibn Arabi (Lapidus 1992, 21). According to the Sufi view of divinity, the universe is nothing but a manifestation of the Divine. God is one and infinite, yet the multiple divine attributes of God are present in his creation and therefore within all human beings. The analogous reasoning that words establish builds upon this paradox that there exists "unity in diversity, and diversity in unity" ("All is One, One is All"). The master's referencing of this apparent contradiction allows his discourse to enlarge the meaning of makam in a way that facilitates a new thinking about the tonal structure of a mode and the relations between different notes that make up its scale and tonal center. Even if the analogy used here might seem to collapse mode to a single note, the narrative strategy is intended to generate a perceptual modification in students in hearing the mode in a new way and to shape their playing accordingly. As Salih Hoca expressed in the following part of his sohbet, what matters is the state of awareness that meaning(s) energized by the analogy engender(s) in listeners. He says:

> To imagine that all sounds are contained in one single pitch is not an illusion, but something to be discerned. As we live our lives in this world, we constantly make judgments about what the after-life might be like. Whether our judgments are true or wrong is not what matters. But to be in a state that helps us imagine those things in this life is important. Being in that state endows us with good manners [*adab*]. To imagine that "unknown" gives us direction, integrity, modesty, decency. It is such imagination that will enable you to perform that perfect improvisation [*taksim*], to play a melody beautifully.

Note how the pivotal role that imagination plays in configuring students' learning is explicitly underlined and valued here. The narrative deliberately uses the words "to imagine" and "to contemplate" in creating its analogy, rather than dressing up its key message in a more precise and logical form ("If *a* happens, then *b* happens"). This imagining does not mean "merely pretending that something is the case," as Casey reminds us in discussing how imagination is a mental act in its own right rather than secondary to other mental acts, such as perception (1974, 6). According to Casey, "no act of perceiving is wholly unattentuated by non-perceptual elements, among which imaginative activity must be included" (3). In the course of an unfolding sohbet event, the listeners are constantly learning to rely on their imaginative powers in order to induce the meaning of things for themselves.

In our final example, the subject of the skilled knowledge being instructed is pitch sensibility. As chapter 3 has already discussed in detail, the true competence of a ney player lies in his or her ability to hear and articulate correctly the pitch intervals in a melodic line so that the tonal presence of a makam can be established adequately. This is no easy task given the discrepancy between the notation system and the actual practice, on the one hand, and the material features of the reed, on the other. Rather than taking instructions directly from the score or from the reed, the player must rely on his or her aural knowledge in calibrating the right interval between any two notes. Given the tremendously important role that cultivating this aural sensibility occupies in the mastery of makam music, a great deal of Salih Hoca's sohbets revolved around this topic. The narrative below is from one of his many speech performances devoted to the importance of intonation. Here, spoken words generate a certain knowledge of pitch as something that possesses a relational and not an absolute value. They encourage also a way of thinking about tonal relationships by reflecting upon one's intersubjective relationships with other people. According to Salih Hoca, managing both "relationships" requires a good judgment of the right distance between any two notes/selves. This is how his words unfold:

> We need to think of pitches as zones [*bölge*]. The pitch *dik kürdi*, for example, has its own territory. When we look at a piece of music, first we need to analyze those zones and then try to express its pitches correctly. The mastery of Niyazi Hoca lies in his enviable tonal precision. If we take Turkish music as a music of relationships [*münasebet musikisi*], the essential thing we need to grasp is each pitch's relationship to another. The secret of learning this music lies in understanding those relationships. Let's remember Niyazi Hoca's definition of music. "Music is the spiritual relationship between any two notes," he says. Now, there is always a distance between any two notes. Music theory calls that distance "interval" [*aralık*]. But if we think of that distance as "interval," we will never become freed from the rules of theory. If we treat that distance as relationship [*münasebet*] then we might be able to search for those spiritual relationships between notes.
>
> This definition of music applies to many things. Aren't there also ethical measures in life? Just like pitches, we too have a relationship with one another. Distances, relationships, matter in every sphere of our lives. Think about your partner, your child, your work life. There is at least one key similarity between the world of sounds and of human beings. Managing both entails skillful judgment of the right distance between any two notes/selves. If one works out those relationships correctly, one lives a life composed of beautiful melodies, then it becomes a correct life.

In these examples, the narratives allow a vast range of parallels to be discerned between music and social life. The mechanics of sohbet work in its bringing into mutually affecting relationships three or more organizing clusters of metaphor: musicianship, Sufi Islamic theology, and everyday practice and sociality. There is no straightforward "march" from music to spirituality or from the recounting of an everyday life situation to an artistic judgment. Yet by rendering these separate clusters of metaphor as mutually "related," sohbet manages to "teach" not by prescribing but by way of conveying in which multiple possibilities of meaning can be retained. The creative devices of metaphoricity and wordplay constantly demand from listeners that they intuit the meaning of spoken words beyond and behind surface of plain language. An artistic principle or a technical instruction comes to be imagined in the form of a virtuous behavior; the sonic interval between two notes receives its meaning from the relationship between two selves. Words do not dive straight into the "message," but rather instruct through suggesting possible resemblances and relations between different practices or between different life situations: "the primacy of the relation substituting for the primacy of things [alone]" (Velho 2007, 81). The analogous reasoning organizing the speech "expands the horizon of knowledge by making actual what were before only potential meanings" (Marks 1978, 254).

Further, the kind of verbalizing that orients these verbal performances is akin to a "language-game," to use Wittgenstein's term. What we see is a "complicated network of similarities overlapping and criss-crossing," characterized by Wittgenstein as "family resemblances" (1961 [1953], 66–67). Words, in this sense, "do not have distinct, sharply delineated meanings" (Ortony 1975, 46). The words makam, pitch, note, and seyir acquire their meaning according to how the metaphoric language makes use of them in that moment (and how listeners bestow their own interpretation on them). Because speech facilitates here a way of sensing one thing in the image of another, it potentially enables new perceptions of both. By showing us one thing as another, a dimension of meaning to which we may have been deaf can become available for our attention. This perceptual modification emerges not because each new analogous relation introduces a new knowledge but because it offers a new perspective for thinking about it. As Fernandez notes, this is why metaphors are forceful: "their aptness lives in their power to change our moods, our sense of situation" (1986, 52).

The modification, in other words, is not necessarily in *what we see* but happens more in *how we see* (and *hear*). Benjamin has captured this point in his writing on stories. He says that a story "does not aim to convey the pure essence of the thing, like information or a report. It sinks the thing into the life of the storyteller, in order to bring it out of him again" (1973, 91). In a similar vein, an analogy cannot capture all dimensions of a musical element but makes a certain aspect of it become more easily available to the consciousness of both the teller and the listener. Each time a new metaphorical insight is made, a new musical understanding and hearing is potentially enabled.

Of course, listeners can extract meanings differently from an analogy or discover that what was true for a character in an exemplary story is irrelevant for themselves. Clearly there were occasions whereby my fellow talebes did not agree with every interpretation put forward by Salih Hoca's language-games. Let me refer here to how one talebe (female, architect, sixty years old) assessed how she made sense of the metaphoric language of sohbet:

> I am sixty years old and have experienced many things in life. If I take everything Salih Hoca says as my own truths [*doğrular*], this would mean putting

> all of my own aside. But every time I leave the workshop, his sohbet makes me think and reflect on things, even if I might not agree with what he said in that lesson. Sometimes I remember a thing he says or a comparison he draws while I am in the middle of doing something. The other week, in the lesson I tried to play an ornamentation that was beyond me. In explaining that it was too early for me to jump onto that movement and that I should be really concentrating on building up my sound, he gave the example of wearing a fine brooch with the wrong attire. He worded it so well that I now think of this comparison when it fits other situations.

This reflective comment reveals that it is not necessarily an agreement with the intrinsic veracity of the sohbet that makes the speech event effective. The use of language is itself charged with significant perceptual and affective power. Indeed, students often discussed how the speech turned out and commented upon how, when rendered effectively, sohbet performance changed their mood and sense of a situation. This was a regular topic of discussion among those of us who would share the night ferry ride back to the other side of the city after each lesson. For instance, on one particular occasion during our ferry trip when five of us were discussing how Salih Hoca raised the importance of repetitive practice in the mastery of the ney through recourse to the repetition organizing Ibn 'Arabi's years of namaz practice (see above), one friend remarked, "I don't do namaz, nor do I have to believe in what Salih Hoca says about namaz to appreciate his point. But when he tells a story that really fits into the situation, it sticks in my memory." This evidently suggests that the metaphoric language is central to the pedagogic utility of sohbet. As Ortony has pointed out in terms of the cognitive, sensorial, and emotional force of metaphors, "The vivid imagery arising from metaphorical comprehension encourages memorability and generates of necessity a better, more insightful, personal understanding" (1975, 51). Sohbet, in this sense, is a form of poetic creation. Just as with poetic experience, the rich metaphorization pervading the language of sohbet can move us by affording new insights. "Metaphor is a play on words; poetic image is additionally a play on the word" (Weiner 1991, 13, cited in Downey 2005, 48).

Listeners as Co-creators of Sohbet

> If the teller is to be wise [*arif*], the listener must be mature [*kâmil*]. If those maturities exist in a group of students, or even in just one student, the state [*hâl*] of sohbet arises. There is nothing in me. A listener like that needs to be present, at least one person who is in such a state. To recount, one listener is sufficient. Saintly Kenan Rifai has a beautiful saying on this. He

> says: "I can address all living beings in the universe, but no one might be in the state to hear what I say. There might be only one person able to receive my words, and I can recount to him or her as if I am speaking to the whole universe. If one person does not exist, I can recount to myself." There is still one person there. This is what sohbet is like. Sometimes that state doesn't arise, another time it emanates unexpectedly, and we find ourselves in the sohbet. (Salih Bilgin, 2012)

The verbal improvisation of sohbet cannot be done without the help of its audience. Listeners contribute to the making of sohbet not the least because talk needs at least two parties to be exchanged. But as Salih Hoca sets up for us above, even to emerge, sohbet needs at least one listener who is in such state of attentive listening. The view of the listener as not merely recipient of words but as an active contributor to the act of speaking has been laid out in many anthropological and linguistic works examining various kinds of verbal and nonverbal communication. For instance, according to Mikhael Bakhtin, "A word is territory shared by both addresser and addressee, by the speaker and his interlocutor" (1986, 86). Listeners have been identified as the "co-authors" of any speech act (Duranti 1986) and "co-creators" of meaning, "a dynamic entity that can actively influence the interpretation that will be given a speaker's talk" (Goodwin 1986, 306). The way that Václav Havel considers the role of the audience in a theatrical performance can also be read in this light: "[I]n the theater the work we are watching is not finished, but instead is being born before our eyes, with our help, so that we are both witnesses to its birth and, in a small sense, its co-creators as well" (1983, 255).

In what ways might this attribution of efficacy to the audience be useful in understanding the collaborative role that the talebes play in co-telling the sohbet emerging in ney lessons? The first thing to note is the interpretative work they undertake as listeners. The meaning of an analogy, a story, or even of a nonmetaphoric utterance is never confined to the spoken words improvised by the speaker. Each time a new listening context is established, the members of the audience actively work out the meaning of what is being said. This hermeneutic process of assigning meanings (to texts, sounds, and the like) is, as Duranti points out, not "a passive activity whereby the audience is just trying to figure out what the author meant to communicate." Rather, it is a way of linking what someone said "to a world or context that the audience can make sense of" (1986, 244). Each member of the audience maps the sohbet through his or her own perception.

Further, it should be recalled that the mixed makeup of Salih Hoca's meşk groups constituted an important context of the ongoing listening activity. In attendance were students who were already well acquainted with Salih Hoca's speech acts, as well as others who were unpracticed in the art of listening. Thus, rather than forming a single listening body, each "audience" accommodated members who differed significantly from each other in terms of how much perceptual and bodily modification they had been through in their enskillment process and over what period. The fact that a fresh beginner and a talebe who had been learning for years sat side by side, exposed to the same verbal utterances, meant that in making meaning each listener brought different kinds of accumulated skilled knowledge to bear on the language-game of the sohbet. As I know from my own learning experience through exposure to the transformative potential of sohbet, such meaning making is a very dynamic process. Given the heterogeneity of our lesson groups, speech around a certain core of instructions (the importance of tone, pitch sensitivity, correct posture, and so on) was improvised over and over again in every lesson. Yet its reception would not always be the same. Over time, repetition in listening allowed a new sense of perspective on a piece of instruction, which the listener might have heard already. Salih Hoca himself reflects upon this dynamic meaning-making process, which he had been subject to as a listener, that there was always something new to hear in his master's sohbet:

> I spent twenty years in the company of my hoca. We did great lessons, which did not involve playing at all. There was always sohbet. And there was always something new to hear in those sohbets even when we heard the same thing over and over again. That repetition is good for learning. It is not something to be avoided. A talebe shouldn't be in an expectation that every lesson will say something novel.

The temporality of sohbet, and of apprenticeship more generally, is important in shaping what the listener makes of each speech act situated in time and space. The series of perceptual modifications that the talebe goes through in the skilled learning process constantly generates for them a new listening context where new interpretations of similar speech acts can potentially emerge. As one gradually acquires new ways of hearing, listening, and observing and experiences a refining of their body movements, they can also begin to hear the same analogy or a story in a new light. Suddenly, the same narrative acquires a slightly new meaning or a certain aspect of it becomes foregrounded in the listener's consciousness. The "over time-ness" of the experience of exposure to sohbet is essential for developing what Wittgenstein calls "aspect seeing" or "seeing as." As Duranti discusses by drawing on Wittgenstein's "duck-rabbit image," "meaning-giving consists of a change in attitude or disposition toward something" (2009, 209–10). Based on the intentional modifications we go through, our experience of an object (or sound) and how we see or hear it can change. Suddenly, we might see a different side of it. Through repeated listening and observing, one can also reflect on a knowledge or skill—say, a certain makam—which had been turned into "natural attitude" and reimagine it in some new form. The novelty of the sohbet does not necessarily lie, then, in its referential content. It is the capacity of the listener to cultivate an "aspect seeing" that allows a novel experience of listening to emerge.

The temporality of sohbet is also essential for an ongoing alignment of meanings between the speaker and the listener, as well as between co-listeners. What sohbet says and what effect it generates do not emerge from the speaker's actions alone in this sense but are, rather, "constituted within a collaborative process of interaction that includes the audience as a very active co-participant" (Goodwin 1986, 284). As the listeners grow into sohbet, a synchronicity of meanings begins to emerge around the rhetorical devices employed during the speech events. This synchronization does not suggest that listeners come to agree with everything that the speaker says; by contrast, true disagreement, and not confused incomprehension, can happen once a shared understanding of the speech emerges. What is involved over time is that students learn to bring their own interpretations of utterances or narrative devices into an alignment with that of the speaker and of other co-listeners who had been exposed to learning through listening over a longer duree. Such alignment is most powerfully noticed when a newcomer breaches those shared understandings, as often happened with "first-day" conversations.

That sohbet, like any speech event, is a joint achievement of the speaker and co-listeners is something that master speakers are profoundly and intimately aware of. What good sohbet makers are also aware of is that sohbet must be made appropriate to its audience in order to turn out well. When to strike the right note, how much meaning to give away, which metaphors and analogies to utilize, how to bring listeners into a state of tension (and relief) or to deliberately create an ambiguity—or even contradiction—of meaning are all improvisatory acts the speaker performs according to his or her immediate audience. In fact, there is quite often a dimension of skillful subterfuge in sohbet. This may involve a deliberate obscuring of certain meanings, a partial revealing of what was really meant, a generating of a meaningful contradiction, or an overstating/understating of an insight to be imparted. Skillful speakers can strategically use the language to create such maneuvers in specific sohbet occasions. For instance, in one revealing fieldwork event, I attended a social breakfast at a Küçük Çamlıca teagarden, which was arranged by one senior talebe of Niyazi

Sayın's with the intention of creating a once-in-a-life-time experience for his twenty or so ney students. These were devout Muslim men and women in their early twenties and mostly students at Istanbul's various universities. After the breakfast was finished, Sayın began to address these young ney enthusiasts, who seemed to be aspiring to hear what he thought about the religious meanings of the ney, as the questions asked gave away: Could the ney be conceived of as a musical instrument only? Wasn't it different from other instruments in some way? What was the position of "our religion" on this? Could Sayın say a few words about what kind of relationship he discerned between the ney and *maneviyat* (spirituality)? The unfolding sohbet by Sayın embraced the listeners' concerns yet served only to overturn, rather than reinforce, their prejudgments. By downplaying the status of "uniqueness" assigned to the ney and debunking the "spiritual" discourse cemented in the symbolic meanings of the instrument, his rhetoric created an unexpected insight so as to confound the listeners' expectations. My point is that an interpretation of what Sayın says here (and how he says it) has to first consider the kinds of goal that as the speaker he might have pursued vis-à-vis his intended audience. In this case, prompting in the listeners a state of self-examination or even self-confrontation by way of challenging their established perceptions and beliefs may well have been one overriding goal. The same sohbet conversed with a different type of audience may not yield the same hermeneutical results. Masterful speakers can generate, then, multiple—even contradictory—messages that are peculiar to the time and place of each sohbet event.

What Sohbet Does

> You can make up a missed *namaz*, but you cannot make up the *namaz* of sohbet. Because words are like a flood, they flow over and recede. . . . The same sohbet never comes in its first shape even when the topic is the same. For this reason, sohbets are considered as *âyât-i müteşabihat*.[5] Between them is resemblance but no mimicry. (Filiz 2009, 248)

Returning to one of the core questions of this chapter concerning why spoken words matter so much in this skilled learning practice, we can draw at least three conclusions: first, that through its rich array of narrative strategies, sohbet facilitates in learners new skills of hearing, listening, and musical understanding; second, that in continuously enlarging the potential meanings of correct musical practice, sohbet sets up a context in which listeners are in a position to work out the meanings of and reflect upon a complex of relationality that spoken words weave between music and Sufism (a music-Sufism amalgam), as well as with other spheres of daily life. A third vital function of sohbet pertains to the shared affects that orient individuals in the moment of conversing. This is something significant in its own right, since there is much more to the aural receiving of words than comprehending their referential content. The goal of a successful sohbet is not to persuade its audience about a certain point of view; its goal is to create various affects in listeners so that they can develop a capacity to learn, to be attentive, to eagerly pursue becoming a lifelong talebe, and to surrender themselves to the master's authority. The efficacy of this speech genre lies more in how it affects the listener than in what it says.

Consider the quote above from Neyzen Lütfi Filiz (1911–2007) in his book, *Noktanın Sonsuzluğu*[6] (The Infinity of a Fullstop), which articulates the significant affective dimension of sohbet by constructing an "analogy" based not on a perceived similarity but on a contrast between sohbet and namaz (2009, 248). Clearly, Filiz's statement is open to a multitude of meanings, but one angle it throws on the issue is particularly important for our own purposes here: the value of sohbet, because of its unrepeatability. Unlike in the case of namaz, a practice enjoined upon Muslims as one of the core pillars of Islam, sohbet (if missed) cannot be "made up" or reproduced in another time space. There is, first of all, timeliness (or one-time-ness) in the event of sohbet. Namaz can be planned, but sohbet cannot. It emerges when its timing is right. "This is what sohbet is like," says Salih Hoca. "Sometimes that state [*hâl*] doesn't arise, another time it emanates unexpectedly and we find ourselves in the sohbet." What this suggests is that the mood of the moment defines the timeliness of sohbet. As Heidegger notes, "we always have some mood. We cannot escape having a mood, as we are always being-with, that is, we affect and are affected by others in each moment of our being-in-the-world" (cited in Gieser 2008, 304–5). In the lesson context, a certain question asked or a comment made by a student, a virtue demonstrated in someone's playing, or failing to display a certain etiquette constantly shapes the "atmosphere" in the room, triggering various kinds of emotional states. Mood is what creates the conditions of sohbet to emerge. It is when the speaker responds to the mood of the moment that sohbet occurs.

Further, there is also timeliness to sohbet that is oriented to its efficacy in momentarily evoking certain emotional responses in listeners. As an Ekberi Sufi who had vast experience of doing sohbet with his own talebes, Filiz intimately knew that, just as one cannot jump into the same river twice (to coin a phrase), the same sohbet can never be replicated. How sohbet affects the listener and the mood of the speaker are all peculiar to that moment. The repetition of words, even if the same topic came up again, may not achieve the same result. The words expressed to me by the sheikh Abdul Aziz of the Melbourne-based Mevlevi group, which cohered around weekly held sohbet and mukabele, illuminate this point: "Sufi sohbet is an energy exchange, and it occurs spontaneously in the moment, and this immediacy and relevance to every participant's needs 'in the moment' is what gives it its authentic quality, its power and its purpose or efficacy," he pronounced. For him, this experiencing is "beyond the intellect and ideas, or argument or philosophy, it is the essence of being, of presence." Filiz shapes his analogy slightly differently to allude to this element of timeliness central to the affective capacity of sohbet by describing it as "the greatest *namaz*, which cannot be made up later" (*kazası olmayan en büyük namaz*) (2009, 246). This time, an element of continuity comes to connect these two core Muslim devotional practices, albeit in an order of hierarchy enabled through the analogy's skillful overturning of the orthodoxy.

Salih Hoca's students, too, valued the mood-altering efficacy of his sohbets. "The *hâl* that I am in before I walk into the *atölye* and my *hâl* as I walk out are never the same," remarked one fellow talebe; "When the lesson comes to an end, I am always in a new state [*hâleti ruhiye*]," he exclaimed. Students often commented on the "sincerity" [*samimiyet*] of the speech events developing en route and how listening to Salih Hoca's spoken words created in them certain strong and varied emotional responses. "When I am listening, I feel like his words appeal not only to my intellect [*akıl*] but also to my heart [*gönül*]," said Murat, a senior talebe and, thus, an experienced sohbet listener (male, age thirty-nine). When I asked him what particular aspect of the affective quality of the sohbets moved him, he responded by saying:

> You know that expression used in *tasavvuf*, "to speak with the language of *hâl* [*hâl dili*], not with the language of words [*kâl dili*]," that's how Salih Hoca talks, with a language of *hâl*. Let's imagine for a moment that I am sitting in Hoca's chair, speaking to the talebes using exactly the same words that Hoca would have used. Would it be the same sohbet? Of course not. To have an effect upon us, words must come out of the mouth of someone who had already experienced what those words convey. If you advise someone to act in a certain way, and if you hadn't embodied that knowledge [*adab*] yourself [*o şey bünyende değilse*], your words won't be of any worth.

In reflecting upon what charges sohbet with such affective power for him, Murat distinguishes between a "language of *hâl*" and a "language of *kâl*," a distinction often made by Sufis. The point is that, the morally transformative efficacy of sohbet lies not merely in its referential content. The speech is felt to be effective because what it conveys is experiential knowledge, best epitomized by the Arabic word *adab*, which Ira Lapidus describes as "the correct knowledge and behavior in the total process by which a person is educated, guided, and formed into a good Muslim" (1984, 39).[7] That is, for Murat, the ethical sensibilities that Salih Hoca's words communicate do not just exist in his "talk" but are manifested in his own bearing and conduct. It is the non-intellectual power of the speech event that Murat is foregrounding here—in other words, the potential of the sohbet event to perform a "language of affect" (hâl). The expression of hâl gains more of the quality of a character trait than a meaning of a feeling state or mood, though the two are deeply interrelated.[8] According to Al-Ghazali, hâl—"state of soul"—is that attribute (*vasf*) or character trait that can be experienced instantly and momentarily in the form of an emotional state (for example, a state of repentance, patience, gratitude, and the like) (cited in Sherif 1975, 113).

The cultivation of certain states of mind, or of a sentimental education, is essential to the practice of sohbet. Sohbet constructs emotions. This is something significant in its own right, as Kirkwood discusses in depth by referring to the discursive practice of telling parables, which serve as vital teaching devices in many religious traditions. Kirkwood (1983) remarks:

> If a narrative succeeds in evoking a certain mood or state of awareness, sometimes it is the resulting feeling, not a conceptual message, which is to be valued and cultivated. Of course, if a parable alters the listener's mood, this would not preclude the possibility that the conceptual meaning of the story is also important. But to view feeling response as merely a motivation for an ultimate change in thinking or acting would be incorrect. (66)

The underlying theme of the argument here is that certain moods or emotional states such as "equanimity, mental quietude, awe, [and] devotion" "are not just the means, but the ends of spiritual discipline" (66). Thus when a parable succeeds in briefly altering the mood of the listener or evoking one of these states of awareness in them, it accomplishes its task. Similarly, Hirschkind makes the point that for the Muslim he worked with in Cairo, the affective responses that sermons invoke in listeners ("fear of God" seems to be a particularly important one in his ethnography; see also Mahmood[9] [2005, 140–45]) are "actions in and of themselves" (2006, 90), constituting "the affective conditions of virtuous conduct" (74). He refers to them as "ethical affect" (74). The efficacy of sohbet, too, can be conceived in this light. The affective responses it creates in listeners are at the same time the kinds of virtues that are understood to be fundamental to becoming a skilled practitioner of the ney: reflection (*tefekkür*), self-interrogation (*muhasebe*), patience (*sabır*), humility (*tevazu*), discernment (*basiret*), serenity (*dinginlik*), thankfulness (*şükür*), surrender (*teslim*), and love (*muhabbet*). Over time, exposure to sohbet can also enable the listener to more habitually perform such qualities of action.

Let me conclude this section with a final sohbet narrative from Salih Hoca in which he reflects upon what he conceives as the most important of all emotional states that sohbet potentially generates: *muhabbet* (warm affection; or love). He says:

> Ney playing is a technical matter. You learn how to move your lips, your fingers in a certain way, this and that. But to make music, to do justice to the pitches, you need to be fed by other sources. You need sohbet. . . . Sohbet generates *muhabbet*, and *muhabbet* is the essence of ney learning. No other pleasure in the world can have the taste [*lezzet*] of *muhabbet*. When you are in that state, you learn from your hoca continuously, regardless of whether you play the ney or not. Learning can only occur if you breathe the same air as your hoca [*aynı havayı teneffüs edersen*]. Taking a lesson is not all that important, but being in the presence of your hoca, sitting side by side with them, is.

A deepening feeling of affection between a hoca and talebe constitutes the greatest potentiality of sohbet as well as the foundation for life-long commitment to learning. Over time the acts of listening, conversing, and sharing close company ("to breathe the same air," "to sit side by side") build up a powerful emotional and spiritual connection between participants. Sohbet, in this regard, is conducive for relations of intimacy, enabling the subjects to become companions in the experience of listening and conversing. Herein lies its major efficacy. As Silverstein remarks, just as "companionship is intimately linked to conversation, conversation engenders companionship" (2008, 126).[10] His translation of sohbet as "companionship-in-conversation" (121) (rather than simply as "conversation") captures more fully its nuances and social implications.[11] In fact, this relationship between the two terms, sohbet [*suhba*] and companions [*sahaba*] is also a semantic one in the Arabic language (both words come from the same trilateral root, s-h-b), the latter referring to the companions of Prophet Muhammad who passed their lives in his service and company. "Sohbet is what, by definition, *sahaba* do" (Silverstein 2008, 127).

In claiming that the ney cannot be taught without sohbet, that "without sohbet, the shell can be learned but not the essence" (see the quote at the outset of this chapter), Salih Hoca does not only have the referential content of this verbal practice in mind (what sohbet says). Just as important is the affective capacity of sohbet (what it does), including the powerful emotive registers it potentially creates between the meşk subjects: the talebe's love, surrender, and loyalty to his or her hoca, and the hoca's love and care for the talebe. These emotive registers do not form a mere backdrop *to* skilled learning.[12] What emerges from Salih Hoca's words above is a conception of love, conceived as more than an emotion. To love has a direct bearing on learning because there is a sense here that to love is to grow in one's capacity to be influenced by the one toward whom such affection is felt ("When you are in that state, you learn from your hoca continuously regardless of whether you play the ney or not.") We encounter this conception of love [*muhabbet*] as an inclination [*meyil*] of the heart, as "a metaphysics of influence" (Silverstein 2008, 130) in Sufi poetry and philosophy. For Sufis, muhabbet is the most effective path to God.[13] As Helmut Ritter remarks:

> There is a spiritual power which is suited above all others to promote the soul's concentration on another being, to suppress and eliminate all other ties and interests, to make that being into the center of one's feelings, and from within this emotionally laden center to dominate all aspects of life and to determine all expression in life a power which is more effective than any other efforts at overcoming restraints and hindrances, which can traverse the distance of a day's travel in minutes and performs achievements of high aspiration where all other efforts fail. The power in question is love. It provides the mystic with assistance to attain his goal, closeness to God, and to achieve union with Him. (2003, 358–59)

"Without love, there is no meşk" (Aşk olmazsa meşk olmaz), says a Turkish proverb: equally, without sohbet, there can be no meşk. By thinking about sohbet as a form of improvisation, this chapter has sketched out some of the essential ways in which musical learning happens in sohbet. The acts of teaching by word of mouth and listening perform important educative and affective tasks, which are conducive for becoming a skilled practitioner. In the next chapter I discuss more explicitly what has been an implicit topic running throughout this chapter: In what ways is learning through sohbet imperative for the ethical constituting of the subject? How does musical apprenticeship socialize learners into new ways of being and relating to other selves? This is what we turn to in chapter 6.

CHAPTER SIX

Music and Ethical Modification

THE PROCESS OF BECOMING A NEYZEN entails a disciplining of the kinesthetic body in ways far beyond technical adeptness. Through repeated practice and long-term exposure to listening—both musical listening and listening to sohbet—as well as observation and imitation of more experienced students and teachers, learners attain new sensory-motor capacities and modification of corporeal and affective dispositions. All of these have efficacious influence in students' ethical lives by accentuating certain ways of being and acting in the world. Insofar as ethics is deeply embedded in our ordinary lives (Lambek 2010) as well as in our relations with other selves (Sidnell 2016), it is the correct term (or perhaps the most fulsome) to signify certain core dimensions of studio life. In this chapter I explore these processes whereby the skilled practice of mastering the ney potentially changes learners' moral selves by sponsoring in them certain ethical sensibilities and ways of relating to others (and to the city), an event that I frame here as ethical modification. Ethical modification suggests not the holistic construction of selfhood but more the creation for students of a reflexive practice. Talebes learn to perceive what constitutes good musical practice, even as they also examine, and potentially modify, how they relate to the surrounding world.

How might we gain a handle on the transformative power of this art pedagogy to cultivate not only new artistic but also ethical perceptions in practitioners? The question is informed by the recent interest in the subject of ethics in anthropology, popular enough that Michael Lambek (2010, 5) diagnoses an "ethical turn" in the discipline (see also Keane 2015; Robbins 2012; Faubion 2011; Laidlaw 2002). One feature of this concern is the explicit attention it gives to the relationship between morality and everyday human practices, or what Lambek calls "ordinary ethics." Inspired by the conception of ordinary language by J. L. Austin and Ludwig Wittgenstein, "ordinary ethics" "is relatively tacit, grounded in agreement rather than rule, in practice rather than knowledge or belief, and happening without calling undue attention to itself" (Lambek 2010, 2). Joel Robbins (2012) notes the preoccupation of this new ethical turn in anthropology with issues of human freedom, which involves a rejection of presumptions concerning the determining of human behavior by social structures or inculcated modes of perception in favor of a more empirical exploration of people's exercise of the practice of freedom. For him, a paradox characterizes this new concern: as a discipline, anthropology has for countless societies sketched out "the kinds of normative social routines that provide some of the moral foundation of life everywhere" (2012, 1), yet it has rarely focused on ethical character formation per se or on the scope individuals have to ethically constitute themselves.

Perhaps Robbins's assertion was already historically dated? Inquiry into moral practice from the perspective of "ordinary ethics" has a longer pedigree in the anthropology of Islam. For instance, drawing on the work of Talal Asad (1986), both Mahmood (2005) and Hirschkind (2006) have developed an account of ethical self-fashioning among Muslims participating in "piety movements" in Egypt, paying explicit attention to the relationship between ethics and the body as a locus for self-making. In this view, bodily practices (for example, praying and veiling [in Mahmood's work], and taped-sermon listening [in Hirschkind's work]) are understood as vital "developable means" for fashioning an ethical subject, working as "a technology of the self" (Foucault 1997). As Mahmood writes, "the specific gestures, styles, and formal expressions that characterize one's relationship to a moral code are not a contingent but [are] a necessary means to understanding the kind of relationship that is established between . . . what one is, what one wants, and what kind of work one performs on oneself in order to realize a particular modality of being and personhood" (2005, 120). For the Egyptian sermon listeners, for example, it is through participation in listening that one comes to cultivate various affective and pious dispositions (such as humility, repentance, or fear of God) conducive for "ethical self-improvement" (Hirschkind 2006, 74).

Informed by an Aristotelian understanding of ethics, both of these anthropological analyses of the constitution of Muslim subjectivity are relevant in thinking about how the performative body comes to be a "theater" for the ethical modifications required in becoming a skillful neyzen. The artistic dispositions and ethical sensibilities that skilled learning fosters are interwoven, an understanding that often finds explicit articulation within meşk contexts. "Meşk cultivates personality, not persons" (Meşk şahıs degil şahsiyet yetiştiriyor), remarks Neyzen Süheyl Ünver (1898–1986), conveying a widely shared conception that in this practice *musiki* and *ahlâk* (ethics) is inseparable.

Although masters recognize that the open-ended processes of artistic/ethical constitution of the self are intertwined, these processes can be juxtaposed in different kind of ends-means relationships. As Neyzen Sadrettin Özçimi, also a fine *ebru* (water marbling) artist, said to me: "Our art traditions are transformative [*dönüştürücü*]. They are for disciplining [*terbiye etmek*] the soul [*ruh*]," referring to those art traditions that had especially flourished in Sufi disciplinary contexts and had been taught through meşk. As he went on to explain:

> Meşk is not just teaching an artistic skill. It is also about teaching the student the *ahlâk*, the spirituality [*maneviyat*] of that art, teaching them how to approach that art. We know that these art traditions [referring here to calligraphy, music, and ebru] were used in the tekkes. Why were they used? With the aim of softening the soul [*ruhu yumuşatmak*] and bringing it to an appropriate state [*hâl*] so that it can be shaped. Can you shape a hard dough? This is what art is intended for, to mold the soul so that it can be shaped. If you are able to use art to cultivate good morals in human beings, then it becomes a correct [*doğru*], a beautiful [*güzel*] art.

Özçimi's words communicate a strong conviction that the musical practice serves as a means for ethical cultivation. Accordingly, to discipline the self (*nefs*), the body must also be trained. The intentional modifications that meşk enables are understood here as conducive to giving the soul a new shape, predisposing it to the development of desired ethical sensibilities. For Özçimi, the achievement of artistic excellence should not be conceived as an end in itself—or at least not as its only end. But it is *the* way to obtain the "real" end—that is, the perfecting of one's moral self. Conversely, as Niyazi Sayın suggests, this relationality works also the other way around: the embodied ethical modifications that skilled practitioners acquire over time are precisely the means for becoming a true artist. As Sayın uttered in one conversation: "'Music is food for the soul,' they say. But in reality, it is the other way around. Only a virtuous [*erdemli*] soul can do music well," adding that for the ney to give a good sound, first its player needs to "sound" well. The latter, according to Sayın, is fashioned by a wide range of things, from where one lives, to each and every practice or habit that constitutes one's everyday life. He said:

> When it comes to the question of how one attains excellence in art, we need to consider one's way of life as a whole. The neighborhood [*muhit*] we live in, our social relationships, all of these have both material and moral entailments for us. If you plant a flower and watch it grow each day, that too teaches you something. We have to constantly work on ourselves. I am eighty-seven years old now but I am still learning. I am a talebe. "From cradle to grave," [Beşikten mezara] says our Prophet. I will continue to learn from cradle to grave.

Undergirding both Özçimi's and his master Sayın's discourses is an understanding of ethics as imbued in a person through practice. Accordingly, just as with musical skill, virtuous dispositions do not exist a priori but are actualized through repeated activities ("techniques of the body" [Mauss 1979]). Both comments align, in this sense, with a conception of habitus (*malakat* in Arabic) as laid out by Islamic scholar Ibn Khaldun (d. 1406), which foregrounds the role of outer practice and repetition in the formation of habit. In this view, the doing of any skilled activity adapts the soul with an attribute (*şifa*), giving it "a special coloring that forms it" (Lapidus 1984, 53).[1]

Following this, the ethical principles informing this character formation exist in more than ney masters' discourse. They inhere in the musical practice—that is, through learning to play the ney in a certain way—including skilled learners' participation in the broader sociality of the community of practice. Let me proceed with a musical example to illustrate this point. As chapter 2 has already discussed at length, privileging the value of a good sound over the playing of melody is one of the core perceptual modifications that the artistic practice demands from learners. No other skilled action in ney playing comes before building up a forceful sound from the reed. Novices must delay the step toward playing a melody and commit themselves instead to blowing single notes until a desirable tone begins to emerge.

To reflect upon my own learning experience, coming to approach sound as a type of slow knowledge and the perfecting of sound as a virtuous act in its own sake constituted one new sense of perspective that I gained through attendance at sound-work. This is a practice that values the attitude of proceeding inch by inch, mastering one step at a time. This sensibility of "doing less but doing it well" was not only specific to the aesthetics of sound, it also informed all of the craft's skilled actions, from mastering makams to learning to improvise. For example, Salih Hoca encouraged me to spend eight months on makam *Suzinak*. Other students, too, were required to master the soundscape of a single piece. Ethical action here requires an attentiveness very different from that privileged by the pressures to be productive that pervade many of our daily practices. In our accelerated world, value is more often directed to the importance of *what* is produced rather than to *how* it is produced. For instance, the pedagogical methods organizing most modern systems of formal education are, in the main, designed and implemented with an explicit focus on aims, objectives, outputs, and outcomes where developing a skill as swiftly as possible and working on multiple tasks characterize the types of "habits" being fostered (Harris 2007). By contrast, the musical practice here demands a different pace and a different "calculation" of means and ends in order to reach excellence.

Finally, with its rich texture of metaphors and analogies, Salih Hoca's verbal articulations always acted as vital aids in generating new insights about the potential meaning of an embodied action, facilitating new ways of approaching music, artistry, and skilled knowledge. To briefly illustrate, foregrounding how sound has itself as its own end, Salih Hoca addresses me in one lesson, saying: "Think about melody as 'beauty' [*güzellik*] and proper sound as 'good character' [*iyi huy*]. Physical beauty is transient, but good morals stay with one permanently. You can get tired of listening to a beautiful melody, but you never get tired of a good sound. That always draws one's attention to itself." I explore the relationship between language and ethical modification later, but the key point to highlight here is how, by drawing attention to virtues internal to the "externals" of skillful playing (in other words, sound expression, techniques of ornamentation, phrasing, or articulation, and so on), the teaching method at work here continuously encourages learners to consider what makes a particular action or aesthetic element good musical conduct, a pondering that also entails ethical reflexivity. Thus, even if imitation is the key technique at work in becoming a musician, not all learning happens silently or "under the radar" of consciousness.

Embodiment and Musicianship

As Shawn Lindsay notes in his "Hand Drumming" essay, "the learning of a new skill presents a threat to the habitus in that it entails a reworking and revitalizing of the body's corporeal schema" (1996, 202). To acquire an embodied mastery of a practice one must undergo, through repetitive training, a series of corporeal modifications. Among other things, this entails inhabiting the bodies in new ways through cultivating certain modes of comportment and gestures that are socially meaningful to the musical community of practice.

Because new students come with already habituated ways of existing in the world, their comportment is immediately discernible by experienced students and teachers alike. "You recognize the intention of a novice the moment she or he comes through the door," remarked ney master Bülent Özbek, who runs his own studio in the bustling district of Kadıköy. According to Özbek, the way a person sits, his or her bearing, and how he or she speaks reveal whether someone genuinely want to become a talebe or have come simply to kill time. "You know the fabric" (Kumaşı anlıyorsun), he said, adding empathetically that, either way, a hoca was responsible for taking everyone seriously: it was up to the novice to decide whether the learning activity was for them or not. Just as students and teachers perceive the intention of a potential new student as imparted through how he or she enters the room, sits, stands, or walks, the changing performance of one's bodily comportment comes to index how far one has progressed along the learning path. Many teachers expressed a similar opinion that the best talebes were those who re-ordered their bodily comportment correctly. For instance, in one revealing conversation, Neyzen Ali Tüfekçi, lecturer in the ney-teaching program at the State Conservatory for Turkish Music at Istanbul Technical University, was sharing his concerns about the changing educational life at his institution where he himself had undertaken musical training back in the 1990s as a talebe of Neyzen Süleyman Erguner. Pointing out the implications of a change driven by a shift toward a growing standardization of the curriculum, he noted:

> The conservatorium has changed a lot; what being a talebe means has changed too. When we were students, you learned through the master-apprentice relationship. But now there is a fourteen-week curriculum, and a student knows which makam is to be covered, say, in week seven. Some hocas are trying hard to preserve meşk, but the system isn't allowing us to teach like that anymore. Everything has become standardized, so has the talebes and the pitches [*perdeler*] they play. There is no love [*aşk yok*], just an artificial meşk [*sadece suni bir meşk*]. But, of course, exceptional talebes exist. Currently, I am working with eight students, and one of them signals that he has the potential to become a good talebe. When I look at him, I see my own earlier self. The way he sits, the way he walks—he always leaves the room walking with his back toward the corridor—his character, his expression of respect for his hoca, his polite manners [*efendiliği*] and modesty [*mütevaziliği*]. Unlike other students, he doesn't ask questions like "*Hocam*, what are we doing next week?" He is patient and meticulous [*intizamlı*].

Note here how the understanding of an ideal talebe is closely tied to a repertoire of virtues embedded in a certain mode of comportment, etiquette, and manners, all of which have an ethical import. The bodily "signs" that the student is said to give away, which ultimately make him stand out among the cohort of students Tüfekçi is working with, are related in the first place not to his adeptness of skill but concern precisely his ways of holding his body, style of expression, listening mannerisms, and ways of acting, each imparting a morally sound intent. In recounting the virtues he recognizes in his student's embodied presence and actions, Tüfekçi is not framing them as a mere reflection of the person's moral character but as a certain kind of attitude toward practice. It is through such gestures and actions that the talebe demonstrates a genuine intention, a "seriousness" (see Lambek 2015) of purpose in becoming a committed talebe.[2] To demonstrate a capacity to comport the body in a fitting manner is to intentionally orient oneself toward the act of learning—a comportment toward learning. Without such orientation or attitude, how can learning be effectively—and affectively—achieved? Tüfekçi goes on to explain this point further by reflecting upon his earlier self while a neophyte at the conservatory. He remarks:

> These things matter. When I used to be a talebe, I would never sit down until Hoca told me to do so. I would recognize his arrival from how he closed the door of his car. I knew his number plate by heart. Only when you are in such state, you begin to learn the ney. Sometimes Hoca would be busy with something else in his office or someone would drop by to chat with him in the middle of our lesson. I would be told to fetch tea. Having prepared so well, being so eager to learn, I would feel so frustrated in those situations, but we were not in a position to say anything of course. We had to endure, we had to show patience. These things are also part of learning. You cannot complete the path without such whims. As they say, the dervish who waits for the tekke gets to drink the soup. Years later you drink that soup.

A strong sense of purposiveness and an active effort toward learning are invoked by the actions and mannerisms that Tüfekçi is recalling here. As he explicitly states, the acquired sensory habits, gestures, and sensibilities that help compose a new bodily comportment cannot be separated from what is intended to be achieved. They *are* constitutive of learning. Further, insofar as ethics is intrinsic to our bodiliness, speech, and actions (Lambek 2010[3]), the "outward" deeds have ramifications for the series of ethical modifications one experiences. As Tüfekçi's reflexive comment about what developing those bodily capacities and ways of acting came to mean to him suggests, it is through the disciplining and performing of the fleshy body that the ethical dispositions conducive for becoming a skilled practitioner flourish. These virtues are patience, respect, responsibility, and trust.

More precisely then, how does musical apprenticeship transform the bodily postures and comportment of ney students? Back at Salih Hoca's studio, this learning process occurred through participation in the rich sociality of the place. Learning in the company of fellow students also meant learning from them. Through observing their peers in action, novices gradually begin to fine-tune their previously ill-fitting bodily comportment. In my first lessons I remember feeling out of tune with the collectively orchestrated bodily gestures of the class who sat side by side facing each other along the two long *sedirs*. These included standing up when Salih Hoca walked into the room or acknowledging his presence through repositioning the body; not sitting down with the ney on the lap during the lesson time but leaving it in its case—understood as demonstrating self-control given that exposing too-much eagerness or ambition to play was not received well; exhibiting expectant listening; the affirmation of following the lesson intently through eye contact, nodding, and verbal assent (sohbet events are a joint production of meaning); entering or leaving the room by expressing an implicit attentiveness toward the embodied presence of others. Keeping the body as still as possible was also common, as was the posture of a diminishing—not an expanding—body. Students performed a bodily drawing-in upon themselves so as to not overly project a presence. In one way, all this repertoire of embodied actions came to mean "skillful listening," communicating not only one's attentiveness to learning, but also a sense of esteem and humility before the master. Students always proudly acknowledged how far they had come in mastering how to listen as they reflected upon what made the learning practice most meaningful for them. In fact, certain students never brought their instrument with them during the whole time I spent at the studio, convinced perhaps that they would never become particularly competent in ney playing. Yet I was always struck by their diligence in attending not only their own but also other groups' weekly lessons.

Outside the lesson room, immersion in the rich social life of the studio also provided ample opportunity for students to learn and rehearse essential knowledge of etiquette and appropriate comportment. Such learning occurred through social exchange and interaction not only with their peers and Salih Hoca but also with a larger constituency of skilled practitioners, including the earlier generation of neyzens taught by Salih Hoca (some of these senior talebes used the studio for their own teaching activity), fellow musicians coming over for group rehearsals, masters and students attending other skilled practices (calligraphy, tanbur, and kemençe lessons, for example), the studio's larger circle of friends coming and going, and another group of committed talebes who had become apprentices by way of working in the atelier also. For novices, participation in this broader field of relationships and sociality is a constant source of learning how to behave, how to sit, how to interact with others—all paramount for becoming a legitimate practitioner of the art (Lave and Wenger 1991). Knowing when to talk, how much to talk, and how to formulate an utterance when in the presence of others also involves the fostering of one's humility and sense of respect. Students are expected to become attentive to the embodied presence of others, and to act in accord with the "mood" of the place. Ideally, this self-cultivation is not self-absorbed but demonstrates a caring comportment, sensitive to its surroundings. The skillful comportment of apprentices and senior talebes was best performed in the practice and ethic of *hizmet* (service, care), showing in their attentive attitude an alertness to moment-to-moment emerging necessities in the surrounding environment. This core group of talebes were involved in provisioning the studio by running most of its daily errands, ensuring that there was always freshly brewed tea, and serving others. Well aware of the virtues of developing such ethos of serving others, one of the young apprentices said to me, "To receive *himmet* [spiritual help, guidance], one must do hizmet," reiterating this well-known Sufi motto so as to express a sense of sensitiveness to the morally transformative intersubjective reciprocities undergirding the learning process.

To take a step back here, the concept and practice of hizmet belongs to the core of meşk. While this expression may more literally refer to certain acts or practices undertaken to show care for others, it also captures, in a larger sense, the whole experience of inhabiting the lifelong ethical subject position of a talebe, complete with the emotional entailments such experience comprises, such as owing obedience (*sadakât*) and surrender (*teslimiyet*) to the master's authority. Rendering hizmet is by definition what a talebe does. And because one never ceases to be a talebe vis-à-vis one's own hoca, the responsibility of performing hizmet has no end either. Take Salih Hoca, for instance. Alongside the daily forms of care he showed to his master, his sense of hizmet toward Sayın strongly inhered also in every minute detail of his teaching practice, including his establishing of his own role vis-à-vis his students as an intermediary (*aracı*) only. "This is how Niyazi Hoca showed this to us," "This is how we learned it from him," he would repeat after displaying how to render a certain movement correctly, always putting himself in the subject position of a talebe while declaiming ownership of that piece of musical knowledge. Physically absent, Sayın was there in spirit.[4] In similar vein, Salih Hoca's emphasis on mastering the musical pieces composed by the members of his lineage can also be seen as a rendering of hizmet, inviting students to conceive this learning as becoming part of a community as it connects the living to dead masters.

Here we might discern a moral economy of exchange that the social principle of hizmet ensures within institutions of lineage. Lineages can be seen as communities of hizmet—a chain of hizmet—creating ongoing relationships, which operate on a very similar line to the "gift" in anthropological theory. At a certain point in his or her lifetime, a master artist occupies a dual position as both the provider and the receiver of hizmet. One never stops being both at the one time. As Paul Anderson reminds us, obligation "does not just lead to moral action; it also creates community" (2011, 18). The sense of responsibility and obligation to serve others is not just a means for becoming an ideal talebe but is constitutive of this musical community.

Thus, even if the master-pupil relationship is the immediate context in which artistic enskillment occurs, one grows into knowledge—in other words, knowing how to sit, how to walk, how to behave—through practice, in watching and observing others; in listening; in doing hizmet; in "being-in-the-studio," and in mastering particular ways of playing. The approach I have outlined here does not conceive of ethical practice as knowledge of a corpus of "rules" or "codes" coextensive with a certain culture or acquired in a prescriptive manner. Ethical becoming is not rule following or an inculcation of moral codes. Rather, by returning to Aristotle, we can take ethical modifications to be inextricably connected to training practices that are intended to transform the practitioner.

"You Can't Become a Neyzen If You Don't Know How to Cook"

At Hezarfen students' experiences of gaining ney competency also involved firsthand exposure to a rich repertoire of skilled activities of an extramusical kind. Take cooking, for example, the second-most-important daily activity at the ney school after music! According to Salih Hoca, the path to becoming a neyzen goes through the kitchen. "No matter whether you are a man or a woman, a neyzen should know how to cook," he used to say. In fact, for the majority of my male fellow students, the kitchen of the ney school is where they gained their first proper exposure to cooking. Not only was gender segregation discouraged in all forms of sociable activity taking place at the school, but males in particular were made subjects of socialization into tasks that are traditionally assigned to women.

At the studio hardly a day passed that Salih Hoca did not cook. Cooking with or for his talebes constituted his hizmet to them. Daily occasions of commensality were an important part of the school's everyday life. Cooking was articulated to important dates in the Islamic calendar as well. For example, *iftar* meals were prepared and shared throughout the whole month of *Ramazan*, while special cooking and feasting occasions were held on *kandil* (the five holy

FIGURE 6.1. Cooking preparations at the studio. Photograph by Turgut Y. Dalar.

nights of Islam) to show hospitality to respected members of the community of practice. More-well-off members of the studio sometimes volunteered to take responsibility for provisioning the evening meal. Buying chickpeas, vegetables, or meat for up to twenty people was not cheap, yet in the main Salih Hoca paid for food out of his own pocket, as well as encouraging his students to establish relationships with local vendors (*esnaf*) while taking an interest in seasonal produce and food quality.

Further, teaching expanded way outside the classroom of the ney school, comprising a wide range of activities that Salih Hoca did with his talebes in select places in the city. Daily excursions that involved visiting trades shops in Istanbul's neighborhoods of Tahtakale and Karaköy or wandering around secondhand markets in the city were activities that willing students participated in. Attendance in such place-based (and place-making) activities facilitated in students an embodied know-how about where to find a certain object, craftwork, or even a particular food in the massive urban jungle of Istanbul, about how to discern the quality or value of that thing and how to appreciate the skilled labor that had been invested in its making—in other words, of good craftsmanship. A remark made by one of my fellow talebes is illuminating: "From Hoca I learned how to spend money and what to spend it on," he said. "I have a limited amount of money, but I might spend all of it on a piece of writing [calligraphic inscription]." In an important sense, participation in these spatial practices in and around the city also cultivated in serious learners new urban competencies that involved learning how to talk to people—not to anonymous people, but to a merchant for instance—or how to bargain. Becoming a skillful bargainer implies here a form of entering into or building up a reciprocal relationship with another person as well as becoming an actor in certain circuits of trade and skill.

In another sense, the activities referred to here can also be seen as corporeal practices of personalizing the city or of orienting oneself toward the city. Experiential engagement with Istanbul's landscape also extended to other clusters of places, including Sufi tekkes, the tombs of saintly figures, and Istanbul's neighborhoods with old Ottoman buildings. According to Salih Hoca, an embodied familiarity with the city's "spiritual" (*maneviyatlı*) places was also essential for becoming a neyzen. "You cannot blow the ney if your eye is oblivious to the calligraphy written on the fountain in the Üsküdar Square." (Turkey changed its script in 1925, so not everyone can read the Arabic alphabet.) "If you want to become a neyzen, you should go to Eyüp and walk around its old streets." "If you want to learn the ney, it is good for you to go and sit in the courtyard of the [Mevlevi] *dergâh* in Galata." "A neyzen should make the time to go to Çınaraltı in Beyazıt and visit the secondhand booksellers and beadmakers there." For Salih Hoca, apprenticeship in becoming a neyzen occurred through these activities as much as in playing the ney.

The transformation fostered in becoming a skilled practitioner of the ney involved, then, a new attitude toward the city's urban environment. In being spoken for (and in being visited), certain places in the city were deliberately brought to the attention of students, disclosed as something to be noticed and inhabited. One fellow talebe, a kindergarten teacher, explained to me how, since coming to the lessons, she had developed a new liking for discovering Sufi sites. "I went to Bursa the other weekend and didn't leave a single tomb [*türbe*], a single tekke unvisited there," she remarked, pointing out how such places had not been the focus of her attention earlier.[5] The spatial practices that the ney school sponsored for students were sometimes extended beyond Istanbul. On one occasion, upon finding out that a certain talebe had not yet visited the tomb of the saintly Mevlana, Salih Hoca immediately bought a plane ticket to send the young man to Konya.

These examples demonstrate how this meşk practice enables a new attentiveness toward places, as well as new aspects of the city—fresh urban "affordances" (Gibson 1979)—to dawn for students. The city "emerges for the perceiver in his or her acts of educated and embodied engagement with it, including, of course, with other beings, both human and non-human" (Houston 2015b, 9). Thus to reckon with the city in new ways—to perceive it against the grain of its constitution by capital *and* nationalists (such as the AKP) with their ideologies embedded in the urban environment—can be seen as another vital entailment of the perceptual/ethical modification that learners experience. As phenomenological insight reveals, there is an ethical dimension or particularity in perception.[6]

Further, given that Islamic references part-compose the extramusical practices that individual subjects participate in here, we can also say, following Heiko Henkel, that in enabling the constitution of Muslim spaces, these spatial practices "not only define practitioners as religious Muslims but, in fact, shape them as Muslims" (2007, 64). In his anthropological study on how pious believers seek to inhabit heterogeneous, industrial, and secular contemporary Istanbul "in a Muslim way," Henkel writes that the old city, with its Ottoman mosques and tombs, are "not part of a mold in which Muslim lives are naively shaped but, instead, [are] chosen points of reflection, poetic references" (67). Consciously "place-making" Istanbul as Islamic is effected "by foregrounding Muslim elements and backgrounding other elements, by designating certain elements as significant and others as unimportant, and by visiting felicitous Muslim spaces" (58).

In fact, the places that Salih Hoca directs his students' attention to are also the very places that are objects of a "project of creating Muslim space" (58) for Henkel's interlocutors. Yet unlike with the latter, what this process of relating to the city in new ways reflects—or aims for—is not a pietization of those selves. Instead, the ney pedagogy proposes that the slow process of coming to do this music well requires a methodical immersion in its "life world" through becoming conversant with its related fields of action (in other words, with Islam, with the city, with its dead neyzens, and with art and craft work and their materials). The moral subjectivity-in-the-making here is not a "pious" self but one that involves the whole person.

As the following section will show, Salih Hoca's skillful teaching of the ney through this rich array of activities, from cooking to city visitations, is not without precedents. The pleasurable activities described above were key elements of his own experiences of being a talebe under Niyazi Sayın, revealing how Salih

Hoca's meşk practice has been shaped by his particular learning history. Even if a replication of Niyazi Sayın's methods and relationships is not possible in Salih Hoca's school, there are much more than echoes of them in his organization of his own teaching.

His Master's Sound

There was a calligrapher [*hattat*] Necmeddin Okyay (1883–1976) whom we respected deeply. He was a true instructor [*mürebbi*], a hoca to us. We grew up next to him. When I had developed an interest in learning the ney, he said to me, "There is this Halil [Dikmen] at the Academy [of Fine Arts], painter [*Ressam*] Halil. Let me take you to him." Hoca [Halil Dikmen] was the Director of the Fine Arts and Sculpture Museum in Beşiktaş then, which opened in 1937 upon a directive from Atatürk. Earlier I had wanted to take lessons from other neyzens, but our economic situation did not allow it. The Second World War had finished not long ago, I wasn't in a position to pay for lessons. I had bought a ney for 10 Liras from Osman Dede at Çadırcılar Market in Beyazıt. Necmeddin Hoca took me to Halil Dikmen. This person was a magnificent [*muazzam*] ney player. He was a talebe of Neyzen Emin Dede. He only played the şah ney, never played any other *akort* (tuning). He had this şah ney, 91.5 centimeter-length. I have never, yet, obtained a sound like his from my ney. He had a splendid [*müthiş*] sound. I took lessons from him for fifteen years, every Thursday afternoon. He would play for two to three hours, and I would commit that piece to my memory. I have never heard anyone blowing the ney like him. [. . .]

The morals, the kindness of Hoca, his grace, his humanity. He never complimented me on my playing, not even once. That's how his temperament [*huy*] was. I was in my early thirties back then. I wasn't in a position to say much. He would talk, I would listen. I used to look at those people visiting him at the museum, all very respectable people. There was this fellow talebe who was also taking lessons from Hoca. One day I saw him coming out of the [museum] building. "Did you have your lesson?" I asked him. "I did, but I am giving up," he said. "I realized that I will never get a sound from the ney like the sound of Hoca. But I will continue to come to him to learn morals [*ahlâk*] from Hoca," he said. I will never forget this. Hoca was an incredibly virtuous [*faziletli*] man, incomparable to anyone. He always dressed up respectfully. He had this small bag; he would carry some bread and cheese in it. He smoked a third-class cigarette. May God rest his soul. I have never heard a ney sound like his in my life. Today they say for *gazel* singer [*gazelhan*] Hafız Sami (1874–1943) that his voice can't be fully captured in his

> [phonograph] recordings. The same is true for Halil Dikmen. We have his sound, but it can't be fully comprehended [*anlaşılmıyor*] today. (Interview with Niyazi Sayın, 2014)

These words by Niyazi Sayın provide us with an affectionate and intimate insight about his master Halil Dikmen (1906–1964). Alongside his reverence for Dikmen's artistic brilliance—accentuated here by Sayın's repeated references to the excellence of Dikmen's sound—Sayın also expresses an admiration for his master's ethical qualities, emphasizing how he influenced/advanced his talebes morally, beyond mere musical development. The autobiographical reflections that extensive interviews with lineage musicians facilitated also commonly reveal similar learning experiences, grounded in feelings of deep respect and admiration as much for the moral persona as for the musical artistry of one's hoca. Such insights provide us with crucial firsthand knowledge about how skillful masters teach their talebes not only how to play music well but also how to be. They fulfill in the lives of their talebes the role of an exemplar, providing an inspiring repertoire of practices for emulation.

The significance of the subject position of the master as a source of moral or spiritual guidance has been discussed in certain studies of apprenticeship-based learning in which surrender and loyalty to the authority of the teacher is essential to the learning relationship. For instance, Dalidowicz notes how in the artistic tradition of the *kathak* dance, the role of the guru is much more than teaching the skills and knowledge of the art, involving the leading of the pupil along the path of self-realization (2012, 63). The guru role in this context articulates deeply with the Hindu cosmological idea that the guru is a living medium for God, acting "as an intermediary for this higher more diffuse divine force" (61). Similarly, in his work on learning to play tabla in North India, James Kippen discusses how gurus play a vital role in the "character-training" of their apprentices (1988, 131), which, in this case, involves advice-giving on moral issues.

By contrast, in the learning context discussed here, the exemplary role of the master consists not in their mediation of the divine, nor mainly in verbal advice and admonitions but, at the same time, in their ways of being. A hoca teaches not only with words but also inspires through acts that emanate a blessing (*feyz*[7]) to the talebe. James Faubion's (2011) account of "ethical becoming" delineated in his *An Anthropology of Ethics* is helpful here. In his analytical framing, ethical becoming concerns more broadly the ways in which one comes to occupy a certain ethical subject position. Placing a strong emphasis on pedagogy, Faubion emphasizes that pedagogues do more than set out certain normative rules to be followed by others (he calls this "themitical" ethical action); but because they come to inhabit and maintain their subject positions so well, they are able to act as an *exemplar* with a capacity to convey values and ideals of how to be and how to live (2011, 51–52). Ethical becoming is an on-going dynamic process in this sense and encapsulates the possibility of change, that is, of ethical modification (45–46).

Thus, differently from how Kippen frames it, the "character-training" of the skilled practitioners that I discuss here is not just limited to learning about or being exposed to the moral viewpoints of one's guide in responding to ethical issues. In their comportment, demeanor, rhetoric, and actions, skillful masters are seen worthy of emulation, capable of "serving at once as existential guide" (Foucault 1997, 233–34).[8] As one of Sayın's accomplished talebes remarked, "Even the way Hoca [Sayın] walks on the stage is a source of learning morals [*ahlâk*] for us. There are so many [artists] who appear on the stage with much arrogance [*kibir*]. But Hoca enters the stage in complete humility [*tevazu*]. His body says to his audience: 'I have an addressee [*Bir muhattabım var*]'" (personal conversation with Bülent Özbek).

The autobiographical reflections by other ney musicians who learned directly or indirectly from Sayın often expressed a similar appreciation of his ethical sensibilities—and not merely of his unequalled virtuosity—accentuating the ways in which Sayın has maintained his subject position as a hoca so well. To provide just one example, in the following comment Neyzen Ömer Erdoğdular foregrounds how his master's virtue of generosity set him as a model to his talebes:

> I started going to Niyazi Hoca in 1965. He used to live in Üsküdar then, in an old, two-story, wooden house remaining from his father. He was living together with his mother, elder sister, and his sister's daughter. We had our lessons there. Hoca is a highly knowledgeable person, of course. When he was growing up in Üsküdar, he spent time with significant Sufi figures from the late Ottoman years. In his sohbets he would tell us about the Mevlevi dervish Sucu Ali Fâni Dede and Eşref Efendi (1876–1954) whom he respected deeply. He would tell us about the renowned calligrapher Necmeddin Okyay, who was also the imam of the Yeni Valide Mosque in Üsküdar, and Nafiz Uncu Efendi (1887–1958), the imam of the İskele Mosque. Both were great hafız of their time. Hoca used to recount to us how in those years it was hard to pick which mosque to go to in order to do the *teravih namazı* [special evening prayers performed during the month of *Ramazan*], given the incredible voice of the hafız in those days as well as the talents of recitation that they displayed. "It was like going to a concert," he used to say. One had to choose

> whom to listen to that evening. We heard many stories about such valuable figures who occupied a crucial place in Niyazi Hoca's life. Hoca was always generous to us, always hospitable. His house never lacked visitors. It is that generosity, those morals [*ahlâk*] of him that give his ney that exceptional sound. When we used to go to his house, we were not even allowed to take a box of *lokum* with us. "Empty handed you will come," we would be told. He accepted nothing, but only gave to us. It is that generosity that makes up the sound of Niyazi Sayın's ney. (Personal conversation with Erdoğdular, 2013).

The learning biographies of Sayın's students suggest an incredibly rich variety of means through which musical apprenticeship cultivated new ethical horizons in these skilled practitioners. As Erdoğdular recounts above, the discursive practice of sohbet is one such vital means (see chapter 5). Their experiences of becoming a musician also involved firsthand exposure to a wide range of skilled activities of extramusical kind. Sayın spent a great deal of time with his talebes, teaching them how to cook, how to saw, how to make prayer beads, how to grow flowers, how to make a ney or a mouthpiece. Visiting secondhand markets, repairing old objects, showing them how to practice the art of ebru, and involving them in bookbinding were all aspects of his lessons. As Salih Hoca noted, "He would want us to know where to eat the best white beans [*kurufasulye*] or where to find the best coffee. Learning where to find the best ebru paint and how much paint to buy were also part of our meşk. We did great lessons with Hoca walking around Tahtakale and Beyazıt."

Similarly, in another account, Neyzen Aziz Şenol Filiz reported how his own experience of musical apprenticeship under Neyzen Fuat Türkelman (1941–1992) back in the 1980s encompassed much more than playing the ney. Filiz recounts:

> Fuat Hoca knew how to write [calligraphic writing]. He was also good at ebru. Back then [1980s], these art practices were not fashionable [*moda değildi*] like today. He was a good craftsman. He knew how to make prayer beads on his lathe machine, he knew how to cut and inlay mother of pearl [*sedef*], and many other skills like these. Outside the conservatory, at his home, we used to spend a great deal of our time together working on these things. The lathe machine would stop working, and we would find ourselves running up and down the hardware market in Karaköy looking for its part. We would spend days going around Istanbul looking for wood suitable for beadmaking. There were times when I'd rather wish that we sat down and played the ney instead. Ney didn't take up more than 30 percent of the whole time we spent together. But none of these events were separate from learn-

> ing the ney. This is what you grasp in retrospect. (Personal conversation with Filiz, 2012).

The biographical accounts recorded here give us clues about broader embodied and practical aspects of the training that these ney players were subject to, all leading ney artists today. The rich array of extramusical activities pursued here do not constitute an exhaustive list of rules or roles that one has to abide by in order to gain musical competency. Nor are they posited as indispensable for becoming an expert neyzen. Yet what emerges from these reflective comments of ney musicians is that the unmediated presence of hoca and talebe in each other's company is an enabling condition for emulating the ways of being and acting of one's master. Emulation begs such shared presence. As one senior talebe of Salih Hoca said to me in reflecting upon the series of ethical modifications that he had gone through: "If you really wish to learn from a *mürebbi* and spend a lot of time with that person, their smell permeates in you [*o kişinin kokusu sana siner*]. The talebe must see his or her hoca, how they dress, what shoes they wear, how they live in their house," underlining how these elements are conducive for coming to occupy the subject position of a talebe fittingly. The emphasis that lineage neyzens give to the face-to-face "atmosphere" of meşk and their critical assessments of other pedagogical practices that lack such quality (for example, method books, online courses, ney-teaching DVDs, and the like) should be understood in the light of this point. Being in the company of one's hoca, receiving his words, watching him in action, and doing things with him provide the conditions for the birth of a desire in the talebe to emulate his teacher.

Without this side-by-side-ness of the hoca-talebe "ensemble," the strong affective ties that make possible the *rabıta* (relation) between them, too, would not exist. *Rabıta* is an intersubjective bond built upon feelings of surrender, dedication, and reciprocal trust, mirroring a "guidance relationship" as Qureshi (2003, 63) notes for the *mürşid-mürid* connection found in Sufi Islam. And yet as with all things intersubjective—phenomenologically understood, a capacity to participate in the intentions and emotions of the other person—the hoca-talebe dyad is not devoid of friction. Tensions, disagreements, misunderstandings, and misfiring are as much constitutive of it as surrender and devotion. Salih Hoca will tell you himself that many talebes have left in the past. Not everyone's motivations are aligned with the affective-ethical conditions of meşk, which requires intense, lifelong socialization. As I witnessed in the course of my own fieldwork, those not willing or able to invest in the emotional labor that comprises the hoca-talebe bond did not stay long at the studio. One acquaintance of mine with whom I shared the evening ferry rides across the Bosporus for almost half a year decided in the end that subjection to a hoca was not for her, perceiving this type of commitment to learning as impinging upon her agency. But this decision was also sparked by a more everyday event of miscommunication concerning the reciprocity of exchange in the studio. Sometimes, discontinuities happened due to personal conditions. Given that most of my fellow talebes were adults busy with family and work responsibilities, not all could cope with the demands of this intense sociality and daily interactions at the studio.

Over and beyond these situations, relationships at times fell apart in the face of difficulties that are inevitably part of any close intersubjective relationship. Similar to a parent-child bond, the hoca-talebe relationship is formed in dependency. The talebe relies on the authority of the hoca not only for artistic knowledge but also for his or her self-esteem and for a sense of recognition of his or her own legitimacy as a neyzen. To negotiate or deal with feelings of vulnerability and inferiority aroused by this emotional dependency on the master is also at the heart of the intersubjective quality of meşk. Potentially, the long trajectory of musical apprenticeship involves moments of conflict or even breakdown. And just as a continuing hoca-talebe bond can be the most powerful source of emotional and spiritual meaning in the life of a talebe, the falling apart of that relationship can be felt as a devastating blow for the rejected talebe. One ney player I met during my fieldwork, who was unable to restore his relationship with his hoca after six years of intense "discipleship" (his expression) under him, described his experience as the most traumatic event in his life. "I had completely surrendered myself to Hoca. This emotional bond is very important in meşk. You pay your hoca the respect that you may not even pay to your own father," he stated.

What this shows is that lineages are not only self-recruiting social institutions, but they are also self-pruning. The temporal succession of a lineage is fragile, as there is always a possibility that the affections of the hoca-talebe bond might come to an end. Thus, at any one point, a lineage only reflects the social webs of "successful" meşk relationships. If the hoca-talebe relation is an accomplishment, so is a lineage.

Language and Ethics

Given that musical apprenticeship at Hezarfen required participation in a thriving speech "economy" both during and outside the lesson time, a more detailed look at how the use of language fosters ethical modifications in learners is needed.[9] Before doing so, it will be instructive to reiterate a couple of related points made earlier. In chapter 5 I emphasized the central place of sohbet in skill acquisition. A key idea centering this book is that spoken words are not merely instrumental in describing skilled action but are constitutive of learning. Speech—and here I am mainly referring to sohbet as the key speech genre of this teaching practice—achieves this in a number of ways. First, as we have already seen, there is an explicit instructional intention in the give and take of sohbet, a cognitive dimension connected to its pedagogical substance. Second, through its rich rhetorical devices and techniques, speech fosters in learners perceptual modifications pertaining to music, as well as to social relations and actions constituting daily living, by its skillful weaving of analogous connections between them. Third, an efficacious sohbet transforms listeners emotionally, setting them in a new mood or altering their *hâl* (affective state). As the comments by those talebes who had been exposed to the pleasurable experience of listening to Salih Hoca's sohbets revealed (see chapter 5), the perceptual modifications enabled by listening cannot be separated from this intense affective force of sohbet.

This third point is explicated in Hirschkind's study on the Islamic piety movement in Cairo, which explores the way that speech and audition work as a means of ethical self-improvement for Egyptian male pietists. Sermons, according to Hirschkind, evoke in listeners "the primary affective conditions of virtuous conduct" (2006, 74). "Fear of God," for example, seems to be understood by the Muslims that he worked with as a particularly vital "ethical response" to be cultivated so as to live and act in accord with standards of Islamic piety. The ways in which sermons develop the receptive capacities of listeners—not necessarily their cognitive but their affective and "gestural" capacities—is central to the argument that Hirschkind makes concerning how his Muslim interlocutors construct themselves as ethical subjects. He writes:

> Sermon oratory recruits the body of the listener in multiple ways. Beyond its referential content, the sermon can be seen as a technique for animating and organizing a stratigraphy of bodily experience and for endowing the human compound with gestural potential. . . . Sermons impart not simply moral lessons but affective energies of ethical potential, a background of sensory and motor skills considered by those I worked with to be necessary for inhabiting the world in a manner appropriate for Muslims. (2006, 98)

While Hirschkind's exploration of the relationship between affective orientations and moral action is useful for thinking about the ethical entailments of sohbet, I want to give more weight to language than he does in considering the important role it plays in enabling various perceptual and ethical modifications in the skilled practitioners of the ney. The dualistic distinction that Hirschkind's ethnography maintains between what he identifies as the "cognitive" and "sensory" dimensions of listening puts language in an ambiguous position in relation to ethics. There are "two contrasting modes of sensory organization," he says: "one purely intellectual, the other ethical and grounded in the honed patterns of sensorimotor responsiveness" (97). In this assessment, which discriminates between the cognitive and sensorial dimensions of listening at work in the course of sermon audition, the ethical is sealed off from the "intellectual" content or "cognitive" work of speech, becoming tied rather narrowly to the sensorial-affective domain.[10]

By contrast, to acknowledge that listening is not only a cognitive act but also involves vital sensory dimensions does not require a binary juxtaposition between its different registers (cognitive, emotive, and sensorial). The ethical is central not only to how listeners are emotionally affected or moved by the performance of speech but also to what they make of its "message" in the cognitive sense. As Lambek points out in his outline of *ordinary ethics* in his introduction to the edited collection of that title, ethics is embedded in language, including its vocabulary and semantics, among other elements. The ethical insight, he asserts, is deeply rooted "in the categories and functions of language and ways of speaking, . . . in specific nouns and adjectives, verbs and adverbs, or adverbial phrases respectively, thus in the shared criteria we use to make ourselves intelligible to one another, in 'what we say when'" (2010, 2). There is an ethical quality to our modes of speaking and modes of being/acting.

As we have seen in chapter 5, one salient feature of the spoken language organizing Salih Hoca's speech acts is his extensive use of metaphors and analogies. Through skillful manipulation of familiar words, he addresses his audience with a language that conveys its message by continuously weaving analogous relations between musical knowledge and other domains of social life. Simply stated, this is what metaphors do: they convey meaning by making comparisons, drawing out a likeness or affinity between two or more different things. Yet following Ahmed, we can discern the pedagogic efficacy of metaphoric language as lying not merely in its potential to transfer meaning through comparison but also in its potential to *create* and *explore* meaning. The centrality of metaphor (and paradox) in the processes of meaning-making by Muslims is examined in Ahmed's thought-provoking book *What Is Islam: The Importance of Being Islamic*. Metaphors, Ahmed says, are a "means of meaning-making" (390), and "they are also *uses* (that is, *means*) and *meanings* of Islam" (393).

How did this meaning-making work? Let me examine speech acts from two separate lessons. While each communicates the same insight of the importance and virtue of obtaining a "thick," full sound from the ney, they do so by building their own metaphorical pathways. Salih Hoca remarks:

> The real ney is this ney, friends [*pointing at his own body*]: this ney [*pointing at the ney in his hand*] is a symbol. We should aim to get a good sound from this ney [*pointing at his own body*] so that this ney [*pointing at the ney in his hand*] also sounds good. Achieving a beautiful sound is a precious thing. This is because there is a real neyzen who blows into this ney [human being], a neyzen who plays us. "I breathed life into you, and now you breathe life into the things I said," says that neyzen to us. So we should speak good things and carry out good works. And if we are playing this instrument, we must also do it well. We must get a good sound out of the ney.

On another occasion he says:

> Here our goal is to make a good sound on the ney. We should continue to work on this even if the Day of Judgment was to come tomorrow. There is a *Hadis*, as you know: "Even if the end of time is upon you and you have a seedling in your hand, plant it," the Prophet said. The intention here is certainly not tree planting in and of itself. Whatever you are doing, you should continue doing it until the end, and do it the best you can. For instance, if your job is to make a ney, you should strive to make a better ney, and you must make sure that none of the neys you make are identical with each other. Are we identical? "In many-ness I found oneness." [*Kesrette buldum vahdeti.*] Who said these words? [*One of the talebes replies here:* "Niyazi Mısri."] Only from multiplicity can oneness emerge.

Each one of these speech acts foregrounds and backgrounds particular aspects of the same "message," affording listeners a new perspective or experience in perceiving its meaning and force. In the first speech act, the virtue of establishing a good sound gains its meaning(s) from the analogous relationships drawn out between the "instrument-ney" and the "human-ney," and, second, between the "human-neyzen" and the "True neyzen": just as the neyzen blows breath into the ney, the Essence blows life into the human-ney. The analogy is extended to gaining a beautiful sound from the instrument and to getting a good "sound" from life.

In the second example the spoken language moves from the known to the unknown in a slightly different manner, this time by crossing back and forth between sound work and other enterprises (tree-planting, ney-making, and so on) that one expends labor on in life. The perfecting of each requires commitment and persistence, and *doing the best one can do today.* One meaning accrues to another. The speaker demands from listeners a new exploration of meaning by interrelating the individuality and uniqueness of each ney and of the individuality and uniqueness of each Divine creation. Their perceived likeness seems to emerge here: just as Divine creation sets out an example for making a good ney, the latter act of creation—the material world—itself stands as a metaphor for the former (the Divinity). The metaphoric relation proposed here expresses the fundamental Sufi idea—the idea of Akbarian Sufi philosophy—that all things in the material world are the manifestations (*tecelliyat*) of the Essence. To put it differently, the Seen world in which we live "is a figural or metaphorical representation (Arabic: *majaz*) of Real-Truth [of the Unseen World]" (Ahmed 2016, 20). The reciting of the poetic line by the seventeenth-century Sufi Niyazı-i Mısri, "In many-ness I found oneness," only makes sense (in terms of this speech act) in relation to this thought. It evokes and alludes to the core Akbarian idea of "Unity of Being" (*vahdet-i vücud*), which has been central to the teachings of many Sufis, from Attar to Ibn Arabi. In this instance, it is precisely the use of metaphor that allows the language to retain and express these complex meanings—in other words, the complexity of Revelation in Islam—in an explorative mode.

In these examples, rather than merely declaiming the rules one needs to abide by in order to play the ney, speech fosters a way of knowing music by bringing it into a mutually effecting relationship with the Sufi conceptualization of the world (in other words, Sufi epistemology), petitioning listeners to reflect on both. In this process, neither of the entities brought into a shared relation of meaning (music and Islam) collapses into the other, nor does one gain primacy over the other. Each makes a certain aspect of the other (more) knowable. It is precisely this semantic capacity of metaphors and analogies that makes them the best-suited means for producing knowledge in this Muslim music-making context. Ahmed's insight concerning the affordances of the *semantic capacity* of metaphor is instructive here. Metaphor, he says,

> enables words—and *the users of words*—to go beyond a single level of meaning (the literal) so as to generate complex meanings (and complexes of meanings) beyond the literal limitations of formal definitions. . . . Metaphor does not seek to determine or prescribe the meaning of "truth," but instead allows "for the *multi-dimensional exploration of meaning(s)*." (2016, 390–91; original emphasis)[11]

What is achieved here is a way of knowing music *and* Islam whereby the complexity and polyvalency of each can be retained, explored, expressed, and communicated. The aim is not to confine their significance to one/true meaning and mobilize it but instead to leave it open—not contraction but expansion of meaning(s). In fact, while the analogous reasoning at work here potentially enables a new sense of what is entailed by the metaphor, it does so without actually naming which particular attributes or characteristics of those elements (in other words, the Divine creation) are being brought into a relation of meaning. Salih Hoca recognizes them as unnamable and wishes to retain them precisely as such.

In the light of this, the pedagogical value of sohbet in this learning context (and in societies of Muslims) should be found simultaneously in the conditions of listening that it enables and in the semantic capacity of its deeply metaphorical language by means of which knowledge can be explored and communicated in an explorative mode. This is why metaphors are indispensable to sohbet. The musical pedagogy cannot accomplish its task—that is, an exploration of possible meanings—without the aid of these language tools.

In sum, here the ethical is tied up with the power of language to enable multiple, and always different, perspectives and moods, a new sense of situation.[12] Each listener (and the speaker) explores the meaning of these language-games according to their own capacities to know, which are charged with ethical import. Ordinary perception is already ethical. As Ortony states: "In the process of comprehending the statement I in some sense 'reconstruct' the event described and I do so by bringing to bear a great deal of what I already know, not just about the language, but about the world. . . . What I invoke is largely experiential, perceptual and cognitive, and to this extent generally similar, but probably almost never identical, to what others invoke" (1975, 47). Our meaning-making is mediated by our horizons of the past.

Yet although one might always extract from the metaphor a different meaning according to one's own present concerns, over time, listener(s) can also come to cohere around the possibilities of meanings that similar speech acts invoke in them. As I discussed in chapter 5, sohbet involves an always-emerging alignment of meanings between the speaker and the trained listener and is an event, therefore, of both individual and collective meaning-making. Through exposure to listening, one can begin to give new insights and perspectives to speech, and start to address the skilled practice—and the world—in new ways. This perceptual modification is an ethical modification.

CHAPTER SEVEN

Musical Islam

IN THIS FINAL SHORT CHAPTER let us move away from the ethical transformations at work in the studio and redirect discussion to the pressing and more general issue of Muslim ethics, as addressed in the fields of music production and Islamic piety. Up until now we have seen how the language, the ethics, and the practices of learning the ney seem imbued with an Islamic ethos. But how does this music-making explicitly relate to Islam?

This question is important not just because, clearly, there is a relationship between them. It is important also because the recent scholarship in both anthropology and Islamic studies examining Muslim art practices appears overly invested in one particular version of Islam, one based on legalistic reasoning and authoritative texts (in other words, the Qur'an and hadith) and is heavily concerned with issues of the authorization and even permissibility of music/art *in* Islam. Much of this work elaborates on the relationship between music and Islam using terms such as piety, Muslim moral subjectivity, and the Islamic discursive tradition. One conceptual and epistemological implication of this framing is that scholars, encouraged by their informants, investigate how the practice of art is justified if it addresses and communicates a religious message or becomes a means for transforming individual subjects into better ("more pious") Muslims. But what of other dimensions and forms of Muslim music-making that not only lack such a mission but are also actually at odds with the project of art as piety mobilization or as missionary apologetics?

For the skilled practitioners at Hezarfen, music-making pursues neither of these aims. Here, music practice is not driven by an ambition to convey an Islamic message, even as some novices take up education in the ney with the aim of becoming better Muslims. Indeed, if they enroll with such a desire, they are strongly discouraged from continuing in it. During the course of my fieldwork I witnessed numerous occasions of this kind. "Pious" students would come. When asked why they wanted to learn the ney, newcomers often predictably connected the ney to Islam, claiming an "Islamic" quality for it. Dissatisfied, Salih Hoca would try to disabuse them of their overestimation of the religious significance of the ney, reclaiming its musical status instead and asking the person to consider whether this was the right place for them.

Yet as the ethnographic descriptions of the ney pedagogy in the preceding chapters have revealed (especially in Salih Hoca's speech making), this musical practice does facilitate for learners and master musicians a particular way of engaging with Islam, shaping their subjectivities *as* Muslims while also fostering in them new sensory and artistic perceptions and skill-based capacities. Before bringing *Musical Ethics and Islam* to conclusion, my aim is to give more weight to this significant dimension of musical apprenticeship, addressing how it trains students in a *musical Islam*. This involves fostering in them an explorative way of knowing both music *and* Islam—a way of knowing one through the other. Let me begin by sketching out an overview of some general shared traits (conceptual and empirical) in the broader literature that examines music and Islam.

Art as Apologetics

Partly in response to the rise of Islamophobic discourse in Western contexts and elsewhere, a revitalized interest in Muslim music-making has investigated whether and how music is integral to Islam, as well as what Muslims do with it. This interest is partly situated within, and stimulated by, broader contemporary debates in anthropology and other disciplines concerning public piety, the emergence of new Islamic consumerist lifestyles, media and religious art productions, and practice-oriented projects of pious "self-cultivation" that Muslims engage with in their everyday lives. There is now a rich array of case studies across diverse socioreligious settings investigating, among other things, how Muslim theologians and religious leaders debate the permissibility and appropriateness of music (Otterbeck and Ackfeldt 2012); the ideological and social control of the artistic sphere by states or Muslim leaders in different national contexts (Berg 2014; Winegar 2014); the ways in which music (or art more generally) serves as a resistance tool (Alagha 2016); as an avenue for subverting the secular public sphere (Barendregt 2012); and as a vehicle for religious outreach, political mobilization, and for creating an Islamic community (Boubekeur 2007; Hill 2016). Supplementing these research questions is growing attention to the efficacy of art practices and music in cultivating pious selves (van Nieuwkerk 2013), and in fostering a religious identity, global or other, among Muslim subjects.

While this research program oriented to study of the public sphere, piety, and the moral implications of Muslim music and art practice is diverse, several unifying analytic, conceptual, and epistemological concerns are discernible. To begin with, in this literature we find an overemphasis on those art-related discourses and practices that are driven by an overt mobilizing urge and a missionizing intention to use music/art as a tool for communicating a moral-religious message. Much in these practices can be summarized under the technical term of apologetics—that is, artistic endeavors done in justification or defense of Islam. Depending on the object of study, the kind of mobilizing intention undergirding the Islamic practice under scrutiny might vary, of course. For example, studies focusing on ruling elites and political-religious leaders have shown that the instrumental use of art might take the form of a "civilizing" project stirred by an ambition to educate young people and to "inculcate them into a certain social collective," as Winegar's (2014) work involving state actors and Islamist intellectuals in contemporary Egypt illustrates (or see Düzen [2018] on the youth-directed "civilizing" project of the AKP Government in Turkey). On other occasions, the use of music by power holders might be geared toward political resistance and mobilization, particularly in contexts of conflict. This is a key theme in Berg's study on the self-production and use of music by Hamas as an avenue for "spread[ing] political messages to the people," as well as "to mobilize and exhort to action" through the transformative power of music to change people's mood and foster a shared identity (2012, 305). Similarly, writing on the Lebanese Hezbullah, Alagha documents the selective utilization of music by the organization's cadres as a tool for "Islamic revival and cultural resistance" that aims to "revitalize the *umma* and wake it up from its hibernation" (2016, 176). In both of these cases, the use of music is legitimized only if it exists within the frames of what is considered to be halal according to Islam and if there is an Islamic advantage or benefit (*maslaha*) connected to it (168).

Missionary and missionizing music also figures as a common trope in another line of research that takes Islamist and piety movements as its object of study. A number of studies have analyzed Muslims' creative engagement with religiously approved musical genres such as *nasyid* or *anashid* ("chants" or "recitations") (see, for example, Berg 2014; Barendregt 2012; ter Laan 2016; Joulili 2012) in which we often find an explicit quality of *da'wa* (or *dakwah*, "bringing closer to Islam"). Here again the mobilizing intention defining the "*da'wa* music" or "sonic *dakwah*" (Barendregt 2012, 320) might take a variety of forms: "to propagate Islam as a social ideology" and "to contest colonization and the perceived ongoing political and economic repression by the West," as Barendregt (2012, 319) notes for a missionary movement in Malaysia; or "to teach and educate the audience about the proper way of leading a Muslim life," as in the case of Islam-inspired music that ter Laan (2016, 87) looks at in Morocco.

A somewhat similar explicit pedagogical purpose emerges in many analytical inquiries devoted to examine the political aspects of Islamized popular music forms, such as rap, hip-hop, or punk music. For example, portraying Muslim hip-hop artists in the United States as "verbal *mujahidins*" Alim examines how Islam shapes these artists' actions as "socially and politically conscious Hip Hop beings involved in a movement for change in the world" (2006, 46). This "Muslim verbal *jihad*," Alim notes (excitedly), has the potential "to create a counterhegemonic discourse that 'threatens' the ruling class and their ideas" (46).

This research program has contributed to knowledge about the transformation that Islamist and pietistic movements and in some cases Islamist authorities (see Otterbeck 2012) and even artists have undergone in the past two decades, by documenting their changing discourses concerning music as well as their emerging influence on the production of pious art (see George [2009] on Indonesia). According to Karin van Nieuwkerk, these changes attest to the general development of "a pious cultural sphere" (at least in Egypt) where the rhetoric of "art with a mission," "halal songs," "respectful art," and "purposeful art" circulate widely. As her work with Muslim preachers, artists, and pious Egyptians shows, instead of declaring art to be unlawful, Muslim authorities now take a more accepting attitude toward it, even if only to approve and accommodate those art practices that have a mission. Her assessment of their pedagogical intent is important, if directed toward the creation of pious subjects and moral improvement (2013, 192). Van Nieuwkerk analyzes this shift in the attitudes and strategies of Islamist movements concerning art as evidence of the emergence of a "new form of religiosity" (205) among the middle class and as "an expression of the transformation of Islamism into 'post-Islamism'" (203).

This highlighting of "new" forms of Islamic religiosity through the trope of "post-Islamism" is notable for how it articulates new class formations, Muslim lifestyles, and consumption patterns. However we also find in such religious practices a continued orientation toward one particular Islamic "discourse formation" (Foucault 1994), that of "legalistic" Islam. Whether the ethnographic focus is on the discourses and practices of religious leaders and scholars, on Muslim activists (past or present), or on Muslim artists, there is a strong tendency in these studies to identify and explicate a normative mode of Islamic discourse and reasoning. Another word for this is what Kelsay (2007) calls "sharīa reasoning," a discourse based on jurisprudential argumentation and on the scriptural texts of Islam which is overly concerned with the authorization of "correct" practice—in other words, as what counts as "*halal*/proper/legitimate" and "*haram*/indecent/illegitimate" in line with authoritative Islamic texts.[1]

This tendency is further reinforced by the centrality of the Asadian formulation of Islam as a "discursive tradition" in many of these studies. According to Asad, "If one wants to write an anthropology of Islam one should begin, as Muslims do, from the concept of a discursive tradition that includes and relates itself to the founding texts of the Qur'an and the Hadith" (1986, 14). A "tradition," he argues, "consists essentially of discourses that seek to instruct practitioners regarding the correct form and purpose of a given practice" (1986, 14). To be sure, this recommendation has informed the critical enquiries of a body of anthropological work on Islam, prominent among them Mahmood's (2005) and Hirschkind's (2006) focus on the Egyptian piety movements and, more particularly, on the religious lives of those Muslims self-consciously committed to fashioning themselves into more "Islamic" ethical selves through practices such as veiling, attending mosque study groups, and listening to sermons. What becomes occluded by this overly textual and legalistic framing of Islam for studying Muslims' music-making is the epistemological and methodological implications that it has for thinking about *nonlegal* Islamic discourses that are different from those offered by these partisans of Islam. Their implication by default is that to be Muslim is to be normatively oriented.

There is by now a fruitful discussion in studies of Islam and Muslim life concerning some of the problems magnified by this apparent overinvestment in the conceptualization of Islam as "discursive tradition." For Shahab Ahmed, the problem with Asad's formulation is that it is "*prescriptive*" and overtly concerned with the "authoritative prescription of the correct: that is, [with] *orthodoxy*" (2016, 272).[2] One effect of this conceptualization of Islam as an "*orthodox-izing*" discursive tradition, he says, is that "authoritative, prescriptive and exclusivist discourse—including authoritative, prescriptive and exclusivist reasoning—becomes, by definition, (more) Islam/ic than non-authoritative, and non-exclusivist discourse/reasoning" (274). "Can we not conceive of other forms of authority," Ahmed asks, "that not only are *not* prescriptive, but are actually at odds with prescriptive authority?" (282, original emphasis)

Ahmed's point is instructive here because the discourses and practices that are constitutive of the community of practice that I am discussing are precisely of that "non-authoritative," "non-prescriptive," and "non-orthodoxizing" kind. Before I discuss this further, let me take stock here and summarize the dominant features informing this literature. First, note its concentration on the apologetic and missionary impulses that drive the artistic practice in question. Second, it possesses a tendency to subordinate artistic practice, apprenticeship, and meaning to religious concerns and politics. And third, it over-engages with questions around the legality and permissibility of the art practice under discussion. Equally important, it implies (whether it explores it or not) that a certain mood or affect characterizes or foregrounds the (music) practice of Muslim artists: an anxiousness, defensiveness, or activist/pragmatist attitude toward the very relationship between art and Islam. By contrast, the musical practice under discussion here is not an Islamized version of popular and essentially non-Islamic music—rap, metal, or rock—being employed to convert or convict. It has a different historical weight to it, related to a genealogy instituting a musical repertoire, style, and lineage (of master musicians) upon which contemporary masters innovate.

"We Aren't That Type of Muslim"

The musical life in Hezarfen presents us with a mood that is very different from the affect characterizing many other forms of Muslim musical practice that have been the focus of recent scholarly work. While their analyses foreground the serious question of their informants' concern whether and how music is legitimate according to the traditional texts of Islamic jurisprudence, a complete lack of anxiety or interest in these questions characterizes the practice there. To be sure, Islamic scriptures were extensively worked into the fabric of Salih Hoca's discursive performances. Quotations from the Word of God and reports of the sayings and deeds of the Prophet Muhammed were recited in his speech acts. However, there was no intention to justify or defend the connection of music with Islam, to apologize for Islam through musical mission, or even to assert the absolute truth of those scriptures themselves. Instead, scripture and poetry were referred to when they were helpful for thinking about music, and music was used to bring out new meanings of the Qur'an. The Islamic discourse about music, or to put it the other way around, this musical discourse about Islam, is nonmissionary, if not anti-missionary.

What does it mean, then, to participate in this project of *musical Islam*? And what "type" of Islam is it? Given that Salih Hoca was uninterested in definitional claims or debates, it was only in response to a student mentioning a debate that he stumbled upon on a music blog that the issue emerged. The question concerned whether it was sinful to play the ney before doing ablutions. Salih Hoca guffawed for a moment, and then responded:

> We aren't that type of Muslims (*Biz öyle Müslüman değiliz*). Here the issue is the perspective from which one looks at music. What we see in music from the window we look through is a vehicle that helps one travel to God. The paths to God are many. You can travel to God by bus, by bicycle, or on foot. But some vehicles are so powerful that they can help one traverse that distance in the fastest way, like love [*muhabbet*], like music.

This response is striking for a number of reasons. First of all, it is a non-exclusivist statement that recognizes a multiplicity of ways of being and living as a Muslim. It does not seek to claim that any one of these different modes is right or wrong or that one is more "authentically" Islamic than another. Instead, it acknowledges, in the first instance, that, historically Muslims have taken a variety of paths as a means of relating to the Divine and of exploring Divine Truth. Second, it posits a particularly clear self-definition about the "self": to say "We are not that type of Muslim" is to pronounce at the very same time "We too are Muslims—but of another sort." Third, because his answer here is not governed by an urge to recommend one particular form of authority as somehow (more) "standard" or "orthodox" (than others) in terms of Islam; it is a non–orthodox-izing statement at its best. Thus is it not driven by an intention to prescribe which mode of religiosity (a way of traveling to God) ought to be chosen over another. By contrast, rather than proscribing, its language of analogy leaves it to listeners to work out and *explore* the meaning for themselves. And fourth, while it is a nonprescriptive and non–orthodox-izing statement, it is not devoid of implied normativity. In claiming that vehicles such as music and muhabbet are especially forceful in enabling one to "travel to God," its discourse posits its own preferential values about living as a Muslim.

Equally interesting, what is the type of Muslim that Salih Hoca says "we" are *not*? Given the immediate context in which this response came about—the preoccupation of some Muslims to ascertain whether or not ablution is obligatory before ney playing—the statement about what "we are not" takes a position in the main against a rule-centered Islamic discourse, one that is overly concerned with regulation, correction, and prescription of appropriate behavior. This is not to say that Salih Hoca's assertion deprecates legalistic Islam (*sharia*) or its primary sources Qur'an, hadith, sunnah, and so on. Instead, while it fully recognizes a variety of modes of authority as being operative in Islam, the overriding concern here is not the identification of orthodoxy as the defining goal of living a Muslim life. In fact, what often made Salih Hoca lose his patience with those who utilize the prescriptive truth-claims of law in their own interpretations—in an attempt to establish what is orthodox and what is heresy—is their fixing of their own theological constructs onto what it means to be and/or live as Muslim to the exclusion of all other perspectives (in other words, dismissing other perspectives as "nonstandard" and "heterodox"). The antiplural and antiliberal rhetoric often employed by Islamic *da'wa* movements (Mahmood 2005; Hirschkind 2006) epitomizes such a dismissive tendency, complemented with an authoritative urge to address and correct other Muslims about their own ways of reaching the Divine, as well as to refute those who deviate from "orthodoxy." Informing the statement "we are *not* that type of Muslim" is a sentiment of dissatisfaction and disagreement with such exclusionist Islamic discourses. This sentiment was expressed more clearly in Salih Hoca's continuing response to the debate about the "*sharia* of ney-playing." He went on to say:

> There are these Wahhabi sympathizers who dictate that *levhas* [calligraphic inscriptions] should be taken down from mosque walls. "Such things didn't exist during the time of Prophet," they claim. Imagine what type of religion Islam would be if we wiped music or calligraphy out of it! We don't worship these arts. They do service [*hizmet*] to us. For example, the inscription over there says "Allah is the best companion [*refik*]." This one here says "From Muhammed accrued love [*muhabbet*]." Now we look at these writings, and use them to enrich our souls. How? Both for their visual aesthetics and for meaning-making. It is no coincidence that the Ottoman-Turkish Islamic arts developed mainly in the tekkes. The most influential calligraphers, poets, and writers of literary works came out of the tekke.

These words give us further clues about both the type of Muslim that Salih Hoca says "we are *not*," but also about what type of "we" is implicated here: Muslims who take music (as well as calligraphy and love) as a means for meaning-making and exploring divine knowledge. What is high on the agenda of these Muslims is precisely the potential of music to facilitate an experiential encounter with and knowledge of God. Justification of this is the famous hadith—and the Sufi motto—which Salih Hoca often iterated in his sohbets: "Whosoever knows himself knows his Lord."

In this, the emphasis is placed on the endeavor of *exploration* and not on prescription, a useful distinction that Ahmed makes in discussing different kinds of disciplinary projects and modes of authority that have been historically at work in Islam. "Explorative discourse," he explains, "does not seek to *prescribe* a single meaning" in terms of Islam, but rather "*explores a range of possible meanings as Islam* and is prepared to leave those meanings both unsettled and unsettling" (2016, 284; original emphasis).[3] "Exploration is precisely the business of setting out into the unknown, the uncertain, the unexperienced, the unsettled, the new" (282).

Ahmed's critical insights are useful for thinking about the essential tasks that the disciplinary practices of sohbet and meşk set out to do: "to *explore and expand the dimensions of the meaningful*" (286; original emphasis). So when Salih Hoca communicates knowledge about the virtues of a certain musical principle by way of moving crisscross between music and Sufi epistemology, he is doing no less than exploring meaning(s) in terms of Islam. Because he is bringing into his analogies what he recognizes as meaningful of Islam, his words can be also usefully understood as a way of speaking *as* a Muslim about *what it means to be a Muslim*.

Further, while this Islam-infused musical pedagogy has entailments for both enskilling learners in musical knowledge and for shaping their subjectivities as Muslims through a range of ways (through its creative use of sohbet or by fostering a certain kind of relationship with the urban environment, for example), neither of these respective processes (or ends) is given primacy over the other. Nor, for that matter, is one reduced to or subordinated to the other. In fact, the intricate confluence of music and Islam in this apprenticeship context can be likened to a relationship of *analogy*: each helps explore meaning about the other, to explore the meaningful.

Urging us to consider the *explorative discourses* in our conceptualizations of Islam, Ahmed writes:

> The notion of "Islam" that gives normative and constitutive primacy to legal discourse is the "default" conceptualization of the majority of scholars today (even if it is often unacknowledged by them), and is certainly the habitual one in the popular consciousness of the majority of contemporary Muslims and non-Muslims alike. . . . The primacy that is given to the constitutive determinacy of legal discourse over other discourses serves to *distort our perspective* and effectively prevents us even from *recognizing*—let alone understanding—that, historically, Muslims have constructed normative meaning for Islam in terms that allowed them to live by and/or with norms other than, and at odds with, those put forward by legal discourse (117; 121; original emphasis).

The noninterest of the recent dominant literature on Islam and music in nonlegalistic projects of Islamic music attests to Ahmed's point. What we can also add to Ahmed's observation is that a failure to acknowledge such explorative discourses as "Islamic" also prevents us from recognizing a particular liberality that actually exists in Islam. Here I use the word "liberal" in the literal sense of the word,[4] to mean "munificence," which implies a generosity in accepting the validity of lives and practices (religious or otherwise) of those different from one's own. The statement "We are not that type of Muslim" epitomizes such a liberalism, for it recognizes the "Muslim-ness" of those who pursue paths different from its own even as it calmly asserts its own path to be legitimate and orthodox.

Finally, let me finish by noting that if there are in practice (and theory) different ways of being Muslim, we might acknowledge also that there are different ways of being "liberal." Mahmood (and others) recognize and decry the universalizing of one core aspect of liberalism, its assumption that *autonomy* (literally, to give oneself one's law) and a will for freedom are of prime importance in the making of a liberal subject. She also recognizes that the goal of autonomy might come into conflict with Islamic piety movements that value submission to God and to Islamic scripture in which divine law has been revealed. And yet as a number of writers have pointed out (see, for example, Houston 2004), in a Kemalist context the self-fashioning activity of religious Muslims also involves a practice of autonomy, as activists reflect upon and critique the nationalist ethos of state-Islam, choosing to make something else of their religion.

Equally important, the practice of Muslim music-making explained in this book, which as we have noted herewith may be understood as encompassing some core features of liberalism (for example, anti-illiberal, anti-totalitarian), does not necessarily aim at the fabrication of an autonomous subject in its pedagogical practice. To put it differently, music education here can be understood as liberal, but "*not that type of liberal*" who views all forms of submission to authority—apart, of course, from submission to the authority of the liberal state itself—as invalid, undemocratic, hierarchical, totalitarian, and so on, on the grounds that the autonomy of the individual must always prevail. The community of practice analyzed here recommends an ethics of surrender, submission, and fidelity on the part of the talebe and values the role of relationality and the experience of intersubjectivity (in other words, the transcending of individual "agency") in the process of ethical formation. The fostering of a will that chooses to surrender to an "authority"/another self is also an enactment of active agency. In brief, investigation of freedom and autonomy that might orient Muslim ethics does not have to come at the expense of the juxtaposition of Islam with what Mahmood calls "secular-liberal polity." As Schielke notes, "what we see," in Mahmood's work, "is a critique of idealized secular and liberal self-understandings by means of their juxtaposition with an equally idealized Islamic tradition" (2010, 8).

In conclusion, in grappling with the varied ethical formations of Muslims, we encounter both idealized understandings and messy practices. Sometimes we learn about autonomous Egyptian Muslims who constitute themselves as pious subjects against (Kemalist) state-Islam, and liberal Muslim musicians who value the act of dependency on others (and God). An anthropology of Islam that orients itself to the rich everyday lives of Muslims in their particular social-historical context must find simplistic the intellectualism of self-affirming theories of Western and Muslim difference. By contrast even as it studies how local Muslims adopt, appropriate, or reject the ideological positions of intellectuals, anthropology must orient itself to ethnographic interpretation of the ways in which the people it studies shape their worlds on their own terms.

Conclusion

IN THE PRECEDING CHAPTERS, I have sought to describe the breadth and complexity of the transformative practice of becoming a neyzen. Mastering the ney involves bodily, ethical, affective, sensory, and social modifications, an apprenticeship that takes place in the historical present moment. In bringing *Music Ethics and Islam* to an end, let me foreground here some of the key insights that have guided my efforts to faithfully describe the embodied participation in ney learning as a lived experience, as phenomenological investigation is committed to do. In order to allow my description of the unfolding process of teaching and learning to manifest itself on its own terms—and to understand the motivations and purposive attitudes of individual actors in their own terms—I have sought to work here from microscopic particulars rather than reaching for macrocosmic generalities about meanings inherent to human learning. Ethnographic exploration of music education must originate with the lesson.

To reiterate a fundamental insight that phenomenologists consistently make, learning is a transformative event so far as it allows the learner to constitute the thing or entity that is the focus of learning in a new light, thus giving a new meaning to the "world." "Items assume new meanings because of [a] new way of looking at [or hearing] them" (Giorgi 1967, 116). Building musical knowledge, in this sense, enables one to hear the world in a new way. What does this mean for the novice ney player?

As this book has shown, a series of interwoven skilled actions cohere in ney competency from building up a sonorous tone, discerning the best pitch relationships, and learning to hear and feel makams to manipulating the written score and composing a flavorsome taksim. While the musicological theory posits these musical phenomena (pitch relations, makam, and so on) as collective musical meanings or representations possessing an "objective" truth, a different reality emerges in the world of practical learning: for musicians or skilled practitioners, the objectivity of such sonic phenomena (or *akumena,* following Smith [1967]) is constituted out of subjectivity through the intentional acts of the learner.

It is precisely this point that informs music phenomenologist Thomas Clifton's understanding of music as a "constituted object." In *Music as Heard,* he contends that "music is not an autonomous appearance, but the outcome of a collaboration between a person and real or imagined sounds" (1983, 74), where a listening body is "perceiving, interpreting, judging, and feeling" (2). This point concerning perception and subjectivity should also acknowledge the researcher's—the researcher as apprentice—positing of musical phenomena or making of them the factual object of ethnographic investigation.

Throughout this book I have used the Husserlian idea of "intentional modifications" as a conceptual lens to explicate how musical learning fosters new aural and artistic perceptions in neophytes by mobilizing a variety of tools through which knowledge, tacit or verbally articulated, can be acquired. To become a neyzen means to become disciplined in attending the aural phenomena in new ways. Ihde describes this as cultivating *phenomenological listening.* Performing the "perceptual variations" of foregrounding and backgrounding are central to phenomenological listening—in other words, to consciously focus attention to a different aspect of the auditory field—"allow[ing] the phenomena to more and more clearly show [resound] themselves" (2007, 85).

Yet our accounting for the manner in which the ney learners experience perceptual modifications peculiar and particular to Ottoman classical music should also identify the inter-subjective nature of this transformative process. "Subjects, objects, lives and worlds are made in their relations" (Lave 2011, 152). Throughout this book I have maintained that learning a relationship lies at the heart of musical apprenticeship. Crafting knowledge emerges from webs of relations, which involve, first and foremost, the inherently hierarchical yet deeply affective relationship of hoca-talebe.

This relationality or intersubjectivity also extends to artistic lineages into which one is grafted through meşk. Despite the emergence of the recording industry in the early years of the twentieth century that allowed aspiring music practitioners to benefit from audio recordings as key learning supplements, today the genealogical aspect of musical learning still carries prime importance among ney artists. For my interlocutors, doing meşk means learning directly from a hoca who, in the past, had also sat side by side with his hoca, becoming receptive to the force of a suite of transformations (sensorial, moral, affective) orchestrated by the hoca-talebe dyad. This relation might invoke the imagery of learning as achieved by "standing on the shoulders of giants," a metaphor (by sociologist Robert K. Merton) that Richard Sennett finds apt for illuminating the fundamental features of knowledge transfer in science; "first, that the work of great scientists sets the term of reference, the orbits, within which lesser standard scientists revolve; and second, that knowledge is additive and accumulative; it builds up in time as people stand on the giants' shoulders, like those human pillars in the circus" (2009, 79).

Sennett's observations also hold true for how building knowledge works in aesthetic traditions such as the musical disciplinary regime I have discussed here, yet with one crucial difference. The affective-moral economy undergirding the intersubjective world of ney learning demands a set of ethical sensibilities and affective loyalties that are generally different from that of science. As I have tried to show, there is a continuum of emotions energizing the ever-evolving hoca-talebe relationship: the talebe's surrender, devotion, and undivided loyalty to the master, and the master's guidance and care for the talebe. Learning ties the two together in feelings of reciprocal trust and deep affection even as it recognizes and reproduces the power relations intrinsic and peculiar to this relationship. Talebes depend on their hoca not only for their artistic competency and guidance but also for approval and for the recognition of the legitimacy of their own artistic being.

Yet this "surrendering self" or the subjectivity of subordination that learning produces should not be interpreted as the diminishing of the talebe's agency. Only an interpretive position that treats all kinds of relationality (in other words, everything that somehow transcends individual "agency") as invalid, hierarchical, repressive, or undemocratic would end up with such a misleading assumption. As the autobiographical reflections by ney artists upon their own creative and ethical formation reveal, the disciplinary regime voluntarily entered into does not produce subjects who are copies of their teacher, passively inculcated into a musical style or competence; rather, the disciplinary subjection experienced here conditions a new capacity (autonomy) to act and improvise on their own. To improvise, to innovate, to create anew, one must first undertake rigorous training, accompanied through subjection to a master.

Other studies also have noted the enabling and productive nature of those learning practices grounded in what are often considered to be the rigid structures of tradition. Dalidowicz's study on apprenticeship in the South Indian dance form *kathak* that is grounded in a similar relationship between *guru* and *shishya* is worth quoting here, given the attention it gives to the temporal flow of the learning process and to how a failure to take temporality into account breeds simplistic conclusions about agency. "When viewing the *guru-shishya parampara* from a single snap-shot in time, to the uninformed observer the picture might indeed seem oppressive," she says (2012, 242). "The temporary suspension of agency that occurs in *guru-shishya* holds a larger purpose, the crafting of a new body, becoming an adept performer and the *expansion of agency*" (243; emphasis added). Dalidowicz describes this "peculiar relationship of experiencing autonomy within the subordination to one's guru" as "an assisted empowerment" (249). These ethnographic perspectives on the kind of agency that emerges from learning practices in which surrender and subordination remain virtues shed light on the problematic radical distinction that liberal thought makes between autonomy and heteronomy (only to champion the former). In it there is a failure to envisage the possibility that any positive aspect of ethics may be constituted out of intersubjectivity.

Inquiry into learning practices and their associated meanings must also recognize the situatedness of educational "regimes" of bodily transformation in larger histories. As I have tried to show in this book, the checkered social life of the ney over the twentieth century itself provides us a lens with which to explore relations between art traditions and larger sociopolitical processes in Turkey, including hegemonic state projects. Chapter 1 discussed how the Republican state's making of a revolution in music and its sweeping cultural reforms aimed at transforming every sphere of social life during the foundational decades of the Republic had direct ramifications for art practices, pedagogical methods, and citizens' participation in art worlds.

Similarly, a complex intertwining of sociocultural forces and politico-economic arrangements has provided the enabling conditions for the ney revival today, shaping the instrument's use and meaning in new ways. As an institutional place, Hezarfen itself is one productive outcome of these conditions. Understanding ways of coming to know requires us to consider the larger generative forces that knowledge practices are situated within, even if such forces are unable to prevent individuals from perceiving their past, present, and future horizons in contrasting ways. The continuity of the neyzen lineage central to this ethnography demonstrates this.

And finally, to end where I began, driven by a "desire to do a job well for its own sake" (Sennett 2009, 8), a craftsman or woman knows that learning also involves learning from things themselves. Empathetic to the idiosyncrasies of each ney, a good neyzen knows how to take the reed seriously, to do justice to its materiality, so as to skillfully craft a pleasurable musical ethics.

Let the ney have the final word:

> At every gathering I play my lament.
> I'm a friend to both happy and sad.[1]

Notes

Introduction

1. Sennett (2009, 9) writes that to become a craftsman is to cultivate an ethical norm that desires "to do a job well for its own sake."

2. The term *meşk* is also used in calligraphic training where it implies both the act of practicing writing and the exercise sheets (*karalama*) used in this craft.

3. For the most comprehensive historical account of meşk, see Cem Behar's (2012) landmark study, *Aşk Olmayınca Meşk Olmaz: Geleneksel Osmanlı/Türk Müziğinde Öğretim ve İntikal*. In the latest edition of this book, Behar also gives an account of meşk in the present (161–93).

4. First established in 1975 under the name of the State Turkish Classical Music Choir, it was renamed in 2012.

5. As Moran says, "All perception takes place under a number of horizons which are implicit structural aspects of our original experience itself. . . . Husserl is particularly aware that perception is a temporal process; it does not take place wholly in the present but is oriented towards future experiences and at the same time is an experience of enduring or continuing from past experiences. There is also a 'horizon of the past,' the potential to awake recollections" (2000, 162).

6. There are as many as fifteen million Kurds in Turkey (around 15 percent to 20 percent of Turkey's population). See Houston (2008). On Kurdish music, see Aksoy (2006).

7. To avoid reproducing the exclusionist vision of the Turkish nation-state ideology, in this book I will use the expression "Ottoman classical music" to refer to this urban musical tradition. Ottoman music-making was a multiethnic practice in which Greek, Armenian,

Jewish, and Christian Arab musician communities actively participated. The term was subject to much polemical debate over the twentieth century, and a number of labels have been applied to it—for example, "court music" (*saray müziği*), "*Enderun* music," "*alaturka,*" "Turkish art music" (*Türk sanat müziği*), "classical Turkish music" (*klasik Türk müziği*).

8. The reed cane suitable for ney-making is known as *arundo donax*, native to the Mediterranean Basin, which grows abundantly in warm, moist climates. In Turkey, reeds from the cities of Hatay, Aydın, and Adana are most sought after among the ney producers. For more information on the reed cane, see Tammer (1993).

9. A series of work has examined musical instruments' entanglement with commodification (Keister 2004), globalization (Baumann 2000), mass tourism, and with "world music" projects (Keister 2004; Neuenfeldt 1994). See also the special issue edited by Karl Neuenfeldt (1998) in *World of Music* under the title "Old Instruments in New Contexts."

10. While the word *maneviyat* (essentially an Arabic word) is most commonly used for "spirituality" in the context of ney music learning, *ruhaniyat* (also essentially Arabic) and *spiritüalite* are other expressions that figure in contemporary Turkish speech. Derived from French, the latter is used in disciplines such as psychology, counseling, and healing practices.

11. Anna King (1996, 343) notes that the term encompasses, for example, "an approach to God, a religious practice, a devotional path, a discipline, a creative energy, a sense of awe and mystery, a distinctive religious ethos or mode of experience, an inner moral orientation, the ethical transcendence of self, mystical awareness, the sense of the numinous, an appreciation of the mysteries and depth of human experience."

12. On sound symbolism, see Feld and Brenneis (2004); Harkness (2013).

13. See Feld (1994); Frith (2000).

14. It is not surprising that the most famous exponents of this Sufi music genre, subsumed under the title of "world music," are all ney musicians, including artists like Kudsi Erguner, Mercan Dede, and Omar Faruk Tekbilek.

15. Author's translation. See https://www.tccb.gov.tr/cumhurbaskanligi/kultursanatodulleri/2014.

16. On the topic of neo-Ottomanism and AKP, see Yavuz (2016).

17. Translated by Reynold A. Nicholson (1926) in Schimmel (1980, 210).

18. The musical form used during the ritual activity of the Mevlevi order. It is the longest and most complex form in the Ottoman music tradition, which contains four parts called *selam*.

19. *Āl ʿImrān* 3:185.

20. Following the 2015 Presidential Arts and Grand Culture Awards, a new award category was introduced under the title "traditional arts" (*geleneksel sanatlar*). *Hattat* (calligrapher) Hüseyin Kutlu, and the *ebru* artist Feridun Özgören (also a ney player) were recipients of this award in 2015 and 2016, respectively.

21. On this particular Sufi epistemology, see Ahmed (2016, 329–43) and Chittick (1989).

22. The special importance that Sayın attributes here to the human creation is epitomized in the famous utterance of the thirteenth-century Sufi mystic Yunus Emre: "We loved the creatures because of their relation to the Creator" (Yaratılanı sevdik yaratandan ötürü).

23. Ahmed's observation about the lack of sufficient attention among scholars on the explorative discourses of Muslims as opposed to prescriptive discourses is important. He notes that when "Muslims act and speak *exploratively*—as opposed to *prescriptively* . . . they are somehow not seen to be acting and speaking in a manner and register that is representative, expressive and constitutive of Islam" (2016, 303).

24. Qur'anic verse (*Bakara*) 2:195.

25. Mahmood writes that "bodily behavior does not simply stand in a relationship of meaning to self and society, but it also endows the self with certain kinds of capacities that provide the substance from which the world is acted upon" (2005, 27).

26. Tim Ingold elucidates the limitations of the presumptions of the cultural transmission model, noting how "the concept of transmission is linked to a genealogical model that separates the acquisition of knowledge-as-information from its practical enactment, and is not for that reason appropriate to describe the ways in which people ordinarily come to know what they do" (2011b: 1). Knowledge, he says, does not come ready-made. Rather, skilled practitioners "*grow into it*, through a process of what might best be called 'guided rediscovery'" (2011a, 162). See also Gieser (2008) for a critique of the transmission model.

27. In the field of anthropology, ethnomusicology, and education, there is a rich array of case studies on craft apprenticeships (Coy 1989; Yen 2005), on skill acquisition in music and dance traditions (Gill 2017; Weidman 2006; Sudnow 2001; Kippen 1988; Neuman 1990); on the making of professional practitioners in boxing, building (masons), capoeira, and shipbuilding (Wacquant 2004; Marchand 2009; Downey 2005; Simpson 2006), and on situated learning (Lave 2011; Lave and Wenger 1991), which take up an apprentice-style methodology. Within anthropology, the body of research on apprenticeship has been variously influenced by phenomenological approaches (Husserl 1970; Merleau-Ponty 1962; Jackson 1989; Csordas 1994), insights from studies of embodied learning and habitus (Mauss 1979; Bourdieu 1977), and by the anthropology of the senses (Stoller 1989; Howes 2003).

28. These felt tensions between anthropological analysis and apprentice-style learning are clearly not mine alone. For two other interesting discussions, see Dow (1989) and Cooper (1989). Dow, an anthropologist who apprenticed in shamanism, confesses that had he concentrated on developing "the proper spiritual relationship" with his master, he would have become a better shaman and a worse anthropologist (207). Cooper, too, provides useful insights into the problems of the dual agendas of doing fieldwork and apprenticeship, describing the incommensurability of these agendas as inducing an "enforced schizophrenia" (138).

29. Niyazi Sayın is an important figure in this book, and not just because he is undisputedly one of the great neyzens. A wide consensus exists among ney artists that one can

speak of the ney history in terms of "before and after Niyazi Sayın." Over and beyond this, an important aspect of his life as a musician involved his dedication to the craft of ney teaching. Many of the neyzens we meet in this study were either past members of his artistic lineage or his students.

Chapter One. A Biography of the Ney

1. Available at http://www.side-underwatermuseum.com/gallery.

2. While firmly rooted in the capital city, this music tradition extended over the major cities of the empire such as Edirne, Bursa, Izmir, and Salonika in the east, and Urfa and Diyarbakır in the southeast (Behar 2015, 16).

3. On the history of Ottoman classical music tradition, see Behar 2015; Wright 1992; Greve 2015. A revised version of Behar's essay in his book *A Short History of Ottoman/Turkish Music Tradition (1603–1839)* is available in the English in Suraiya Faroqhi, ed., *The Cambridge History of Turkey, Volume 3: The Later Ottoman Empire (1603–1839)* (Cambridge: Cambridge University Press, 2006), 393–408.

4. Among Aziz Dede's accomplished students are Rauf Yekta Bey, Ziya Santur, and Emin Dede. Also a composer, Aziz Dede's instrumental compositions (including a peşrev in the makam *Hicaz* and two *saz semaisi* in the makams *Uşşak* and *Yegâh*) are highly respected in the classical repertoire.

5. Following Aziz Dede's death in 1905, Emin Dede continued his meşk practice with Sheikh Hüseyin Fahreddin Dede of the Bahariye Mevlevihanesi and later with Hakkı Dede of the Galata Mevlevihanesi. Upon the death of Hakkı Dede, he was given the Mevlevi title *Dede* and assigned as the chief neyzen of this convent. Emin Dede also composed peşrev and saz semaisi and was known to be an expert of the *Hamparsum* notation, a skill he mastered from Rauf Yekta Bey (İnal 1958, 176).

6. In addition to the Mevlevis, other Sunni tarikats using musical activity involved the Halveti, Kadiri, and Rufai orders. On the liturgical music of Sufi tarikats during the Ottoman period, see Ergun (1943); Feldman (1992).

7. The earliest Mevlevi ayin (set in the makam *Bayati*) whose composer is known is attributed to Köçek Mustafa Dede (d. 1683). The composers of the three earlier ayin pieces—referred to as "*beste-i kadîm*"—set in the modes *Pençgâh, Dügâh*, and *Hüseyni* are unknown. More than sixty ayin compositions exist today, only ten or twelve of which predate the nineteenth century.

8. On the Mevlevi mukabele, see Gölpınarlı (1963); on a comparative analysis on the performative dimensions of the mukabele before and after 1925, see Behar (2014; 2015, 177–98).

9. "The iconographic evidence suggests that the mouthpiece may have appeared in the later 16th century" (Feldman 1996, 121). The first detailed technical descriptions of the ney mouthpiece as well as of the construction of the ney were provided in the eighteenth century by the French translator Charles Fonton in his "Eastern Music" (*Şark Musikisi*) essay. See Behar (2008, 164–65).

10. Some of the key representatives of this style in the twentieth century are neyzens Hayri Tümer (1902–1973), Gavsi Baykara (1902–1967), Burhaneddin Ökte (1904–1973), Halil Can (1905–1973), Süleyman Erguner (1902–1953), Neyzen Tevfik (1879–1953), and İhsan Aziz Bey (1884–1935) (Behar 2008, 121).

11. The politics of Turkification followed two main strategies. First, all Muslims were identified as "Turks," including, for example, Kurdish speakers who constituted the largest Muslim ethnic minority in Turkey. The second main strategy to ensure the ethnic homogeneity of Anatolia involved the forced expulsion of non-Muslim minorities, particularly Greeks, Armenians, and Jews (see Keyder 1987). Among other strategies used as part of the project of Turkification were the campaign called "Citizen, Speak Turkish!" in 1928; the conscription of non-Muslim men to the military as reserve forces in 1941; the discriminatory Capital Levy Tax of 1942 (see Aktar 2000); and the events of September 6–7, 1955, a state-initiated riot against non-Muslims in Pera, Istanbul.

12. For a comprehensive summary of Kemalism as a political-social program, see Houston 2015a.

13. Kurdish and Alevi music, too, were among the musical genres that the Kemalists sought to eradicate in this period.

14. Ethnic-Turkist discursive practice is another one. See Ayas (2014) for an examination of the nationalist discourse targeting Ottoman music, condemning it for being "non-national" and "contaminated."

15. Gökalp uses an inaccurate word here. There are no "quarter tones" used in Ottoman-Turkish music system. Instead, there are microtones, obtained through the dividing of an octave into twenty-four unevenly positioned tones. Further, in claiming that these notes are a source of any "problem" for melodic construction, he is oblivious to the shared modal elements and untempered tones used in both Ottoman music and Anatolian folk music—although the latter is not "Eastern" in his discernment.

16. See Stokes (1992) for a fascinating discussion on how Kemalism's positivist-modernist discourse on the "rationality" of music hailed the folk music instrument, *saz*, as a "logical" and "systematic" instrument.

17. The 1926 curriculum plan of *Darül Elhân* lists the following instruments being taught at its Eastern music section: violin, kemençe, ney, tanbur, santur, oud, and kanun (Kaya 2016, 14).

18. *Darül Elhân*'s Committee for Repertory Classification and Establishment (*Musiki Tasnif ve Tesbit Heyeti*) began its notation of the classical repertory in early 1920s. Initially, the committee consisted of three significant Ottoman music figures: Rauf Yekta Bey (1871–1935), Hâfız Ahmet Efendi (1869–1943), and İsmail Hakkı Bey (1866–1927). In later years Ali Rıfat Çağatay, Suphi Ezgi, and Mesut Cemil also joined the committee. These experts notated the repertoire pieces that they had mastered through the means of the traditional pedagogy (Rauf Yekta Bey and Hâfız Ahmet Efendi were both talebes of Zekai Dede [1825–1897]). Without their work, a large number of compositions—around a thousand pieces were published—would not have survived. The committee continued its

work until the 1960s. These *Darül Elhân* publications continue to maintain their prestige today as a primary source of reference.

19. Having replaced Turkish Hearths (*Türk Ocakları*) in 1932, the Republican People's Party (CHP) established in their place the People's Houses, constituting "the first government-sponsored body to take a serious interest in vernacular literature, music, and dance, to teach these in a systematic way, and to interpret them through publications and staged performances" (Öztürkmen 1992, 186). According to Karpat (1963), by 1940 their number had reached 379.

20. For a history of ethnographic representation and how fieldwork was used in the service of nationalism in Turkey, see Houston (2009). Both Istanbul Municipality Conservatorium (beginning with 1925) and the newly founded State Conservatorium in Ankara were directly involved in this mission of collecting and archiving folklore melodies. The State Conservatorium continued to organize field expeditions once a year from 1937 to 1957. On state-sponsored folklore, see Bates (2016).

21. In the oral and aural setting of meşk, the practice of beating *usûl* (rhythmic mode) played a vital role in the disciplining of the talebes' attention. By beating their hands on the knees and thighs ("*diz dövmek,*" "*usûl vurmak*") apprentices would commit the musical piece into memory. More than a mnemonic technique, this learning ritual was also symbolically charged, denoting the hard work and perseverance of the learner. In the absence of notation, this pedagogical method facilitated the transmission of the musical repertoire, a practice that continued up until the mid-twentieth century (see Behar 2012, 19–24). Although notation has replaced this technique of memorization today, usûl vurmak has not completely vanished. In some of the ney lessons I attended during my fieldwork, it coexisted with the musical score.

22. Among his well-known talebes are Halil Dikmen, Hakkı Süha Gezgin, Halil Can, Süleyman Erguner, Hayri Tümer, and Emin Kılıç Kale. For biographical information, see Ergun (1943); Ayvazoğlu (2008).

23. Zoe Griffith (2011) makes a similar observation about the important role that meşk pedagogy played in the survival of Islamic calligraphy, another art form that was rendered "contradictory" by the modernist thrust and positivistic imagination of Kemalism. She describes the surprising continuation, and even thriving, of calligraphic art under the Republic—partly because the Kemalists tolerated the use of Arabic script in this art practice for "decorative" purposes.

24. In a short 1981 essay titled "Musical Meetings in Homes" (*Evlerdeki Musiki Toplantıları*) composer and vocal artist Alâeddin Yavaşça lists some of the houses where regular meclis gatherings were held in Istanbul in the post-Republic period. See also Neyzen Kudsi Erguner's autobiography (2005, 23–31) on musical gatherings at Özbekler Tekkesi in Üsküdar in the 1950s, a place which Erguner describes as "the fertile soil of [his] formative years" (31).

25. According to the results of research conducted by the periodical "*Radyo*" on the monthly broadcasting hours of music programs on Ankara Radio, the "classical Turkish

music" programs occupied 220 minutes, while symphonic music and opera music programs occupied 1,290 and 320 minutes, respectively (Kütükçü 2012, 81).

26. See *Udi* Cevdet Kozanoğlu's (1896–1986) memoirs (1988).

27. Similarly, the kemençe artist Cüneyt Orhon (1926–2006) reports that when he joined the Ankara Radio in the late 1940s, religious music was still treated as a "taboo" (Aksoy 2009, 261).

28. It is difficult to argue that a consistent official policy toward religious music was laid down in this period. Following the 1950s, under the rule of the reformist Kemalism of the Democrat Party, certain acts sympathetic toward religious musical performance were taken up, such as the regular broadcasting of the *mevlid* form (a popular poem by Süleyman Çelebi on the Prophet's birth and life, recited at significant ritual events) on the radio, and the restoring of the recitation of *ezan* (call to prayer) in Arabic. In 1932, Mustafa Kemal had ordered the translation of the ezan and Qur'an into Turkish.

29. On the history of the Mevlevi mukabele reinstituted in Konya after the early 1950s, see Neyzen Selami Bertuğ's memoirs (Ağaoğlu 2013).

30. See, for example, *The Mystic Flutes of Sufi: Preludes to Ceremonies of the Whirling Dervishes*, JVC World Sounds, 1988.

31. In the 1990s, the members of this duo, Birol Yayla (tanbur and guitar) and Aziz Şenol Filiz (ney) recorded two albums (*Yansımalar*, 1991 and *Bab-ı Esrar*, 1995) released by the record label Kalan Müzik. These albums were extremely influential in the popularization of the ney, as confirmed by many young ney enthusiasts during my fieldwork.

32. Early examples include the album *Zikir*, by jazz percussionist Okay Temiz and Neyzen Aka Gündüz Kutbay, released in 1989, and the fusion-jazz performance by Süleyman Erguner and Butch Morris in 1992 at the Akbank Jazz Festival.

33. This revitalized and transformed genre of popular Sufi music productions has been a catalyst for the ney's revival among Turkish urbanites today—an admission that neophyte ney players happily made in the course of my fieldwork. Ney masters also (less graciously) verified the effect of the new Sufi music on the high demand for ney learning in Turkey, a phenomenon they interpreted as the commodification of the instrument alongside the broader commercialization of Sufism both domestically and globally.

34. The nature of Sufi music and where and how it can be performed is hotly debated not only among ney artists committed to the Ottoman classical music tradition but also among "world musicians." For example, in one polemical exchange between Neyzen Kudsi Erguner and Mercan Dede in the *Yeni Şafak* newspaper (published under the title "Where Does the Ney Fit?" [*Ney Nereye Yakışır*]), we find Erguner arguing that for music to be labeled "Sufi," it must feature the Sufi repertoire.

35. The Mevlana Museum in Konya was the most visited venue in Turkey in 2007, with 2.5 million visitors. http://www.kulturvarliklari.gov.tr/TR,43336/muze-istatistikleri.html.

36. Available at http://mistikmuzik.org/?page_id=1441.

37. The touristification of the "sema" extends beyond Turkey's borders. The Ministry of Culture and Tourism also sponsors the tours of its whirling dervish ensemble outside

Turkey. One sema performance I attended in Sydney in 2008 accompanied a promotional tourist film, complete with complimentary bags filled with tourist maps of Turkey and knickknacks displaying the Mevlevi imagery alongside the sacred symbols of the nation. On the transformation of the Mevlevi mukabele from a spiritual event into a "performance" or "show" under the Turkish Republic, see Behar (2014; 2015).

38. No single narrative captures this striking contemporary interest in the ney. Its current thriving status articulates more generally with the profound transformation of Turkey since early 1990s, facilitated by the economic liberalization program, the deregulation of state-controlled media, the pluralization of new communication technologies, the emergence of new lifestyle and consumption habits, and the expansion of culture industries.

39. In the face of this growing demand for neys, the price for the instrument has become more varied, ranging from 50 to 2,000 Turkish Liras. In commercial outlets neys are branded under the names "mystic ney" or the "Sufi flute," occasionally complimented with ney training DVDs. PVC-made neys are not rare, either. Makers of the instrument have also changed the ney's design to accommodate the aesthetic preferences of the customers. New decorative styles have emerged, which involve the inscribing of various images on the body of the ney, most commonly a whirling-dervish figure or a calligraphic inscription, as many ney makers I visited in Istanbul and Konya reported.

40. The full name of this organization that provides free public training is the Istanbul Metropolitan Municipality Art and Vocational Training Courses (*İstanbul Büyükşehir Belediyesi Sanat ve Meslek Eğitimi Kursları* [İSMEK]). Similar institutions also exist in other Turkish cities under different names. İSMEK commenced its activities in 1996. In the period 2012–15, the number of students enrolled in ney courses was recorded around 4,500 to 5,000 (personal conversation with an İSMEK official).

41. See *Diyanet*'s 2013 summer programs in Konya: http://www.yenihaberden.com/konyada-yaz-kuran-kurslari-basladi-7453h.htm.

42. Since 2000s ney method books have also become more available (see Erguner 2007; Karadağ 2013; Kaya 2011).

43. Notation figures as a teaching aid in Salih Bilgin's meşk practice with his master, Niyazi Sayın, as well as in Sayın's own meşk practice with Halil Dikmen. Dikmen's master, Neyzen Emin Dede, was famous for his musical literacy skills. He was well versed in the Hamparsum notation and, as I was told firsthand by Niyazi Sayın, he was quick to integrate notation into his teaching practice. To restrict the definition of meşk to "a non-literate mode of musical transmission" would be to ignore all of these learning relationships.

44. On the problematic binary distinction often made between orality and musical literacy, see also Poulos (2011) and Behar (2015, 161–76). Further, in an essay titled "Text and Memory in Ottoman/Turkish Musical Tradition," Behar (2013) examines a series of examples from the past and present Ottoman/Turkish musical scene to demonstrate how the taken-for-granted oral-written duality is too simplistic. Gill-Gürtan's (2011) article on the "multiple and contradictory" meanings that meşk carries in present-day Turkey is also useful here.

Chapter Two. Breath and Reed

1. For a photographic record of Bilgin's başpares, see Bilgin (2012).

2. Translated by Reynold A. Nicholson (1926) in Schimmel (1980, 210).

3. Schimmel cites another story of the reed that can be traced back to the tale of King Midas of Gordion from the ancient Near East and an Islamic version of it found in the twelfth-century Persian poet Sanai's *Hadiqat al-haqiqat*: "It is said that Hz Ali could not bear all the spiritual wisdom entrusted to him by the Prophet and told it to a lake in the wilderness, and again it was the flute that revealed to mankind some of the Prophet's deepest secrets" (2005, 13).

4. Both the media and the music industry are significant contributors of this meaning-constitution about the sound of the ney. A quick survey of ney-related websites, newspapers, magazines (see the "Ney" magazine catering exclusively to ney students), concert publicity, and CD recordings reveals the generation and dissemination of a widespread discourse about the intrinsic "spiritual" quality of the ney's sound. See the titles of published interviews with ney*zen* musicians: "The Sound of the Ney Is Separation and Yearning!" "Ney, the Symbol of Oneness," "In the Ney We Find Ourselves," "What We Search for Is the Sound of Heaven."

5. In chapters 5 and 6 I discuss the affective and ethical implications of these verbalized instructions and the crucial role that spoken language plays in this musical apprenticeship context.

6. As I explain later, neys come in different sizes according to their tuning.

7. The embouchure technique (known as "bilabial blowing") integral to ney playing requires a partial closing of the mouthpiece hole with the lips. The breath is blown against the inside edge of the tube. As a common experience, a beginner may try for several weeks before getting any sound from the flute.

8. A good analogy for learning how to get a sound from the ney is Polanyi's famous example of learning how to ride a bike. In both skilled actions, verbalization of the kinesthetic movements required for inculcating the proper angle and balance that leads to making sound or riding a bike are practically or "enactively" difficult for the beginner. As Polanyi writes, "We cannot learn to keep our balance on a bicycle by taking to heart that in order to compensate for a given angle of imbalance (a), we must take a curve of the inside of the imbalance, of which the radius (r) should be appropriate to the square of the velocity (v) over the imbalance" (1969, 144).

9. What is considered "correct posture" varies among ney musicians. For example, the postural element of resting one arm on the upper leg (see figure 2.1) is unique to Neyzen Niyazi Sayın's style, a visual as well as corporeal signature of the ney-playing style he developed. We should also note that different forms of playing positions were historically in place among ney players. In the visual illustrations from the Ottoman period it is common to find ney players sitting on the floor. See, for example, the illustration of "Surnâme" of the Ahmed III period (1720–30) and the image of an *ince saz* ensemble drawn by Charles Fonton (d. 1793). (On visual analysis regarding Ottoman instruments and music-making, see Pekin 2003). In addition, the position of standing was not uncommon during the

Mevlevi mukabele, a sign of respect shown for the saintly Mevlana. This symbolic ritual was retained in the public sema ceremonies held in Konya until the early 1970s during which Neyzen Halil Can and later Ulvi Erguner took the lead as chief ney players.

10. Expressions about a neyzen's posture are not uncommon—for example, "bearing like a neyzen," "to glance like a neyzen." The latter metaphor also figures in Ahmet Hamdi Tanpınar's novel *Huzur* on the occasion when the novel's characters gather to listen to the neys of Emin Dede and his talebe Halil Dikmen (referred to by the pseudonym "Cemil") (2010, 305).

11. I heard this story first by Neyzen Yılmaz Kale when I interviewed him in his Gaziantep house in May 2012. The story was recounted to him by his father Neyzen Emin Kılıç Kale (d. 1984) who was Emin Dede's talebe.

12. Because in the Ottoman classical music tradition every pitch (*perde*) exists with its own name, I am compelled to provide the original name for each note throughout the text.

13. Some neyzens include the tonal area from low G (*kaba rast*) to F-sharp (*geveşt*) under dem sounds.

14. Note that each of these labels overlaps with the names assigned to the standard keys (*ahenk*) used in the Ottoman-Turkish music system, because of the important function that the ney played in mixed ensembles as a tool of diapason. In addition to these seven types of main-pitch neys, there is also a second category known as *mabeyn* (half tone) neys that are half a tone lower or higher.

15. The source of this quote is an interview that Neyzen Ekrem Vural and vocalist Tahir Engin İçöz—both from Ankara Radio—conducted with Emin Kılıç Kale on October 9, 1983, one year before his death. A transcription of this interview was shared with me by Kale's son, Yılmaz Kale, when I interviewed him in his Gaziantep house. Emin Kılıç Kale acknowledges serving as a talebe for seven masters, including Ahmed Avni Konuk, Rauf Yekta, Ahmed (Irsoy) Dede, Emin (Yazıcı) Dede, Muallim Kazım Bey, Abdülkadir Töre, and Leon Hancıyan.

16. For a phenomenological analysis on how "aliveness" figures in the material life of marble and shapes skilled practitioners' embodied engagement with it, see Leitch (2010). On another note, the dynamism and volatility characterizing the reed's materiality is also manifest in the language surrounding tone: one can catch hold of a good tone (*ton yakalamak*) and lose or drop their tone (*tonunu kaybetmek; tonu düşmek*).

17. As the Iranian ney virtuoso Hassan Kassai declared at the Festival of Ney Players held in Iran in 1991: "The beauty of the ney is its relation to wilderness. So in our approach to how it should be played (or to its tone and pitch production), we should keep nature in mind" (Mohaved 1993, 24).

18. To give a few examples, Salih Hoca, following Niyazi Sayın's tuning technique, shifts the tone hole for *acem* (F) a few millimetres up, given its inclination to sound a little flat in its original place. This adjustment also gives the note its "burning" (*yakıcı*) effect if the player takes advantage of the technique required. In the same way, he shifts the thumbhole up as much as 2 mm. In addition to the reed, final adjustments can also be applied to the mouthpiece in the process of fine-tuning.

19. In most creation narratives the world is brought into being by breath: "When I have shaped him and breathed My spirit into him . . ." (Hijr 15: 29); "Then the LORD God formed the man from the dust of the ground. He breathed the breath of life into the man's nostrils, and the man became a living person" (Genesis 2:7). Breath and the act of blowing are vital metaphors in Sufism. For example, in the *Mesnevi*, Rumi likens humanity to an instrument on which God plays: "[S]/he is the flute, which sings only when the divine breath first fills it" (Schimmel 1975, 166). Similar metaphoric associations can be found in other breath instruments—for example—the flute on Krishna's lips.

20. Gill elaborates on the relationship between the ney and Hû, and on the spiritual meanings that Hû carries for classical neyzens. "*Hû* is not only a metaphor of the *neyzen*'s breathing into the reed as God breathes soul into the human body," she writes. Hû is also "a literal act that replicates and mirrors divine processes as acoustic distribution. . . . *Hû* as sound names God, evokes God's essence, does *zikir*, and serves as a music technique for playing the *ney* that links the contemporary world to the divine (Gill 2017, 83–84).

21. Duranti's take on intersubjectivity is instructive here. He describes it as "acts in which one *actively works* to make sure that the Other and the Self are perceptually, conceptually, and practically coordinated around a particular task" (2010, 28; emphasis added).

Chapter Three. Mode and Mood

1. The term *perde* is used also to refer to a fret on an instrument such as the tanbur. Here, it is used to imply the pitch of a note. Because some names used for makams and perde are identical (*Hicaz, Segâh, Hüseyni,* and so on), makam names are written with a capital letter to avoid confusion.

2. The ney was used for a long time as the reference pitch in ensemble settings. Many ney musicians I spoke with confirmed that this practice continued on radio until the early 1980s.

3. As Sennett writes: "In music conservatoires the master often has trouble putting him- or herself back into the rude state of the pupil, unable to show the mistake, only the right way" (2009, 181).

4. A similar conception of musical modality can be found in the art music traditions in the Middle East, Northern Africa, and Central Asia. The makam system of Ottoman-Turkish and Arab music shares important similarities with the *ragas* of Indian (both North and South) classical music, the *dastgah* of Persian art music, and in various Central Asian musical traditions. In her work on raga, the melodic basis of South Indian music, Weidman (2012) highlights the same conceptual duality.

5. See also Feldman (1996) on makam theory. He identifies seven constituent elements of makam: "(i) The fundamental intervals of music, (ii) the general scale; (iii) the positioning of the particular scales upon the general scale, and hence the relation of 'mode' and finalis, (iv) tetrachords and pentachords (*jins*, 'genre'), (v) melodic movement (*seyir*), (vi) modal combination (*terkib*), and (vii) modulation" (220).

6. For ney-teaching manuals, see Erguner 2007; Kaya 2011; Karadağ 2013. Each of these method books follows a sequence of modes, although their order varies. While *Rast* is

the first makam that Erguner (2007) focuses on in his modal instructions, Kaya (2011) and Karadağ (2013) begin with the makams *Kürdi* and *Beyati*, respectively.

7. *Rast* is described as the "mother of all makams" in Ottoman classical music. Musical instruction generally begins with this mode. Also, when the ney is involved, the scale of this mode corresponds with the natural chromatic scale of the instrument. It is thus a preferred makam in most ney teaching practices.

8. A comma is roughly equivalent to one-ninth of a whole tone.

9. For example, the pitch segâh that the makam *Uşşak* uses is not the same as how the same pitch figures in the modes *Karcığar* or *Segâh*, even if the established music theory and notation indicate each of these different segâh with the same symbol. The player has to know how much to sharpen or flatten the pitch according to the mode in question and according to the location of the pitch in the melodic flow. On the emotive role of good intonation in Arabic *maqam* music, see Racy (2003).

10. There is, of course, more than one technique at work here. For example, as I discuss in detail in chapter 4, when performing a *taksim*, an adept must imagine and fashion a melodic "path" (*seyir*) that conforms to the accepted view of that makam. Similarly, the skilful execution of a mode's characteristic phrases and cadences at critical moments of a performance serves a similar function as a good punch line in a joke. Such artistic actions are vital for consolidating the resonance of a makam and imbuing it with lifelike dynamism.

11. Take the makam *Beyati*, for example. The mode typically likes to emphasize the *Uşşak* flavor on *dügah* (A) and the *Buselik* flavor on *neva* (D). When it extends to the lower register, it likes to take on the *Hicaz* flavor on D and the *Nikriz* flavor on *çargâh* (C).

12. The theoretical and notational conventions of this system were laid down by Suphi Ezgi (1869–1962) and Hüseyin Sadettin Arel (1880–1955) in their respective work: *Ameli ve Nazari Türk Musikisi* (Practical and Theoretical Turkish Music), published in five volumes between 1933 and 1953, and *Türk Musikisi Nazariyatı Dersleri* (Lessons in Turkish Music Theory). The Arel-Ezgi system is not the first attempt to adapt Western staff notation into the transcription of Ottoman art-music genre. In 1921 the late Ottoman composer and music theorist Rauf Yekta proposed a music system based on twenty-four-note-scale (reconceptualizing the method of Ṣafīyy al-Dīn of the thirteenth century) using an amended version of Western notation. It was Yekta's methodological approach that provided the basis for the Arel-Ezgi system (see Feldman 1996; Ayangil 2008).

13. Theorists have attempted to develop alternative notation systems, among them Mildan Niyazi Ayomak, Yalçın Tura, Mustafa Ekrem Karadeniz, and Kemal İlerici (see Ayangil 2008).

14. On this topic, see Popescu-Judetz (1996); Ayangil (2008, 445). Niyazi Sayın confirms that his meşk practice with Halil Dikmen involved *Hamparsum* notation.

Chapter Four. Improvisation and Journey

1. The expression *taksim* literally means "division." See Feldman (1996) for other meanings of the word.

2. Cantemir's treatise *Kitâb-i İlmü'l Musiki ala Vechi'l-Hurufât* provided a detailed account of taksim. The text makes a distinction between verbal and instrumental forms of taksim, introducing lengthy explanations about how taksim performance should be executed (see Feldman 1996; Cantemir ca. 1700). Among other key figures of Ottoman music who wrote about modal improvisation are Hızır Ağa (d. 1795?), Charles Fonton (d. 1700s), Aldülbaki Nasir Dede (1765–1821), and Haşim Bey (1815–1868).

3. Necdet Yaşar recounts that his first joint improvisation with Sayın took place at an informal musical gathering they attended at Necmettin Hakkı's house in 1950. Their first joint *taksim* was broadcast on Istanbul Radio in 1956. http://www.muziksoylesileri.net/cms/index.php?option=com_content&task=view&id=294&Itemid=45. Some of these musicians' joint improvisations were released by Kalan Müzik in 2006.

4. A ten-disc collection of Cemil Bey's instrumental works was released by Kalan Müzik in 2016.

5. Today, most contemporary ney players in Turkey underline the fact that Sayın achieved on the ney what Cemil Bey achieved on his own instruments, creating a new performance style renowned in particular for its exceptional pitch sensitivity and virtuosic versatility.

6. Available at http://www.muziksoylesileri.net/cms/index.php?option=com_content&task=view&id=294&Itemid=45.

7. See Kallimopoulou on the influence of this trio's performances in the musical landscape of Greece in the late 1970s and 1980s, "introduc[ing] a new performance style characterized by small ensemble sound and a strong focus on instrumental repertoire and improvisation" (2009, 118).

8. Another biographical example that Poulos provides in relation to the significant role of joint listening sessions attended by musicians making "joint improvisation" involves Mesut Cemil and his musical companion Ruşen Ferit Kam (1902–1981).

9. One of the key conclusions emerging from Stubbs's musical analysis of these seyir examples is the shared understanding that organizes Sayın's and Özgen's knowledge of each makam. Although their renderings of seyir are different, there are deep similarities between the melodic fragments (motives and progressions) employed by both artists.

10. The problematic popular conception of improvisation as something that occurs "intuitively" or "on the spur of the moment" has been revisited in several ethnomusicological studies, alongside their critique of the juxtaposing of improvisation and composition as two opposite poles; see Nettl (1974). Nooshin's (2003) work on improvisation in Iranian classical music demonstrates, for instance, how a memorization of the canonic repertory is a vital starting point for improvisation.

11. See Signell (2004, 127) for a list of stereotyped phrases identified with a variety of modes.

12. On the emotional impact of modal improvisation in the context of Arab music, see Racy (2000; 2003) and Shannon (2003).

13. Modulation also figures as a key compositional device in the precomposed classical music repertoire. For instance, the *Neva Kâr*, the magnum opus of the renowned Otto-

man composer Buhurizade Mustafa Itri (1640–1712) is one of the greatest examples of the vocal repertoire, making excellent use of modal and rhythmic modulations. *Miraciye*, a religious work by *Kutb-i Nayi* Osman Dede (d. 1730) is another fine example of how modulation can serve to create a rich tonal landscape. The melodic composition of this piece accommodates thirty different makams.

14. A recording of this taksim is available in Sayın's *Sadâ* album (2001). This album is a compilation of some of Sayın's taksims originally recorded during the 1960s and 1970s.

15. This work compiles the notated transcriptions of Sayın's improvisations published in his *Sadâ* album.

16. Racy refers to these two constituent elements of the taksim performance as the "extreme poles of significance" (tradition/convention-innovation). The first pole, he outlines, encompasses "the conventional, normative, stable, and shared facets of Arab culture" (2000, 309), whereas the latter pole "represents musical phenomena that transcend the realm of common practice," allowing for "freedom and individuality" (310). For the ney musicians whose ideas inform this study, these two elements complement each other rather than forming binary sets. It is disciplining in the tradition that allows freedom and individuality, and innovation builds upon the conventional rather than canceling it out.

17. See also Duranti and Burrell (2004) for an analysis of personhood and jazz improvisation.

Chapter Five. Master Speakers, Master Listeners

1. A problem of "translation" emerges in the writing of this chapter. As in the case of converting a taksim melody into a score, taking sohbet excerpts from Salih Hoca's lessons and putting them into a written form strips these performative speech events of their affective power.

2. See Poulos (2018) for a study on private musical assemblies (*meclises*) during the early Republican period, and the central place of sohbet, alongside poetry and music, in these convivial house gatherings of Ottoman/Turkish musicians and music aficionados.

3. See Hirschkind (2006) for a discussion on the therapeutic and morally transformative virtues of listening.

4. The sohbet extracts quoted throughout this chapter are Salih Hoca's own words unless suggested otherwise. They were recorded during the lesson sessions (2012–2015) and translated into English by the author.

5. In Qur'anic exegesis there are two types of verses (*âyet*): *muhkem* verses, which have one determinant interpretation, and *müteşabih* verses, whose meaning is open to multiple interpretations.

6. This four-volume book is a compilation of Filiz's sohbets on Sufism from 1983 to 1988.

7. Nancy Christiansen (1997) makes this point in regard to the mastery of rhetoric during the British Renaissance. To be able be a skillful orator one needed to go through a process of character fashioning and to master the right decorum, a line of reasoning and

practice that blurred, as Christiansen notes, "the boundaries between speech and action, thought and performance" (1997, 298).

8. According to Al-Ghazali, when an attribute (*vasf*) becomes permanent (a disposition), it is called "station" (makam), and when, on the other hand, it instantaneously occurs as a state, it is called the "state of soul" (hâl) (cited in Sherif 1975, 113).

9. A discussion on the relationship between affective orientations and moral action is also central to Mahmood's analysis of ethical self-cultivation. She notes that for the mosque participants, "the process of cultivating and honing a pious disposition . . . centered not only on the practical tasks of daily living . . . but also on the creation and orientation of the emotions such a disposition entailed" (2005, 140).

10. Silverstein's work also demonstrates the role of the face-to-face sohbets in evoking intimacy and compellingness in listeners, which are lacking in the mediated (radio) sohbets his study also examines (2008).

11. By the same token, Michael Jackson underlines the primacy of social implications of storytelling over the "intrinsic truth" of the story told. He writes that "the truth of stories emerges from a *relationship* between teller and listener: in the social bond they forge between the generations or those who come to share in them. . . . What matters most are the truth effects of telling stories, the empathy they generate, the exchange of experience they enable, and the social bonds they mediate" (1998, 180–81, original emphasis).

12. On the importance of emotions as a catalyst for learning, see Milton (2002); Gieser (2008). According to Milton, emotions are essential "learning mechanisms" (2002, 59). Gieser (2008), too, understands emotions as "tools" that learners use when observing and imitating knowledgeable others. Emotions contribute to the process of scaffolding and skilled acquisition in a number of ways, through "filtering attention" (Milton 2002), through allowing a better retention of the knowledge acquired, and through enabling novices to "enter into an *empathic* relationship with a skilled practitioner" (Gieser 2008, 299).

13. Al-Ghazali refers to muhabbet as the most important of all states because in it, one is "penetrated with love of God" (Rouget 1985, 268). See Trix (1993) for the meaning and significance of muhabbet in the context of the Bektashi order. Trix describes muhabbet as a kind of "attunement," "an increasing coordination of hearts," between the mürşid and talib (1993, 150).

Chapter Six. Music and Ethical Modification

1. This formulation of habitus differs from that sketched out by Pierre Bourdieu (1977) in one important way. Bourdieu's "socially informed" body is assembled for the most part in unconscious ways. His envisioning of the acquisition of bodily habits as beyond individual's attention is not helpful in explaining how training regimes such as musical apprenticeship work as a mode of embodied and reflexive perceptual modification.

2. A typical example often recounted by neyzens is an anecdote about Sayın turning up at Halil Dikmen's door (at Museum of Painting and Sculpture in Beşiktaş) half an

hour before the agreed lesson time, revealing, for those musicians familiar with Sayın's biography, the kinds of embodied qualities that a talebe should exemplify.

3. As Lambek puts it, "Ethics is part of the human condition. . . . [G]iven our consciousness, our socialization and sociality, and our use of language, we are fundamentally ethical" (2010, 1). Everyday comportment is another key focus of the conception of "ordinary ethics" as Lambek discusses (2010, 2–3).

4. Ayvazoğlu's biographical book, *Neyin Sırrı* (The Secret of the Ney), documents a similar sensibility as evident in the teaching practice of Neyzen Halil Dikmen, who, through similar verbal exclamations to his talebes, would establish the presence in his own ney master Emin Dede during his meşk sessions.

5. Spatial activities were also the focus of ney pedagogy at some other lesson sites. For example, the ney lessons offered at the Turkish Islamic Arts Library involved occasional visits to the tombs of key figures of Ottoman classical music such as Tanburi Cemil Bey, Hafız Sami, Neyzen Emin Dede, and Saadettin Kaynak. This religious-cultural *dernek* (association)—the lessons were held at the Hekimoğlu Ali Paşa Mosque in Fatih district—was one of the busiest lesson sites in Istanbul at the time of my fieldwork, where instruction in Islamic calligraphy, miniature, water marbling, and Ottoman language was also offered. At the time of my fieldwork, roughly two hundred students were taking up ney lessons at this place (among a total of seven hundred students).

6. Houston's fascinating study on political activism and place perception in Istanbul in the 1970s illuminates these points. His analysis shows how activism's constitution of a new attitude toward the city involves "an ethical/sentimental education (of activists), the cultivation (in activists) of an ethical sensibility that would notice (or infer) particular aspects of the urban environment—poverty, injustice, and inequality—or be moved by certain dimensions of people's lives" (2015b, 8).

7. The expressions of "feyz" and "*feyz vermek*" (to give *feyz*) are commonly used in meşk contexts. *Feyz*, an Arabic word, literally connotes blessing (*bereket*). According to some Sufi interpretations of Islam, the act of visiting (*ziyaret*) the graves of saints is also understood as a means to receive *feyz* from saintly figures (*pir*).

8. My discussion of exemplary ethics differs from some other examples of anthropological discussion on exemplary ethics such as by Caroline Humphrey (1997) and Hirschkind (2006). These studies are concerned with the question of how the discourse of historical exemplars plays a significant role in the formation of a moral self.

9. On language and ethics, see Lambek (2010). Lambek argues, "Ethics is, in the first instance, neither a comportment of social life nor a specific category of human thought but entailed in all speech and action" (2010, 29).

10. In fact, in expressing what makes listening to sermon tapes a meaningful activity for them, Hirshkind's informants themselves often comment on the "intellectual" force or substance of what they hear without necessarily separating this from the affective power that sermons have on them. For instance: "The shaykh teaches you about Islam, what it requires of you, so you won't make errors," comments one informant (2006, 68), while another person says: "You learn things you didn't know, and this is useful. . . . Listening

to a tape of sermon is a way of reinforcing what you've learned." (74). In these examples, listeners appreciate the power of tapes in terms of what its speech contains and conveys.

11. The Qur'an, of course, is also full of analogies and allegories, as it says (for example) in the Sura An-Nur 24, in the Light verse 35: "And Allah speaks to mankind in allegories, for Allah is Knower of all things."

12. We can induce an analogy between the skilled practice of calligraphy in Islam and metaphors. In calligraphic writing, the same word or expression can be rendered in many different forms (scripts, style, background design, color, and so on). According to Osborn, each outward manifestation (*zahir*) of the written word or phrase reveals occluded or "hidden" depths of its inner meaning (*batin*). Calligraphy, Osborn says, is a technology that not only "seeks to express the *batin* through the *zahir*" (2005, 17) but also "uses the visual structure of letters and the aesthetic representation of phrases to explore meaning and expand the significance and presence of a text" (19). This efficacy of visual form-giving in writing can be likened to the capacity of an ingenious analogy or metaphor in spoken language. See also Şenay (2017) on how calligraphy works as a means for reinterpreting, recomposing, and reperforming God's words.

Chapter Seven. Musical Islam

1. Take, for example, the introduction to a special issue titled "Music and Islam" (Otterbeck and Ackfeldt 2012) in *Contemporary Islam*. The authors' interrogation of the relationship between music and Islam only considers theological debates about the permissibility of music in Islam even if they themselves acknowledge that theologians are only one segment of society. This law-centered conceptualization of Islam gives normative primacy to the canonical texts of the Qur'an and the hadith as *the* "authoritative" sources of Islam.

2. "A practice is Islamic because it is authorized by the discursive traditions of Islam, and is so taught to Muslims" (Asad 1986, 15).

3. Examples: the creative projects of Sufism such as poetry, art, and music.

4. Dictionary definition: "Willing to respect or accept behavior different from one's own; open to new ideas." https://en.oxforddictionaries.com/definition/liberal.

Conclusion

1. From Mevlana Jalal-ud-din Rumi's *Masnavi-yi Manavi*. Translated by Helminski (1998).

Glossary

arabesk—a Turkish- and Kurdish-language popular music genre that gained nationwide appeal in Turkey in the 1970s and the early 1980s. Its musical aesthetics are characterized by Arabic-influenced melodies and rhythms, large string ensembles, as well as folk and pop music elements.

ayin—the formalized ritual of a *tarikat.*

bağlama—a long-necked lute with three to seven strings and movable frets, usually associated with Turkish folk music.

başpare—small mouthpiece affixed at the top hole of the ney in order to obtain a clearer sound from the instrument. Though başpare is traditionally made of buffalo horn, hard tropical wood and heavy plastic are other commonly used materials.

dem—literally, "breath"; used to refer to the sounds of the ney from *kaba rast* (low G) to *yegâh* (D).

dergâh—tekke, especially one with a tomb attached to it.

ebru—the art of paper marbling, a well-developed aesthetic practice in the Muslim world. Its technique involves applying paints (oil or acrylic) onto the water surface.

ezan—call to prayer.

fasıl—modal suite form in Ottoman classical music; also used as a musical genre in *gazino*.

feyz—divine effulgence.

gazino—a Turkish nightclub type.

hadith—a saying or tradition of Prophet Muhammad.

hafız—one who memorizes and recites the Quran; cantor.

hat—the art of calligraphy (performer of: *hattat*).

hikaye—narrative telling of accounts.

hoca—master, teacher; the honorific term for a hereditary master of Ottoman-Turkish classical music.

Hû—an intensive added to Allah, meaning "God himself."

ilahi—hymn.

kamış—reed cane (scientifically, *Arundo donax L.*) used in making the body of the *ney*.

kamışçı—reed harvester.

klasik kemençe—*lyra politiki* (also called *armut kemençe*)—three-stringed fiddle used in Ottoman classical and light art music as well as in folk music traditions from coastal towns in the Aegean region of Turkey.

kundüm—a small double drum played with small sticks called *zahme*.

kutup—axis, pivot, or pole; highest rank in the mystical hierarchy.

makam (*maqam* in Arabic)—modal system of Ottoman-Turkish and Arabic art music; also used to designate a single modal unit within the broader makam system (for example, *makam Hicaz*).

meşk—master–pupil learning process based on imitation, repetition, and memorization.

mevlevi ayini—musical suites performed during the Mevlevi ritual of mukabele.

mevlevihane—lodge used by Mevlevi dervishes.

mukabele—the ritual event of the Mevlevi order that involves the sacred whirling prayer of the Mevlevi dervishes.

müezzin—one who calls to prayer.

muhib—sympathizer of a tarikat.

mürit—disciple of a sheikh.

mürşid—spiritual guide.

mutrip—the group of "musicians" performing in the Mevlevi mukabele.

namaz—the Islamic ritual prayer performed five times a day.

na't—poem in praise of the Prophet.

nefs—literally, "breath," "self"; in Sufism it refers to the sensual or bodily self, or ego.

ney (performer of: *neyzen*)—a reed or PVC plastic end-blown flute with a mouthpiece, six top holes, and one thumb hole. Neys come in several sizes, each tuned to a specific tonal center employed in Ottoman art music.

neyzenbaşı—in the Mevlevi mukabele the chief ney player, who is also the chief of all the musicians.

perde—musical note; also used to refer to a fret on an instrument such as the tanbur.

peşrev—literally, "fore-going"; a multipart instrumental prelude, played in the Ottoman *fasıl*.

piyasa—commercial market.

rabıta—relation.

sema—spiritual audition, ecstatic ritual practice of Sufi order.

semazen—dervish who performs the sema.

seyir—tonal "path" followed in a makam.

silsile—chain of initiates.

sohbet—in everyday Turkish, *sohbet* means conversation. It is a key Sufi disciplinary practice that denotes a spiritual conversation between a mürşid and disciples.

taksim—a free-tempo melodic instrumental improvisational form.

talebe—literally, the one who seeks, demands knowledge; pupil.

tanbur—(performer of: *tanburi*)—an eight-stringed long-necked, fretted lute with a hemispherical body, found only in Turkey. Can be plucked or bowed (*yaylı*).

tarikat—the Sufi path as a whole.

tasavvuf—the esoteric and initiatic tradition of Islam.

tavır—artistic style. Ney musicians mostly use this term to refer to the instrumental style of an individual player. The term *üslub* (also style), on the other hand, is generally used to describe a shared, collective style such as that of a lineage.

tekke—dervish lodge; place of meeting or residence for members of a tarikat.

türbe—mausoleum of a saint.

ûd—(performer of: *ûdi*)—a short-necked bowl lute found throughout the Near East and North Africa. The ûd is fretless and has eleven strings.

usûl—rhythmic modal system of Ottoman classical music.

vahdet-i vücûd—the Sufi doctrine of unity of existence, which holds that nothing in the universe has existence independent of God, that all is God's revelation.

zikr—devotional acts in Islam whereby short phrases or prayers are repeatedly recited to remember God.

Bibliography

Ağaoğlu, Yavuz S. 2013. *Neyzen Selami Bertuğ'un Anılarından Belgelerle Hazret-i Mevlana'yı Anma Törenleri (1942–1974)*. Konya: Konya Büyükşehir Belediyesi Kültür Yayınları.

Ahmed, Shahab. 2016. *What Is Islam? The Importance of Being Islamic*. Princeton, N.J.: Princeton University Press.

Aksoy, Bülent. 2009. *Cüneyd Orhon Anlatıyor: Radyo Günlerim*. Istanbul: Pan.

Aksoy, Ozan. 2006. "The Politicization of Kurdish Folk Songs in Turkey in the 1990s." *Music and Anthropology* 11. http://levi.provincia.venezia.it/ma/index/ma_ind.htm.

Aktar, Ayhan. 2000. *Varlık Vergisi ve Türkleştirme Politikaları*. Istanbul: Iletişim.

Alagha, Joseph. 2016. "Shi'a Discourses on Performing Arts: Maslaha and Cultural Politics in Lebanon." In *Islam and Popular Culture*, edited by Karin van Nieuwkerk, M. Levine, and M. Stokes, 169–86. Austin: University of Texas Press.

Algar, Hamid. 1992. "Devotional Practices of the Khalidi Naqshbandis of Ottoman Turkey." In *The Dervish Lodge: Architecture, Art, and Sufism in Ottoman Turkey*, edited by Raymond Lifchez, 209–27. Berkeley: University of California Press.

Alim, Samy. 2006. "Re-inventing Islam with Unique Modern Tones: Muslim Hip Hop Artists as Verbal Mujahidin." *Souls: A Critical Journal of Black Politics, Culture, and Society* 8 (4): 45–58.

Anderson, Paul. 2011. "'The Piety of the Gift': Selfhood and Sociality in the Egyptian Mosque Movement." *Anthropological Theory* 11 (1): 3–21.

Asad, Talal. 1986. *The Idea of an Anthropology of Islam*. Washington, D.C.: Center for Contemporary Arab Studies, Georgetown University.

Avery, Kenneth. 2004. *A Psychology of Early Sufi Samā: Listening and Altered States*. London: Routledge.

Ayangil, Ruhi. 2008. "Western Notation in Turkish Music." *Journal of the Royal Asiatic Society of Great Britain and Ireland* 18 (4): 401–47.

Ayas, Güneş. 2014. *Musiki İnkilabı'nın Sosyolojisi: Klasik Türk Müziği Geleneğinde Süreklilik ve Değişim*. Istanbul: Doğu.

———. 2015. "Alâeddin Yavaşça ve Meşk Ahlakı: Yaşayan Bir Geleneğin Sosyolojik Analizi." *Sosyologca* 9:81–96.

Aydemir, Murat. 2010. *Turkish Music Makam Guide*. Istanbul: Pan.

Ayvazoğlu, Beşir. 2008. *Ney'in Sırrı*. Istanbul: Kapı.

Bakhtin, Mikhael. 1986. *Speech Genres and Other Late Essays*. Translated by V. W. McGee. Austin: University of Texas Press.

Barenboim, Daniel, and Edward Said. 2004. *Parallels and Paradoxes*. London: Bloomsbury.

Barendregt, Bart. 2012. "Sonic Discourses on Muslim Malay Modernity: The Arqam Sound." *Contemporary Islam* 6 (3): 315–40.

Bates, Eliot. 2012. "The Social Life of Instruments." *Ethnomusicology* 56 (3): 363–95.

———. 2016. *Digital Tradition: Arrangement and Labor in Istanbul's Recording Studio Culture*. Oxford: Oxford University Press.

Baumann, Max P. 2000. "The Local and the Global: Traditional Musical Instruments and Modernization." *World of Music* 42 (3): 121–44.

Behar, Cem. 1987. *Klasik Türk Musikisi Üzerine Denemeler*. Istanbul: Bağlam.

———. 1993. *Zaman, Mekân, Müzik: Klâsik Türk Musikisinde Eğitim (Meşk), İcra ve Aktarım*. Istanbul: Afa.

———. (2005) 2008. *Musikiden Müziğe. Osmanlı/Türk Müziği: Gelenek ve Modernlik*. Istanbul: YKY.

———. (1998) 2012. *Aşk Olmayınca Meşk Olmaz: Geleneksel Osmanlı/Türk Müziğinde Öğretim ve İntikal*. Istanbul: YKY.

———. 2013. "Text and Memory in Ottoman/Turkish Musical Tradition." In *Ottoman Musical Intimacies, Balkan Musical Realities*, edited by Risto Pekka Pennanen, Panagiotis C. Poulos, and Anastasia Theodosiou, 3–13. Helsinki: Suomen Ateenan-instiuutin säätiö.

———. 2014. "The Show and the Ritual: The Mevlevi *Mukabele* in Ottoman Times." In *Medieval and Early Modern Performances in the Eastern Mediterranean*, edited by Arzu Öztürkmen and Evelyn Birge Vitz, 515–33. Turnhout: Brepols.

———. 2015. *Osmanlı/Türk Musikisinin Kısa Tarihi*. Istanbul: YKY.

Beken, Münir Nurettin. 1998. "Musicians, Audience and Power: The Changing Aesthetics in the Music at the Maksim Gazino of Istanbul." PhD diss., University of Maryland.

Benjamin, Walter. 1973. "The Storyteller: Reflections on the Works of Nikolai Leskov." In *Illuminations*, edited by Hannah Arendt, 83–107. London: Fontana.

Berg, Carin. 2012. "Tunes of Religious Resistance? Understanding Hamas Music in a Conflict Context." *Contemporary Islam* 6 (3): 297–314.

Berkes, Niyazi. 1964. *The Development of Secularism in Turkey*. Montreal: McGill University Press.

Berliner, Paul. 1994. *Thinking in Jazz: The Infinite Art of Improvisation*. Chicago: University of Chicago Press.

Bessman, Jim. 2002. "For This Tailor-Made Virtuoso, the Nays Have It." *Rhythm* (May 2002). http://www.omarfaruktekbilek.com/for-this-tailor-made-virtuoso-the-nays-have-it.

Bilgin, Salih. 2012. *Zanaattan San'ata Başpare*. Konya: İl Kültür ve Turizm Müdürlüğü Yayını.

Bohlman, Phillip V. 1997. "World Music and World Religious: Whose World?" In *Enchanting Powers: Music in the World's Religions*, edited by Lawrence E. Sullivan, 61–90. Cambridge, Mass.: Center for the Study of World Religions.

Boubekeur, Amel. 2007. "Post-Islamist Culture: A New Form of Mobilization?" *History of Religions* 47 (1): 75–95.

Bourdieu, Pierre. 1977. *Outline of a Theory of Practice*. Cambridge: Cambridge University Press.

Bryant, Rebecca. 2005. "The Soul Danced into the Body: Nation and Improvisation in Istanbul." *American Ethnologist* 32 (2): 222–38.

Can, Halil. 1966. "Dini Türk Musikisi Lügatı." *Musiki Mecmuası*, no. 220.

Casey, Edward S. 1974. "Toward a Phenomenology of Imagination." *Journal of the British Society for Phenomenology* 5 (1): 3–19.

Chittick, William C. 1989. *The Sufi Path of Knowledge: Ibn al-Arabi's Metaphysics of Imagination*. Albany, N.Y.: SUNY Press.

Christiansen, Nancy L. 1997. "Rhetoric as Character-Fashioning: The Implications of Delivery's 'Places' in the British Renaissance *Paideia*." *Rhetorica* 15 (3): 297–334.

Clifton, Thomas, 1983. *Music as Heard: A Study in Applied Phenomenology*. New Haven, Conn.: Yale University Press.

Cooper, Eugene. 1989. "Apprenticeship as Field Method: Lessons from Hong Kong." In Coy, *Apprenticeship*, 137–48.

Coy, Michael W., ed. 1989. *Apprenticeship: From Theory to Method and Back Again*. Albany, N.Y.: SUNY Press.

Csordas, Thomas J. 1994. *Embodiment and Experience: The Existential Ground of Culture and Self*. Cambridge: Cambridge University Press.

Dalidowicz, Monica. 2012. "Learning Kathak: Crafting Bodies and Selves in the Guru-Shishya Parampara." PhD diss., Macquarie University.

Dow, James. 1989. "Apprentice Shaman." In Coy, *Apprenticeship*, 199–210.

Downey, Greg. 2005. *Learning Capoeira: Lessons in Cunning from an Afro-Brazilian Art*. Oxford: Oxford University Press.

Duranti, Alessandro. 1986. "The Audience as Co-author: An Introduction." *Text* 6 (3) 239–47.

———. 2009. "The Relevance of Husserl's Theory to Language Socialization." *Journal of Linguistic Anthropology* 19 (2): 205–26.

———. 2010. "Husserl, Intersubjectivity, and Anthropology." *Anthropological Theory* 10 (16): 16–35.

Duranti, Alessandro, and Steven P. Black. 2011. "Language Socialization and Verbal Improvisation." In *The Handbook of Language Socialization*, edited by Alessandro Duranti, Elinor Ochs, and Bambi B. Schieffelin, 443–63. Malden, Mass.: Wiley-Blackwell.

Duranti, Alessandro, and Kenny Burrell. 2004. "Jazz Improvisation: A Search for Hidden Harmonies and a Unique Self." *Ricerche di Psicologia* 27 (3): 71–101.

During, Jean. 1999. "What Is Sufi Music?" In *The Heritage of Sufism: The Legacy of Medieval Persian Sufism (1150–1500)*, vol. 2, edited by Leonard Lewisohn, 277–87. Oxford: Oneworld.

Düzen, Ekrem. 2018. "Turkey's Nationalist Agenda for Seizing Cultural Hegemony." *Jadaliyya* (available online: http://www.jadaliyya.com/Print/37680).

Eickelman, Dale F. 1978. "The Art of Memory: Islamic Education and Its Social Reproduction." *Comparative Studies in Society and History* 20 (4): 485–516.

Ergun, Sadettin Nüzhet. 1943. *Türk Musikisi Antolojisi*. Istanbul: Istanbul Üniversitesi Yayınları.

Erguner, Kudsi. 2005. *Journeys of a Sufi Musician*. London: SAQI.

Erguner, Süleyman. 2005. *Neyzen: "Süleyman-Ulvi" Erguner*. Istanbul: Düzey.

———. (1986) 2007. *Ney—Metod*. Istanbul.

Faubion, James D. 2011. *An Anthropology of Ethics*. Cambridge: Cambridge University Press.

Feld, Steven. 1982. *Sound and Sentiment: Birds, Weeping, Poetics and Song in Kaluli Expression*. Philadelphia: University of Pennsylvania Press.

———. 1994. "From Schizophonia to Schismogenesis: On the Discourses and Commodification Practices of "World Music" and "World Beat." In *Music Groove*, edited by Charles Keil and Steven Feld, 257–89. Chicago: University of Chicago Press.

Feld, Steven, and Don Brenneis. 2004. "Doing Anthropology in Sound." *American Ethnologist* 31 (4): 461–74.

Feldman, Walter. 1992. "Musical Genres and Zikir of the Sunni Tarikats of Istanbul." In *The Dervish Lodge: Architecture, Art, and Sufism in Ottoman Turkey*, edited by Raymond Lifchez, 187–202. California: University of California Press.

———. 1996. *Music of the Ottoman Court: Makam, Composition and the Early Ottoman Instrumental Repertoire*. Berlin: Verlag für Wissenschaft und Bildung.

Fernandez, James 1986. *Persuasions and Performances: The Play of Tropes in Culture*. Bloomington: University of Indiana Press.

Filiz, Lütfi. 2009. *Noktanın Sonsuzluğu*. Vol. 4. Istanbul: Pan.

Foucault, Michel. 1994. *The Order of Things: An Archaeology of the Human Sciences*. New York: Vintage.

———. 1997. "The Ethics of the Concern of the Self as a Practice of Freedom." In *Ethics: Subjectivity and Truth*, vol. 1 of *Essential Works of Foucault, 1954–1984*, edited by Paul Rabinow, 281–301. New York: New Press.

Fox-Strangways, Arthur H. 1914. *The Music of Hindostan*. Oxford: Clarendon.

Frith, Simon. 2000. "The Discourse of World Music." In *Western Music and Its Others*, edited by Georgina Born and David Hesmondhalgh, 305–22. Berkeley: University of California Press.

George, Kenneth. 2009. "Ethics, Iconoclasm, and Qur'anic Art in Indonesia." *Cultural Anthropology* 24 (4): 589–621.

Gibson, James J. 1979. *The Ecological Approach to Visual Perception*. Boston, Mass.: Houghton Mifflin.

Gieser, Thorsten. 2008. "Embodiment, Emotion and Empathy." *Anthropological Theory* 8 (3): 299–318.

Gill, Denise. 2017. *Melancholic Modalities: Affect, Islam, and Turkish Classical Musicians*. Oxford: Oxford University Press.

Gill-Gürtan, Denise. 2011. "Performing Meşk, Narrating History: Legacies of Transmission in Contemporary Turkish Musical Practices." *Comparative Studies of South Asia, Africa and the Middle East* 31 (3): 615–30.

Giorgi, Amedeo. 1967. "A Phenomenological Approach to the Problem of Meaning and Serial Learning." *Review of Existential Psychology and Psychiatry* 7:106–18.

Goodwin, Charles. 1986. "Audience Diversity, Participation and Interpretation." *Text* 6 (3): 283–316.

———. 1994. "Professional Vision." *American Anthropologist* 96 (3): 606–33.

Gökalp, Ziya 1923. *Türkçülüğün Esasları*. Ankara: Matbuat ve İstihbarat Matbaası.

Gökarıksel, Banu, and Katharyne Mitchell. 2005. "Veiling, Secularism, and the Neoliberal Subject: National Narratives and Supranational Desires in Turkey and France." *Global Networks* 5 (2): 147–65.

Gölpınarlı, Abdülbaki. 1963. *Mevlevi Adab ve Erkanı*. Istanbul: İnkılap ve Aka Kitabevi.

Greve, Martin, ed. 2015. *Writing the History of "Ottoman Music."* Wurzburg: Ergon.

Griffith, Zoe. 2011. "Calligraphy and the Art of Statecraft in the Late Ottoman Empire and Modern Turkish Republic." *Comparative Studies of South Asia, Africa and the Middle East* 31 (3): 601–14.

Halıcı, Feyzi. 1998. *Üstat Hayri Tümer'in Nay Üfleme Metodu*. Ankara: Kültür Bakanlığı Yayınları.

Harkness, Nicholas. 2013. *Songs of Seoul: An Ethnography of Voice and Voicing in Christian South Korea*. Berkeley: University of California Press.

Harris, Suzy. 2007. *The Governance of Education: How Neo-liberalism Is Transforming Policy and Practice*. London: Continuum.

Havel, Václav. 1983. *Letters to Olga*. New York: Holt.

Hendrich, Beatrice. 2011. "Introduction—Beyond State Islam: Religiosity and Spirituality in Contemporary Turkey." *European Journal of Turkish Studies*, no. 13. http://journals.openedition.org/ejts/4527

Henkel, Heiko. 2007. "The Location of Islam: Inhabiting Istanbul in a Muslim Way." *American Ethnologist* 34 (1): 57–70.

Herzfeld, Michael. 1997. *Cultural Intimacy: Social Poetics in the Nation-State*. New York: Routledge.

Hill, Joseph. 2016. "'Baay Is the Spiritual Leader of the Rappers': Performing Islamic Reasoning in Senegalese Sufi Hip-Hop." *Contemporary Islam* 10 (2): 267–87.

Hindemith, Paul. 2013. *Hindemith Raporları 1935/1936/1937*, prepared by Şefik Kahramankaptan. Ankara: SCA Müzik Vakfı.

Hirschkind, Charles. 2006. *The Ethical Soundscape: Cassette Sermons and Islamic Counterpublics*. New York: Columbia University Press.

Houston, Christopher. 2004. "Islamism, Castoriadis and Autonomy." *Thesis Eleven* 76 (1): 49–69.

———. 2008. *Kurdistan: Crafting of National Selves*. New York: Berg.

———. 2009. "An Anti-history of a Non-people: Kurds, Colonialism, and Nationalism in the History of Anthropology." *Journal of the Royal Anthropological Institute* 15 (1): 19–35.

———. 2012. "Anthropology, Autonomy and the Art of Cultural Revolution." *Anthropological Theory* 12 (3): 252–70.

———. 2015a. "Kemalism and Beyond." In *The Oxford Handbook of Contemporary Middle Eastern and North African History*, edited by Amal Ghazal and Jens Hanssen. Oxford: Oxford University Press.

———. 2015b. "Politicizing Place Perception: A Phenomenology of Urban Activism in Istanbul." *Journal of the Royal Anthropological Institute* 21 (4): 720–38.

Howes, David. 2003. *Sensual Relations: Engaging the Senses in Culture and Social Theory*. Ann Arbor: University of Michigan Press.

Humphrey, Caroline. 1997. "Exemplars and Rules: Aspects of the Discourse of Moralities in Mongolia." In *The Ethnography of Moralities*, edited by Signe Howell, 25–47. New York: Routledge.

Husserl, Edmund. 1970. *Logical Investigations*. Atlantic Highlands, N.J.: Humanities.

Ihde, Don. (1976) 2007. *Listening and Voice: Phenomenologies of Sound*. 2nd ed. Albany, N.Y.: SUNY Press.

İnal, İbnülemin M. K. 1958. *Hoş Sada. Son Asır Türk Musikisinaşları*. Istanbul: İş Bankası.

Ingold, Tim. 2001. "From the Transmission of Representations to the Education of Attention." In *The Debated Mind: Evolutionary Psychology versus Ethnography*, edited by Harvey Whitehouse, 113–53. Oxford: Berg.

———. 2010. "The Textility of Making." *Cambridge Journal of Economics* 34 (1): 91–102.

———. 2011a. *Being Alive: Essays on Movement, Knowledge and Description*. London: Routledge.

———. 2011b. "Making, Growing, Learning." Two lectures presented at UFMG, Belo Horizonte.

Jackson, Maureen. 2011. "Crossing Musical Worlds: Ottoman Jewry, Music Making, and Rise of the Nation." *Comparative Studies of South Asia, Africa and the Middle East* 31 (3): 569–81.

Jackson, Michael. 1989. *Paths toward a Clearing: Radical Empiricism and Ethnographic Enquiry*. Bloomington: Indiana University Press.

———. 1996. "Introduction." In *Things as They Are: New Directions in Phenomenological Anthropology*, edited by Michael Jackson, 1–50. Bloomington: Indiana University Press.

———. 1998. *Minima Ethnographica: Intersubjectivity and the Anthropological Project*. Chicago: University of Chicago Press.

Jarjour, Tala. 2015. "*Hasho*: Music Modality and the Economy of Emotional Aesthetics." *Ethnomusicology Forum* 24 (1): 51–72.

Joulili, Jeanette. 2012. "Halal Arts, What's in a Concept?" *Material Religion: The Journal of Objects, Art and Belief* 8 (3): 402–3.

Kale, Emin Kılıç. 1983. Interview with Ekrem Vural and Tahir Engin İçöz, October 9, 1983. Transcription, provided by Yılmaz Kale, in author's possession.

Kallimopoulou, Eleni. 2009. *Paradosiaká: Music, Meaning and Identity in Modern Greece*. London: SOAS (SOAS Musicology Series).

Kaplan, Sam. 2006. *The Pedagogical State: Education and the Politics of National Culture in Post-1980 Turkey*. Stanford, Calif.: Stanford University Press.

Karadağ, Burcu. 2013. *Meşkte Ney Eğitimi*. Istanbul: Pan.

Karadeniz, Ekrem. 1984. *Türk Musikisinin Nazariye ve Esasları*. Ankara: İş Bankası.

Karakayalı, Nedim. 2010. "Two Assemblages of Cultural Transmission: Musicians, Political Actors and Educational Techniques in the Ottoman Empire and Western Europe." *Journal of Historical Sociology* 23 (3): 343–71.

Karpat, Kemal. 1963. "The People's Houses in Turkey: Establishment and Growth." *Middle East Journal* 17 (1/2): 55–67.

Kaya, Ahmet. 2011. *Ney Metodu*. Istanbul: Bayrak.

Kaya, Celal Volkan. 2016. *Darül Elhân Talimatnamesi ve Ders Müfredat Programı*. Istanbul: n.p.

Keane, Webb. 2015. *Ethical Life: Its Natural and Social Histories*. Princeton, N.J.: Princeton University Press.

Keister, Jay. 2004. "The Shakuhachi as Spiritual Tool: A Japanese Buddhist Instrument in the West." *Asian Music* 35 (2): 99–131.

Keller, Charles M., and Janet. D. Keller. 1999. "Imagery in Cultural Tradition and Innovation." *Mind, Culture, and Activity: An International Journal* 6 (1): 3–32.

Kelsay, John. 2007. *Arguing the Just War in Islam*. Cambridge, Mass.: Harvard University Press.

Keyder, Çağlar. 1987. *State and Class in Turkey: A Study in Capitalist Development*. New York: Verso.

King, Anna. 1996. "Spirituality: Transformation and Metamorphosis." *Religion* 26 (4): 343–51.

Kippen, James. 1988. *The Tabla of Lucknow: A Cultural Analysis of a Musical Tradition*. Cambridge: Cambridge University Press.

Kirkwood, William G. 1983. "Storytelling and Self-Confrontation: Parables as Communication Strategies." *Quarterly Journal of Speech* 69 (1): 58–74.

Kozanoğlu, Cevdet. 1988. *Radyo Hatıralarım*. Ankara: TRT.

Krumhansl, Carol L. 1990. *Cognitive Foundations of Musical Pitch*. Oxford: Oxford University Press.

Kütükçü, Tamer. 2012. *Radyoculuk Geleneğimiz ve Türk Musikisi*. Istanbul: Ötüken.

Laidlaw, James. 2002. "For an Anthropology of Ethics and Freedom." *Journal of the Royal Anthropological Institute* 8 (2): 311–32.

Lakoff, George, and Mark Johnson. 1980. *Metaphors We Live By*. Chicago: University of Chicago Press.

Lambek, Michael. 2010. "Toward an Ethics of the Act." In *Ordinary Ethics: Anthropology, Language, and Action*, edited by Michael Lambek, 1–63. New York: Fordham University Press.

———. 2015. *The Ethical Condition: Essays on Action, Person, and Value*. Chicago: Chicago University Press.

Lapidus, Ira M. 1984. "Knowledge, Virtue, and Action: The Classical Muslim Conception of Adab and Nature of Religious Fulfillment in Islam." In *Moral Conduct and Authority. The Place of Adab in South Asian Islam*, edited by Barbara Daly Metcalf, 38–61. Berkeley: University of California Press.

———. 1992. "Sufism and Ottoman Islamic Society." In *The Dervish Lodge: Architecture, Art, and Sufism in Ottoman Turkey*, edited by Raymond Lifchez, 15–32. Berkeley: University of California Press.

Lave, Jean. 2011. *Apprenticeship in Critical Ethnographic Practice*. Chicago: Chicago University Press.

Lave, Jean, and Etienne Wenger. 1991. *Situated Learning: Legitimate Peripheral Participation*. Cambridge: Cambridge University Press.

Leder, Drew. 1990. *The Absent Body*. Chicago: University of Chicago Press.

Leitch, Alison. 2010. "Materiality of Marble: Explorations in the Artistic Life of Stone." *Thesis Eleven* 103 (1): 65–77.

Lewis, Bernard. 1961. *The Emergence of Modern Turkey*. Oxford: Oxford University Press.

Lewis, Geoffrey. 1999. *The Turkish Language Reform: A Catastrophic Success*. Oxford: Oxford University Press.

Lindsay, Shawn. 1996. "Hand Drumming: An Essay in Practical Knowledge." In *Things as They Are: New Directions in Phenomenological Anthropology*, edited by Michael Jackson, 196–212. Bloomington: Indiana University Press.

Lock, Margaret. 1993. "Cultivating the Body: Anthropology and Epistemologies of Bodily Practice and Knowledge." *Annual Review of Anthropology* 22:133–55.

Machover, Tod. 2007. "My Cello." In *Evocative Objects: Things We Think With*, edited by Sherry Turkle, 12–21. Cambridge, Mass.: MIT Press.

Mahmood, Saba. 2005. *Politics of Piety: The Islamic Revival and The Feminist Subject*. Princeton, N.J.: Princeton University Press.

Marchand, Trevor. 2008. "Muscles, Morals and Mind: Craft Apprenticeship and the Formation of Person." *British Journal of Educational Studies* 56 (3): 245–71.

———. 2009. *The Masons of Djenné*. Bloomington: Indiana University Press.

———. 2010. "Preface." In *Making Knowledge: Explorations of the Indissoluble Relation between Mind, Body and Environment*, edited by Trevor Marchand. West Sussex: Wiley-Blackwell.

Marks, Lawrence. 1978. *The Unity of the Senses: Interrelations among the Modalities*. New York: Academic.

Marsden, Magnus. 2005. *Living Islam: Muslim Religious Experience in Pakistan's North-West Frontier*. Cambridge: Cambridge University Press.

Mauss, M. (1934) 1979. "Techniques of the Body." In *Sociology and Psychology: Essays by Marcel Mauss*, translated by B. Brewster, 95–123. London: Routledge and Kegan Paul.

Merleau-Ponty, Maurice. 1962. *Phenomenology of Perception*. London: Routledge.

Messick, Brinkley. 1993. *The Calligraphic State: Textual Domination and History in a Muslim Society*. California: California University Press.

Milton, Kay. 2002. *Loving Nature: Towards an Ecology of Emotion*. London: Routledge.

Mittermaier, Amira. 2012. "Dreams from Elsewhere: Muslim Subjectivities beyond the Trope of Self-Cultivation." *Journal of the Royal Anthropological Institute* 18 (2): 247–65.

Mohaved, Azin. 1993. "The Persian Ney: A Study of the Instrument and Its Musical Style." PhD diss., University of Illinois.

Moran, Dermot. 2000. *Introduction to Phenomenology*. London: Routledge.

Nelson, Kristina. 1985. *The Art of Reciting the Qur'an*. Austin: University of Texas Press.

Nettl, Bruno. 1974. "Thoughts on Improvisation: A Comparative Approach." *Musical Quarterly* 60 (1): 1–19.

Nettl, Bruno, and R. Riddle. 1998. "Taqsim Nahawand Revisited: The Musicianship of Jihad Racy." In *In the Course of Performance: Studies in the World of Musical Improvisation*, edited by Bruno Nettl and Melinda Russell, 369–92. Chicago: University of Chicago Press.

Neuenfeldt, Karl. 1994. "The Essentialistic, the Exotic, the Equivocal and the Absurd: The Cultural Production and Use of the Didjeridu in World Music." *Perfect Beat* 2 (1): 88–104.

———. 1998. "Old Instruments in New Contexts. Case Studies of Innovation and Appropriation." *World of Music* 40 (2): 5–8.

Neuman Daniel M. 1990. *The Life of Music in North India: The Organization of an Artistic Tradition*. Chicago: University of Chicago Press.

Nooshin, Laudan. 1998. "The Song of the Nightingale: Processes of Improvisation in Dastgāh Segāh." *British Journal of Ethnomusicology* 7 (1): 69–116.

Ochs, Elinor, and Lisa Capps. 1996. "Narrating the Self." *Annual Review of Anthropology* 25: 19–43.

Ong, Aihwa. 2006. *Neoliberalism as Exception: Mutations in Citizenship and Sovereignty*. Durham, N.C.: Duke University Press.

Ortony, Andrew. 1975. "Why Metaphors Are Necessary and Not Just Nice." *Educational Theory* 25 (1): 45–53.

Osborn, J. R. 2005. "Islamic Calligraphy as Recitation: The Visual Expansion of Divine Words." *Humanities and Technology Review* 24 (Fall): 15–29.

Otterbeck, Jonas, and Anders Ackfeldt. 2012. "Music and Islam." *Contemporary Islam* 6 (3): 227–33.

Özeke, A. Doğan. 2000. *Neyzenler Kahvesi: Bir Neyzenin Hatıraları*. Istanbul: Pan.

Özkan, İsmail Hakkı. 1984. *Türk Musikisi Nazariyati ve Usülleri: Kudüm Velveleleri*. Istanbul: Ötüken.

Öztürkmen, Arzu. 1992. "Individuals and Institutions in the Early History of Turkish Folklore, 1840–1950." *Journal of Folklore Research* 29 (2): 177–92.

Parla, Taha, and Andrew Davison. 2004. *Corporatist Ideology in Kemalist Turkey: Progress or Order?* Syracuse, N.Y.: Syracuse University Press.

Pekin, Ersu. 2003. "Surnâme'nin Müziği: Onaltıncı Yüzyılda Istanbul'da Çalgılar." *Dipnot*, 1:52–91.

Polanyi, Michael. 1969. *Knowing and Being: Essays by Michael Polanyi*. Chicago: University of Chicago Press.

Popescu-Judetz, Eugenia. 1996. *Meanings in Turkish Musical Culture*. Istanbul: Pan.

Poulos, Panagiotis. 2011. "Rethinking Orality in Turkish Classical Music: A Genealogy of Contemporary Musical Assemblages." *Middle East Journal of Culture and Communication* 4: 164–83.

———. 2018. "At the *House of Kemal*: Private MusicalAssemblies in Istanbul from the Late Ottoman Empire to the Turkish Republic." In *Theory and Practice in the Music of the Islamic World*, edited by Rachel Harris and Martin Stokes, 106–124. SOAS Musicology Series. Abingdon: Routledge.

Prentice, Rebecca. 2012. "'No One Ever Showed Me Nothing': Skill and Self-Making among Trinidadian Garment Workers." *Anthropology and Education Quarterly* 43 (4): 400–414.

Qureshi, Regula. 2000. "How Does Music Mean? Embodied Memories and the Politics of Affect in the Indian Sarangi." *American Ethnologist* 27 (4): 805–38.

———. 2003. "Lineage, Shrine, Qawwali, and Study Circle: Spiritual Kinship in Transnational Sufism." *Religious Studies and Theology* 22 (1): 63–84.

———. 2013. "Sufism and the Globalization of Sacred Music." In *The Cambridge History of World Music*, edited by Phillip Bohlman, 584–605. Cambridge: Cambridge University Press.

Racy, A. J. 2000. "The Many Faces of Improvisation: Arab Taqāsīm as a Musical Symbol." *Ethnomusicology* 44, no. 2 (Spring/Summer): 302–20.

———. 2003. *Making Music in the Arab World: The Culture and Artistry of Tarab*. Cambridge: Cambridge University Press.

Reinhard, Kurt, Martin Stokes, and Ursula Reinhard. 2001. "Turkey." *Grove Music—Oxford Music Online*. https://doi.org/10.1093/gmo/9781561592630.article.44912.

Ritter, Helmut. (1955) 2003. *The Ocean of the Soul: Men, the World and God in the Stories of Farīd al-Dīn 'Attār*. Translated by John O'Kane and Bernd Radtke. Leiden: Brill.

Robbins, Joel. 2012. "On Becoming Ethical Subjects: Freedom, Constraint, and the Anthropology of Morality." *Anthropology of This Century*, no. 5. http://aotcpress.com/articles/ethical-subjects-freedom-constraint-anthropology-morality.

Roda, Allen P. 2014. "Table Tuning on the Workshop Stage: Toward a Materialist Musical Ethnography." *Ethnomusicology Forum* 23 (4): 360–82.

Rouget, Gilbert. 1985. *Music and Trance: A Theory of the Relations between Music and Possession*. Chicago: University of Chicago Press.

Saygun, A. Adnan. 1987. *Atatürk ve Musiki*. Istanbul: Sevda Cenap and Vakfı Yayınları.

Schäfers, Marlene. 2017. "Voice." In *The Cambridge Encyclopedia of Anthropology*, edited by F. Stein, S. Lazar, M. Candea, H. Diemberger, J. Robbins, A. Sanchez, and R. Stasch. http://www.anthroencyclopedia.com/entry/voice.

Schielke, Samuli. 2009. "Being Good in Ramadan: Ambivalence, Fragmentation, and the

Moral Self in the Lives of Young Egyptians." *Journal of Royal Anthropological Institute* 15 (1): 24–40.

———. 2010. "Second Thoughts about the Anthropology of Islam; or, How to Make Sense of Grand Schemes in Everyday Life." ZMO Working Papers, Zentrum Moderner Orient, Berlin.

Schimmel, Annemarie. 1975. *Mystical Dimensions of Islam*. Chapel Hill: University of North Carolina Press.

———. 1980. *The Triumphal Sun: A Study of the Works of Jalāloddin Rumi*. London: East-West.

———. 1990. *Calligraphy and Islamic Culture*. London: Tauris.

———. 2005. "The Role of Music in Islamic Mysticism." In *Sufism, Music and Society in Turkey and the Middle East*, edited by Anders Hammarlund, Tord Olsson, and Elisabeth Özdalga, 8–17. Istanbul: Swedish Research Institute.

Şenay, Banu. 2015. "Artists, Antagonisms and the *Ney* in the Popularization of 'Sufi Music' in Turkey." *European Journal of Cultural Studies* 18 (1): 52–69.

———. 2017. "Textual Ecologies in Islam: Improvising the Perfect Qur'an in Calligraphy." *Journal of Religious and Political Practice* 3 (1–2): 46–56.

Sennett, Richard. 2009. *The Craftsman*. London: Penguin.

Shannon, Jonathan. 2003. "Emotion, Performance, and Temporality in Arab Music: Reflections on Tarab." *Cultural Anthropology* 18 (1): 72–98.

Sheets-Johnstone, Maxine. 2011. *The Primacy of Movement*. Amsterdam: Benjamins.

Sheriff, Mohamed A. 1975. *Ghazali's Theory of Virtue*. Albany, N.Y.: SUNY Press.

Sidnell, Jack. 2016. "Shifting Perspectives." *Anthropology of This Century* 17 (October 2016). http://aotcpress.com/articles/shifting-perspectives.

Signell, Karl. (1977) 2004. *Makam: Modal Practice in Turkish Art Music*. Sarasota, Fla.: Da Capo.

Silverstein, Brian. 2008. "Disciplines of Presence in Modern Turkey: Discourse, Companionship, and the Mass Mediation of Islamic Practice." *Cultural Anthropology* 23 (1): 118–53.

Simpson, Edward. 2006. "Apprenticeship in Western India." *Journal of the Royal Anthropological Institute* 12 (1): 151–71.

Smith, F. Joseph. 1967. "Insights Leading to a Phenomenology of Sound." *Southern Journal of Philosophy* 5 (3): 187–99.

Stokes, Martin. 1992. *The Arabesk Debate: Music and Musicians in Modern Turkey*. Oxford: Oxford University Press.

———. 2010. *The Republic of Love: Cultural Intimacy in Turkish Popular Music*. Chicago: University of Chicago Press.

Stoller, Paul. 1989. *The Taste of Ethnographic Things: The Senses in Anthropology*. Philadelphia: University of Pennsylvania Press.

Stubbs, Frederick W. 1994. "The Art and Science of Taksim: An Empirical Analysis of Traditional Improvisation from 20th-Century Istanbul." Unpublished PhD diss., Wesleyan University.

Sudnow, David. (1978) 2001. *Ways of the Hand: A Written Account*. Cambridge, Mass.: MIT Press.

Tammer, Anthony. 1993. "Construction of the Turkish Ney." *Turkish Music Quarterly* 5 (4).

Tanpınar, Ahmet Hamdi. (1949) 2010. *A Mind at Peace*. Translated by Erdağ Göknar. Brookyln, N.Y.: Archipelago.

Tanrıkorur, Çinuçen. 2003. *Osmanlı Dönemi Türk Musikisi*. Istanbul: Dergâh.

———. 2004. *Türk Müzik Kimliği*. Istanbul: Dergâh.

Tekelioğlu, Orhan. 1996. "The Rise of a Spontaneous Synthesis: The Historical Background of Turkish Popular Music." *Middle Eastern Studies* 32 (2): 194–216.

Ter Laan, Nina. 2016. "'Islam Is There to Make People Free': Islamist Musical Narratives of Freedom and Democracy in the Moroccan Spring." In *Islam and Popular Culture*, edited by Karin van Nieuwkerk, Mark Levine, and Martin Stokes, 81–99. Austin: University of Texas Press.

Toz, Ahmet, I. 2013. *Niyazi Sayın'ın Taksimlerinde İcrayı Oluşturan Elemanların Transkripsiyonu*. Istanbul: Pan.

Trix, Francis. 1993. *Spiritual Discourse: Learning with an Islamic Master*. Philadelphia: University of Pennsylvania Press.

Türken, Salman, Hilde Nafstad, Rolv Blakar, and Katrina Roen. 2016. "Making Sense of Neoliberal Subjectivity: A Discourse Analysis of Media Language on Self-Development." *Globalizations* 13 (1): 32–46.

Üngör, Etem Ruhi. 1973. "Bir Neyzenbaşı ki." *Musiki Mecmuasi, Halil Can Özel Sayısı*, May–June 1973.

Uzel, Nezih. 2006. *Radyoda Bir Gün*. Istanbul: Pan.

Van Nieuwkerk, Karin. 2013. *Performing Piety: Singers and Actors in Egypt's Islamic Revival*. Austin: University of Texas Press.

Velho, Otávio. 2007. "Is Religion a Way of Knowing?" In *Ways of Knowing: New Approaches in the Anthropology of Experience and Learning*, edited by Mark Harris, 64–90. Oxford: Berghan.

Vicente, Victor A. 2007. "The Aesthetics of Motion in Musics for the Mevlana Celal ed-Din Rumi." Unpublished PhD diss., University of Maryland.

Wacquant, Loïc. 2004. *Body and Soul: Notes on an Apprentice Boxer*. Oxford: Oxford University Press.

Weidman, Amanda. 2006. *Singing the Classical, Voicing the Modern: The Postcolonial Politics of Music in South India*. Durham, N.C.: Duke University Press.

———. 2012. "The Ethnographer as Apprentice: Embodying Sociomusical Knowledge in South India." *Anthropology and Humanism* 37 (2): 214–35.

White, Jenny. 2013. *Muslim Nationalism and the New Turks*. Princeton, N.J.: Princeton University Press.

Wilf, Eitan. 2010. "Swinging within the Iron Cage: Modernity, Creativity, and Embodied Practice in American Postsecondary Jazz Education." *American Ethnologist* 37 (3): 563–82.

Winegar, Jessica. 2014. "Civilizing Muslim Youth: Egyptian State Culture Programmes and Islamic Television Preachers." *Journal of the Royal Anthropological Institute* 20 (3): 445–65.

Wittgenstein, Ludwig. (1953) 1961. *Tractatus Logico-Philosophicus*. London: Routledge and Kegan Paul.

Wood, David, Jerome S. Bruner, and Gail Ross. 1976. "The Role of Tutoring in Problem Solving." *Journal of Child Psychology and Psychiatry* 17:89–100.

Wright, Owen. 1992. *Words without Songs: A Musicological Study of an Early Ottoman Anthology and Its Precursors*. Vol. 3, SOAS Musicology Series. London: SOAS.

Yavaşça, Alâeddin. 1981. "Evlerdeki Musiki Toplantıları I-II." *Sanat ve Kültürde Kök* 1 (3–4).

Yavuz, Hakan. 2016. "Social and Intellectual Origins of Neo-Ottomanism: Searching for a Post-National Vision." *Die Welt des Islams* 56 (3–4): 438–65.

Yen, Yuehping. 2005. *Calligraphy and Power in Contemporary Chinese Society*. London: Routledge.

Zürcher, Erik 1998. *Turkey: A Modern History*. London: Tauris.

Index

Page numbers in italic refer to illustrations.

BANU ŞENAY is a lecturer in the Department of Anthropology at Macquarie University, Australia. She is the author of *Beyond Turkey's Borders: Long-distance Kemalism, State Politics, and the Turkish Diaspora.*

The University of Illinois Press
is a founding member of the
Association of University Presses.

Composed in 10.75/13 Arno Pro
with Scala Sans display
by Jim Proefrock
at the University of Illinois Press
Cover designed by Becca Alexander
Cover illustration: *Ney*-s and mouthpieces crafted by
Salih Hoca. Courtesy of Salih Bilgin. Background image
©iStock.com/Strawberry Blossom

University of Illinois Press
1325 South Oak Street
Champaign, IL 61820-6903
www.press.uillinois.edu